SIBERIA
the New Frontier

SIBERIA

the New Frontier

by GEORGE ST. GEORGE

DAVID McKAY COMPANY, INC.   New York

SIBERIA THE NEW FRONTIER

Library of Congress Catalog Card Number: 70-82504

MANUFACTURED IN THE UNITED STATES OF AMERICA

VAN REES PRESS • NEW YORK

Spasi Bog

In Siberia they still sometimes say *spasi bog*—instead of the Russian *spasibo*, or "thank you." (*Spasi bog* means literally "May God save you," and this, of course, what *spasibo* has come from.)

I want to express my profound gratitude to my friends in Moscow and throughout Siberia who rendered me invaluable help in writing this book. Naturally the opinions expressed here, and the responsibility for the book, are my own. But special thanks are due the Novosti Press Agency in Moscow, first and foremost, in persons of Boris S. Burkov, the head of this fine organization; Vadim G. Komolov, the head of its publishing offices; Boris Y. Pistchik, the tireless managing director; Vladimir S. Bruskov, the head of the editorial staff; Alexei N. Kazantzev, his deputy; Alexander E. Porazhniakov, the head of the photo library; and all the men and women of the staff who gave so generously of their time and good will.

There were many fine people in Siberia who welcomed me, too many to mention all, but some of them are due for particular thanks. Alexandra Y. Ovchinnikova, the president of the Executive Soviet of the Yakut Republic; Nikolai V. Bezriadin, the chief editor of *Sovietskaya Sibir* in Novosibirsk; Mark Sergeyev, the foremost poet of Irkutsk; Professor Michail A. Lavrentiev, the guiding light of Siberian science; my good friend Nikolai M. Sibiriakov, the secretary of the Journalists' Union of Yakutia.

I also want to thank my devoted and tireless collaborator, Miss Marina G. Lankpey, who spent untold hours obtaining research material for me.

And my particular thanks go to two young men, Lev Nosov, the crack photographer of the Novosti Press Agency, and Stanislav B. Ilyin, the brilliant young journalist of Irkutsk, my wonderful traveling companions, who shared with me the joys and difficulties of composing this book.

Spasi bog!

GEORGE ST. GEORGE

v

Contents

SIBERIA
the New Frontier

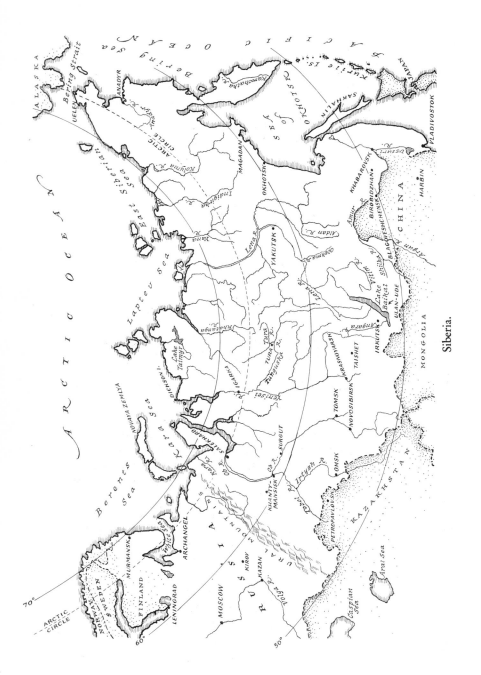

Siberia.

1.

Why This Book?

WRITING prefaces to books is unprofitable. Few people ever read them.

So this is not a preface.

This is just a brief account of the way this book came to be written.

It all started some years before World War I, in what was then the rather small but prosperous merchant town of Irkutsk, in deep Siberia. I am not a Siberian by birth, but I was brought there as an infant. So my first childhood memories are all Siberian.

Any small child's memories are unreliable. They are inevitably silted over with fantasies. It is only much later that one starts to differentiate between them and reality. But usually some days in a child's life stand out clearly, rising out of the haze of memories like little islands. It was on one of these days that the idea for this book was first born.

I remember the house in which we lived in Irkutsk. It was a humbly handsome chocolate-colored wooden affair with wooden gingerbread ornaments covering its entire front. Those filigree decorations were very typical of old Siberia. During the long severe winters Siberian householders would spend hours with a chisel and a saw turning their frozen-in dreams into lace-like designs usually fashioned out of cedar.

Many of these old houses have since been torn down and replaced by functional and unlovely modern structures, but some of them still survive. During my recent trip to Irkutsk—after an absence of over fifty years!—I was pleasantly surprised to see many of them still standing, and happy to learn that some of these surviving beauties will not be demolished, but will be moved intact to an open-air museum of early Siberian architecture to be set up on the shores of Lake Baikal, the "sacred sea" of the Siberians.

The house in which we lived was quite large. Behind it was a yard with the inevitable pigeon-loft: most Irkutians kept pigeons. Not for food, no. An Orthodox Russian would sooner starve to death than eat a pigeon. They were a symbol of the Holy Ghost. Even now, in the era of dialectical materialism, pigeons are not considered edible in Russia.

Our house was owned by a Siberian family, the Karelins. Ivan Ivanovich was a descendant of the *varnaks* ("escaped prisoners"). This represented status in the Siberia of that time. Ever since the Tsars' Cossacks drove the marauding Tartars out of Siberia in the sixteenth century, prisons had been an integral part of Siberian life. Siberia had been used for centuries as the dumping place for undesirables and for political exiles. The old-time Siberians held prisoners in affection: the magic words "I'm a runaway" would open many doors and many hearts all across Siberia.

This is well expressed in what is still the most popular of all Siberian prison songs, "The Glorious Sea, the Sacred Baikal":

> By day and by night from the prison I fled
> All the villagers giving me shelter and succour:
> Women were bringing me water and bread,
> Men filled my pouch with tobacco . . .

This aspect of old Siberia is fading now, but it was very much there when I was a child.

Mrs. Karelin I don't remember at all, though she certainly existed. I know this because the neighborhood knew that she had persecuted her husband, the wonderful Ivan Ivanovich, who was our idol.

He was a remarkable man, this Ivan Ivanovich. During his long and, I suspect, unhappy marriage, he had begot six children, all sons, and had named all of them Ivan, in honor of his father and of his grandfather, who was the original *varnak*. He was the kindest man I have ever met, a compulsive do-gooder who actually gave his only shirt to some wandering beggar. When I first knew him, his only earthly possessions consisted of a pair of patched-up trousers, torn felt boots (which he wore only in winter), and an ancient *barnaulka,* a black goat-skin overcoat common to all Siberia with the exception of Barnaul, the Altai town for which it was named.

They said that Ivan Ivanovich had once been a geography teacher. When I knew him, he had no gainful occupation. Driven out of the house by his spouse and spurned by all the Ivans he had sired, he slept in the pigeon-loft on a pile of old burlap bags in summer, and under it in winter. I don't know how and what he ate; probably his wife gave him occasional scraps and, of course, he had a host of devoted friends in the neighborhood. I don't think I ever saw him eat.

Any injustice or cruelty would send him into a towering rage, and direct action. I still remember a spectacular fight he had

A house in Irkutsk, showing the typical fretwork with which the old Siberians used to decorate their houses.

with the mother of my best friend Keshka (short for Innokentyi, of course, in honor of the only Orthodox saint of Siberia, Saint Innokentyi of Irkutsk) when he caught the good woman smacking Keshka's bottom. Ivan Ivanovich, able brawler that he was, was beaten to a pulp: picking an argument with any Siberian woman was disaster. In those days I never heard of any case of wife-beating in Irkutsk (which was a favorite indoor sport of many men in the Russia of that time), but I saw many a burly man sporting a blackened eye and fat lips as the result of domestic maladjustments.

But if the ladies of our neighborhood were not intimidated by Ivan Ivanovich's terrible temper, it was different with men. I remember that the drivers of freight horse carts were careful not to whip their horses whenever Ivan Ivanovich was in sight. They might have bested him in any man-to-man encounter, but they knew that any argument with him would bring a flock of infuriated women into the fray, and they knew better than to risk that. For Ivan Ivanovich was the darling of our block.

He was probably past 70 when I knew him, but his constitution was as tough as a black taiga bear. He attributed this to having lived his whole life "in truth," and also to his daily plunges into the ice-cold and crystal-clear Angara River. Every morning, in summer and winter alike, he would run out of the yard, stark naked, carrying his goat-skin coat under his arm, and race two blocks to the river and plunge into it—in the winter, through the hole in the ice from which the neighborhood women got their water supply. Then he would jump out, wrap his *barnaulka* around him, and race back to his pigeon-loft. This daily routine was witnessed by admiring neighbors, and a few reckless men followed his example, except during those murderous mornings when the thermometer plunged to forty or so below zero. (Incidentally, this sport is still in vogue in Siberia, its devotees known as *morzhi* or "seals.")

During the short summer, which could be very hot in Siberia, Ivan Ivanovich ran an open-air school in our yard for neighborhood children. His class included boys from five to about nine, all delinquent, and most of them not slated for schooling, which was not compulsory in the Tsar's Russia. So the only education those urchins got came from Ivan Ivanovich and the likes of him. Many political exiles ran similar unofficial schools all over Siberia, creating small centers of local enlightenment in an otherwise largely illiterate country.

Ivan Ivanovich's academic curriculum was just as eccentric as everything else about him. Reading and writing were secondary subjects. The main point of instruction was to prove to the pupils that there was no God, and that Father Nikodim of the neighborhood Church of the Ascension was a crook who fooled simple people.

Now and then the red flat face of our local policeman, Uncle Innokentyi, would appear at the gate. He was a good, kind, hard-drinking man who instinctively hated all trouble. He had the miraculous faculty of disappearing without a trace whenever there was any disturbance in the neighborhood.

"Ivan Ivanovich . . ." he would whine, "not so loud, please. . . . People will think you have, excuse me, ideas in your head . . ."

"Get the blank-blank hell out of here!" Ivan Ivanovich would thunder.

"Ivan Ivanovich—"

"Go and kiss Selivanov's behind, ulcers to his blank-blank soul!"

This was the "coup de grâce" to the poor policeman. General Selivanov was the governor of Irkutsk Province, ruler of a huge domain stretching all the way to the Arctic Ocean. The policeman's usually beet-red face would turn ashen-white at the mention of this dread name, and he would disappear.

Only later did I learn that our policeman, Uncle Innokentyi, was virtually a victim of Ivan Ivanovich, who blackmailed him with Selivanov's name. The blackmail would take the following form: toward evening Ivan Ivanovich would go out into the street and, in a thundering voice, denounce Selivanov. He always used the same formula:

"What is Selivanov?" he would howl in his fog-horn voice. "Selivanov is scum, profanation! It's Lermontov who is life!"

Why he chose to compare Selivanov to the famous Russian poet, and why exactly to Lermontov and not Pushkin, for instance, I never knew, but to me, as to every child in the block, this was a magnificent display of courage. To Innokentyi, the policeman, this must have been a nightmare. Frantically over-

coming his timidity, and holding his sword, which was irrevo-
cably known as *seledka,* or "herring," to his side, he would trot
towards Ivan Ivanovich on his short bow-legs, and whisper something into his ear. Thereupon Ivan Ivanovich would desist and
return to his pigeon-loft. Only much later did I learn the essence
of this magic: Innokentyi kept Ivan Ivanovich supplied with
drink. For Ivan Ivanovich was, in fact, a hopeless alcoholic.
Incredibly, his favorite drink was not vodka, or even pure alcohol, which many Siberians drank undiluted, but the so-called
denaturat—"denatured alcohol"—which was sold for industrial
purposes and was supposed to be highly toxic. The fact that Ivan
Ivanovich drank this dark-blue poisonous concoction made him
a hero in our eyes—to us children this was a proof of his magnificent indestructibility.

Drinking was a ritual with Ivan Ivanovich. He would fill a
tin cup with the evil-smelling *denaturat,* look at it with utter
disdain, and then toss it off in the breathless colossal gulp which
was the proper way of drinking pure alcohol—one had to hold
one's breath in order not to choke. (I was pleasantly surprised
to find, during my recent trip, that this age-old Siberian custom
is still alive in the gold-and-diamond Soviet republic of Yakutia
where the *piteinyi spirt,* or "drinking alcohol," is sold in all wine
stores along with vodka.)

After downing this hemlock-like mixture, Ivan Ivanovich
would screw up his wrinkled face so that his untidy salt-and-
pepper beard assumed a horizontal position, wipe his mouth with
the back of his hand, and croak in a strange falsetto voice which
bore no resemblance to his natural gruff voice at all:

"This is worse than a mother-in-law, ulcers to its soul."

This formula never changed, and it sent us into a rapture of
admiration. ("Ulcers to his—her—or its soul" was an ancient
Siberian oath, and the old-time Siberians used it constantly and
not necessarily in a derogatory sense. Such a phrase, for instance,
as "my wife, ulcers to her soul, is a good woman," would be
thoroughly correct usage in Siberian parlance.)

Summers with Ivan Ivanovich were fun, but it was during
the long and bitter winters that Ivan Ivanovich's true talents
blossomed forth in all their glory.

Since it was much too cold to hold any outdoor classes, or even to denounce Selivanov, Ivan Ivanovich would hole up in his pigeon-loft and, outside of his ritualistic plunges into the Angara, would rarely venture out at all. He would spend his days sitting close to the *mangal*—the makeshift stove made of loose stones piled on a sheet of corrugated iron. With a little fretsaw in his horny hand, he turned out the most beautiful fretwork in Irkutsk, the city famous for its fretwork all over Siberia. His work was much sought after by local householders who supplied him with material, blades for his saw, *denaturat,* and the little food that he consumed, in exchange for the finished product. And indeed only genuine artistic talent combined with poisonous *denaturat* could produce such sheer poetry out of rough cedar planks. (During my recent trip I thought I recognized some of Ivan Ivanovich's exquisite, almost psychedelic designs on some of the old houses in our old neighborhood, but that might well be just my nostalgic imagination.)

But artistic as Ivan Ivanovich's fretwork was, it could not even compare with the products of his alcohol-bemused imagination. Winter was the time when he told us his stories about Siberia.

What stories they were! Undoubtedly in Ivan Ivanovich the world has lost one of the greatest poetic liars ever born. What is more, I am still absolutely convinced that he firmly believed every word that came out of his toothless mouth. It is unfortunate that no tape recorders existed then, and that no one made an effort to write down those marvelous tales. However, since one would have to edit out the profanity, much of their magic beauty would have been lost anyway.

It so happened that I proved to be his best audience. I was magnetically attracted to his inspired lies. For them—only for them—I would even abandon *glyzka,* the favorite winter game of the neighborhood boys. *Glyzka* was more than a game; it was an obsession, a gambling hysteria which gripped every little boy, and even some little girls, in our street. I don't remember the exact rules now, but it was akin to the American game of marbles, except that it was played with hard-frozen horse droppings polished to the highest perfection. A good *glyzka* had to roll far and true over the frozen ground to be effective. It was the maniacal ambition of every boy to accumulate as many *glyzkas* as possible during the winter, and thus emerge a champion.

I never even came close to achieving championship status and, looking back, I don't regret it. Pleasant at it was to win, and accumulate the pile of glistening *glyzkas* under one's porch, it was even more wonderful to listen to Ivan Ivanovich's beautiful stories.

Ivan Ivanovich had two great loves in his life—the love of man and the love of Siberia. He loved his native land as Romeo loved Juliet. He loved everything about it: its endless taiga, its frozen tundra, its mighty frigid rivers, its towering bald mountains, its stagnant marshlands, its plagues of mosquitoes, and even its cruel climate. To him Siberia was more than a huge and empty country—it was the mystical seat of some future *pravilnaya zhizn,* or "correct life," which humanity was to achieve one day when there would be no poverty, no injustice, no suffering, no violence, and probably even no death. He told beautiful lies about his wanderings all over the country (much later I learned that he had never left his native Irkutsk), of encounters with ferocious bears, Ussuri tigers, tremendous packs of wolves, of finding incredibly rich caches of gold and precious stones and whole plantations of the mysterious ginseng, the "root of life" which had the power of making people all but immortal. He told about strange human beings, living on the frozen mountain tops and possessing the secrets of happiness, half saints and half shamans, or witch doctors, who could raise the dead and work wondrous miracles with human souls, eliminating all evil from them. He spoke about the sacred Lake Baikal and the mysteries hidden in its bottomless depths that went to the very center of the earth; about the fire-breathing mountains of Kamchatka; about the lakes lost in the frozen tundra that were the homes of weird monsters, and about hundreds of other wondrous things.

Ivan Ivanovich's knowledge of geography must have been formidable, but he ascribed to Siberia more than mere geographical wonders. To him this was a mystical promised land that was destined to become the home of "good people" when humanity would destroy itself by its cruelty and greed. Then, according to him, Siberia would become the new Garden of Eden, a lush paradise of happiness and plenty, even though he was not quite sure what would happen to its harsh climate.

Strangely enough, Ivan Ivanovich's mysticism had no religious connotation at all. He claimed that it was man and not God who would work this universal miracle, even though, analyzing his words now, I believe that basically he was a true Christian, vaguely of the Tolstoyan cast, in rebellion against the government-controlled church.

"I'm writing all this down, *parya*," he used to tell me, "so that people, ulcers to their souls, can read it when I go back to the taiga."

He called me *parya* which was a mark of special affection. The Siberian word can be translated as "laddie," though it is rarely applied to children.

He would produce a thick old folder tied with a frayed string.

"It will be all in this book—I'm writing every night, *parya*. I'll leave it to you when I go. I'm just waiting for them to call me back—it may come any day now."

I never learned who "they" were and what Ivan Ivanovich meant by going to the taiga. It was all very mysterious, vaguely frightening, and intensely exciting.

It was on a frozen January day that Ivan Ivanovich finally got his call.

The railroad station in Irkutsk was on the opposite side of the river from the city. In our time there was only a flimsy pontoon bridge which was dismantled every autumn during the ice flow and not put back into service until May when the river was free of ice again. Though a serviceable road was laid over the thick winter ice, there were weeks during autumn and spring when there was no solid ice and no pontoon bridge—no connection between the town and the railroad at all. The Angara, probably the most beautiful river in Siberia, was so swift-flowing that it did not freeze over in the usual way. It froze differently. Huge chunks of ice formed on the river bottom, then rose to the surface, creating fearful ice jams against which no bridge could stand. This situation has now been changed by the construction of the hydroelectric dam at Irkutsk, which largely tamed the river.

That particular year—was it 1911 or 1912?—the seasonal

traffic interruption had lasted longer than usual, and the ice road across the river was not open until the beginning of January. Consequently a great number of passengers, and masses of freight, had accumulated across the river. Among the passengers there were several convoys of prisoners consigned to the central jail at Irkutsk from where they would be dispersed to the network of mines operated by convict labor. Usually the convicts would be marched across the river to the town in small convoys. They always passed on our street. In those days leg-irons were still used. No other sound could compare in sheer melancholy to the baleful clinking of many leg-irons. Now the only mention of them is in old Siberian prison songs. But anyone who actually heard this sound could not forget its hypnotic and strangely musical effect.

The noise of approaching chain clanging would always bring people into the street. They had food, tobacco, and copper coins for the prisoners. The guards, looking guilty and miserable in their ill-fitting greatcoats in winter and filthy white shirts in summer, would slow down to allow the prisoners to collect this harvest. No cruel jailers, they were rather brothers in misfortune: service in the Tsar's army was to them like a dreaded prison term. The prisoners shared their bounty with them. The convoy commanders encouraged this practice, because it gave them the opportunity to steal some of the money allocated for the prisoners' food.

Usually the convoys consisted of thirty to fifty men, but on that freezing January day possibly 300 clanging wretches were passing along our narrow street, and the effect was overwhelming. The weather was cruel, and they looked particularly miserable in their gray prison coats.

On several occasions I had seen Ivan Ivanovich watching the passing prisoners, and while his lips uttered curses, his red-rimmed eyes were always moist with tears. Somehow he always managed to have something for them, a piece of bread, an onion, a dried fish, or in summer an apple. But on this particular day he had nothing at all except a tin cup with *denaturat*. But they would not touch it. So suddenly he downed it himself and then did something which struck me as the most magnificent gesture I had ever seen. He removed his torn *barnaulka* and threw it to the passing men. Greedy hands caught it in midair. He had nothing on under it. His torn trousers and the matted gray hair on his chest were scant insulation against the forty-below-zero frost. Before anyone could say a word, he turned and raced back to his pigeon-loft slapping his bare arms against his body.

The next morning Ivan Ivanovich did not run to the river for his morning dip for the first time in many, many years. When I went into the yard, bringing with me my father's old army jacket which my mother had given me to take to Ivan Ivanovich, I saw my friend Keshka. Keshka found time to visit Ivan Ivanovich every morning to bring him some warm bread stolen from his mother's kitchen.

Keshka looked pale and frightened.

"Better go to him, *parya*."

I understood that something was very wrong. Keshka didn't get frightened easily. He was a hardened young hooligan.

I climbed the rickety ladder up to the loft. It was bitterly cold there—the *mangal* was out. Ivan Ivanovich was lying under a pile of burlap bags, shivering, his corrugated old face gray and his nose very long and very white. He tried to smile, but could not manage it. Obviously he was very sick. The sight of his white nose threw me into a panic. I started to fumble with matches, trying to build the fire, and finally I succeeded. Then I put my father's jacket over him, but he did not seem to notice it. His blue lips were trembling as though he were trying to say something. I leaned over him and barely heard his halting words.

". . . to the taiga, *parya*. . . . That folder, ulcers to its soul. . . . You take it. . . . However I don't think I can finish writing. . . . Must go to the taiga today. . . ."

Now I understood the terrible meaning of his words.

"No!" I cried hysterically. "No, no! I'll bring snow—I'll rub your nose! You'll be all right, Ivan Ivanovich!"

"However, it's too late, *parya*. . . . You take that folder . . . finish writing it. . . . Everything I have told you, *parya*. . . . I'm going home . . . to the taiga. . . ."

I don't remember what I answered; probably nothing. But I remember practically sliding down the ladder and running into the street. The sun shone brilliantly and the smoke from the chimneys rose straight up, like pencils—the surest sign that it

was very cold and even the air was frozen into immobility. I
didn't know what I had to do, but I knew that I had to do
something.

The first person I saw was our policeman.

"Uncle Innokentyi! Come quickly! Ivan Ivanovich is very
sick! He's freezing—his nose is white!"

When the policeman climbed up the pigeon-loft ladder the
fire in the *mangal* was burning briskly. He squatted beside Ivan
Ivanovich and gingerly pushed his blue cheek with his fur mitten.
The old man's head just rolled to one side. I was too terrified to
do, say, or even think anything.

The policeman straightened up, removed his fur hat, and
crossed himself.

"It's that *denaturat* that's got him. . . . Better go and call
Father Nikodim, ulcers to his soul."

To me one world came to an end at that moment—a wonderful world filled with smoke and dreams, smelling of glue and
freshly cut wood and pigeon droppings. I don't remember how
they buried Ivan Ivanovich, the man from whom I had learned
the deep meaning of kindness, every dirty word in the Russian
language, and the overwhelming belief that Siberia was some sort
of magical place where one day Ivan Ivanovich's "truth" would
find its home.

But I remember climbing several days later up to the pigeon-
loft which was now bitterly cold and terribly empty, and fum-
bling under the pile of burlap sacks. The old folder was still
there, tied with a string. I could not untie the string with my
mittens, and I bit through it with my sharp young teeth. I remember opening the folder: every yellowed page was blank!
There was only a title, printed in pencil. So Ivan Ivanovich could
not overcome this first and fatal hurdle of so many would-be
writers. Hell must be paved with unused titles.

Ivan Ivanovich's title was short:

Prekrasnaya Sibir'—"Siberia the Beautiful."

Soon afterwards I saw Siberia many times. My father, a railway executive, had a railway car for our private use and we
went in it from St. Petersburg to Vladivostok and back several
times during the next three years—a marvelous trip of eight
days and nine nights. Then, before I had a chance to know the

country better, my father, an accomplished Sinologist, secured a position in China and we left Siberia forever.

Over fifty years have flashed by since then like bright windows of an express train in the night. The currents, whirlpools, and eddies of life have carried me over the planet's geography, which Ivan Ivanovich knew so well without ever leaving his native street. But I have not forgotten Siberia. I have followed her fortunes, her ups and downs, her joys and sorrows, her dreams and anguish from wherever I went, hoping that one day I might go back and see for myself the magic world about which Ivan Ivanovich had no time to write in his folder. Perhaps I would complete his unfinished love story.

Recently I had the opportunity of doing just that.

I didn't find any white-clad shamans on the frozen mountain tops, or monster-infested lakes, or ginseng forests, gold placers, or diamond "pipes." But I did find a new, very young world being born in a very ancient land, and this book is about this world and the people building it.

The word *"Sib-ir'"* (the Russian name for Siberia) means the "sleeping land" in the Mongol-Tartar dialect once spoken in Siberia. But this description no longer applies. I would like to re-christen it "the Awakening Giant."

With apologies to Ivan Ivanovich, may his soul rest peacefully in the frozen taiga which he loved so well.

2.

What Is Siberia?

THIS question is not as facetious as it may sound. There is a good deal of confusion about this term.

This is how the big Soviet Encyclopedia defines it:

Siberia is a part of the Asiatic territory of the Soviet Union from the Urals in the west to the watershed of the Pacific Ocean mountain ranges in the east, and from the shores of the Arctic Ocean in the north to the elevated steppes of the Kazakh Soviet Socialist Republic and the borders of the Mongolian People's Republic in the south. Siberia stretches from north to south for about 3,500 kilometers [about 2,200 miles], and from west to east for about 7,000 kilometers [4,400 miles]. Its area is about 10,000,000 square kilometers [3,830,000 square miles]. In the north, Siberia is washed by the following seas forming a part of the Arctic Ocean: the Kara Sea, the Laptev Sea, and the East Siberian Sea.

The territory of Siberia includes the Yakut Autonomous Soviet Socialist Republic, the Buryat-Mongol Autonomous Soviet Socialist Republic,* the Tyumen, Kurgan, Omsk, Novosibirsk, Tomsk, Kemerovo, Krasnoyarsk, Altai, Irkutsk, Chita and a part of the Magadan provinces, the Mountain-Altai, Khakass and Tuva Autonomous Regions, and six National Districts of the Russian Soviet Federated Socialist Republic [the R.S.F.S.R.].†

Siberia is divided into Western Siberia—from the Urals to the Yenisei river, and Eastern Siberia—from the Yenisei to the mountain ranges of the Pacific Ocean watershed.

* Now the Buryat A.S.S.R.
† Since then, the Tuva has been declared an Autonomous Republic within the Russian Federation, on a par with Yakutia and Buratia.

16

No true Siberian will ever agree with this definition, since it excludes the Siberian Far East.

While administratively and politically this might be correct, to any Siberian the exclusion of the Far East, with such typically Siberian cities as Blagoveshchensk, Khabarovsk, and Vladivostok, is absolutely absurd. Geographically and historically the Far East region, north of Mongolia and to the sea, is part of Siberia, and one of the most interesting and colorful parts, at that. It is an integral part of the Asiatic territory of the Russian Federation; the general composition of its population is no different from that of the rest of Siberia; it has played a very important part in the development of the country. Its economy is organically connected with Siberia, and no inhabitant of the Far East would call himself anything but a Siberian. Such a designation as "Far Easterner" would have no meaning whatsoever in Siberia and, for that matter, anywhere else.

So, for the purposes of this book, the Siberian Far East will be treated as a part of Siberia.

Administratively, this Far East region includes the following Siberian provinces: Amur, Khabarovsk, Primorski (Maritime), Sakhalin, Kamchatka, and the part of Magadan province not included in the encyclopedia definition. This territory includes the Jewish Autonomous Region (a part of Khabarovsk province) and two National Districts—the Koryak and the Chukchi.

A few words about the multinational administrative structure of Siberia. All Siberia is a part of the Russian Federation and is, therefore, a part of Russia. There is a fallacious impression that with the advent of Soviet power the very definition of "Russia" has been politically abolished. While the former multinational Russian Empire is known now as the Union of Soviet Socialist Republics, Russia is the most important part of the Union, and Siberia is an integral part of Russia. The Russian language is the official state language of the entire Soviet Union, and, of course, of Siberia.

Therefore, the most accurate definition of Siberia for our purposes should be "the Asiatic part of Russia," or, more technically accurate, of the Russian Soviet Federated Socialist Republic.

3.

A Brief History of Siberia

SIBERIA is a very old country—and one of the youngest in the world.

The first Siberians known to us lived here as early as 40,000 B.C. Paleolithic (early stone age) settlements have been discovered along the Ob River and the Yenisei River, between Krasnoyarsk and Minusinsk, near Irkutsk, and in Transbaikalia. The remnants of Neolithic settlements (a later stone age) have been found all over Siberia. It is uncertain who these early people were, but about 3000 B.C. the picture becomes clearer. Archaeological findings indicate that people living in the southern regions, along the Altai and the Sayan mountain systems, had European characteristics. They raised cattle and used copper and bronze utensils while the tribes living further north were still living in the stone age. In 2000 B.C. the entire steppe and forest belt between the Urals and Transbaikalia was populated by these cattle-raising copper-and-bronze tribes, but around 1000 B.C. some mongoloid tribes started to drift in from the south. These newcomers brought north with them some signs of Chinese culture.

Until then the social structure had been built around matriarchal families, but the Mongol newcomers brought with them the patriarchy which seemed to be accepted quickly by the native male Siberians. The most northern tribes, however, continued to be matriarchal until rather recent history.

During the period between 1000 and 500 B.C. some bronze utensils found their way to the isolated northern forest regions while the southern tribes began to use iron, and were engaging in some primitive agriculture (in the extreme southern regions there was even artificial irrigation).

The last few centuries before our era were marked by constant warfare between tribes and combinations of tribes, and the rise of tribal aristocracy. Many burial mounds of this era contain imported articles and some examples of local art that testify to the comparative wealth of the dead.

The Sayan-Altai tribes first appear in Chinese historical annals around 300 to 200 B.C. under the collective name of "Dinlings." By this time they had been subjugated by the Huns, and the Altai and the Sayan mountain chains and part of Transbaikalia formed the northern border of the Hun empire. The increased influence of Chinese culture began to appear among the Siberian tribes. Chinese articles and coins have been found in some of the burial mounds of this period. It is possible that the residence of one of the Hun viceroys was located near the present city of Abakan in the Altai where some remnants of Chinese-style buildings dating to about 100 B.C. have been found.

Under the pressure of the Huns some Mongolian tribes started to drift into the Yenisei basin of Siberia either pushing the aboriginal tribes further north or mixing with them.

At the same time in Western Siberia, along the rivers, some cattle-raising tribes started to move north, creating a distinct culture combining the southern and northern elements. These tribes are now known under the collective name of the Ugors. They are the ancestors of the present far northern tribes of Western Siberia.

In the first centuries of our era, the Hun domination started to weaken, and there appeared in southwestern regions new tribes and new combinations of tribes coming from Central Asia, among them some Turki and Kirghis tribes, which in Chinese annals were referred to as the Ha-gias—undoubtedly the ancestors of the present Khakasses of Siberia.

The influence of the Turki tribes with their comparatively high culture based on fairly advanced agriculture started to spread among the multiracial people of southern and central Siberia and ended with their domination of the northern tribes. The subject tribes were forced to pay tax to the new masters in the form of furs, which found a ready market in China. Towards 1000 A.D. the single Kirghis-Khakass confederation along the Yenisei River broke into two small entities. By the beginning of the thirteenth century, Siberia was a crazy-quilt of many multi-racial tribes without any central cohesion.

About this time the Mongol-Tartar expansion took place, organized by the extremely able Ghengis Khan. It was explosive. Within a short time the Mongols spread their domination over much of Asia, including parts of China and India and over all of Siberia, with the exception of the extreme north which they simply did not reach. Then, through Central Asia, they poured into Europe, quickly overrunning all of Russia, at that time composed of many small feudal states, and reaching as far as present-day Hungary and up to the very gates of Vienna. The Mongol-Tartar domination was to last in Russia for almost three hundred years, and even longer in Siberia.

Ghengis Khan's empire was much too vast and too decen-tralized to last, and it broke quickly into a number of smaller khanates, each one, however, powerful enough to exercise its con-trol over subjugated territories. In Russia it broke into two states —Djagatai Ulus which held Central Asia and southern regions of Russia, and the so-called Golden Horde, centered in the middle Volga region and dominating northern Russia and Siberia.

The Tartar rule was extremely loose. It was exercised through Russian feudal princes in Russia, and tribal headsmen in Siberia.

The Tartar domination, even though it set Russia back cul-turally and economically, had one positive facet: it brought about the crystallization of a Russian national spirit: at long last, all the Russians had a common enemy. The Russian princes, though intriguing against one another, were nonetheless moving closer together against the Tartar oppressors, and gradually the role of the Moscow principality became more and more impor-tant. It was becoming a centralizing force. On September 8, 1380, Russian troops, mostly composed of Moscow forces, de-feated the Tartars in the great battle of Kulikovo. This shook the Tartar rule, though it did not end it. However, the process of the consolidation of Russia around Moscow was greatly accel-erated. In 1430 the Tartar rule was finally overthrown, and Russia was loosely united, with the Tartars retreating to their strongholds around Kazan on the Volga. The young Russian confederation was too weak to tackle the Tartars there, and the Tartars continued to make occasional intrusions into the Russian territories. Only under Tsar Ivan IV, the Terrible, did Russia become a truly cohesive state. In the middle of the sixteenth century, Ivan attacked the Tartar strongholds of Kazan and Astrakhan, and drove the Tartars beyond the Ural Mountains.

In Siberia by this time there was the so-called Siberian khanate with the center at Chinga-Ture (now Tyumen), lying on the trade route across the Ural Mountains. Even while under Tartar rule, the Russians had traded for furs with Siberia, then known to them as the Land of Ugor. Now with the Kazan khanate becoming a part of the Russian state, the Siberian Tartars became Russia's neighbors.

The Siberian khanate was not a strong state. It had no support from the native Siberian tribes, and the Khan's throne had several pretenders intriguing against each other.

In this situation the ruling Siberian Khan, Ediger, tried to form a partnership with Russia. Shortly after the fall of Kazan, in 1555, he sent envoys to Moscow offering to enter into the Russian state as an autonomous province, and pay annually one sable skin for each male inhabitant in exchange for the Tsar's help against his personal enemies. After some protracted negotiations this deal was accepted. It is interesting to note that Ediger, probably for the sake of economy, did not claim his suzerainty over any Siberian tribes except the Khanty and Mansi living in the immediate proximity of his capital.

So nominally the Siberian khanate became a part of the Russian state, and some Russian envoys were sent to Chinga-Ture in order to "bring Ediger and all of Siberia to the truth, and to collect the tax in full," to quote a Russian document of that time.

This collaboration did not last long. Ediger was overthrown by Kuchum, his distant relative, who became the new Siberian Khan. Kuchum would have no truck with the Russians. First of all he moved his capital further east to a place called Kashlyk, near the present town of Tobolsk, and then he refused to pay the agreed tax to the Tsar. The relations between the two states became strained. In 1571, the Russian ambassador to the Siberian khanate was murdered. Kuchum declared general mobilization of all his warriors, and started to prepare for an open war against Russia.

By this time, in the basin of the Kama River, a tributary of the Volga, there was a powerful merchant clan, the Strogonovs. One of them is reputed to be the inventor of the famous Russian dish, Boeuf à la Strogonov. The Strogonovs had acquired very large territories close to the Urals, had organized salt mining, fishing, hunting, and other industries there, and had accumulated great wealth, so great in fact that for many years thereafter they were the richest single family in Russia. In effect, they were quite independent of Moscow though nominally recognizing its authority.

Now the Strogonovs were summoned to Moscow and received from the Tsar a deed to all of Western Siberia, providing that they would conquer it at their own expense. This was a brilliant maneuver, since the fur trade with Siberia was becoming very important, and since, in case of Tartar incursion, the Strogonovs would be the first victims in any event.

The Strogonovs organized an expedition of Cossack mercenaries—or anyone who would be willing to fight. The preparations took seven years, from 1574 to 1581, when finally the expedition was ready. The head of the expedition was Ermak Timofeyevich, a man of uncertain origin who was destined to become a celebrated figure in Russian history as "the Conqueror of Siberia."

Altogether, Ermak had 540 men in his "army." To this the Strogonovs added 300 men from their own employees, so the force grew to 840 men. The prospective enemies outnumbered Ermak's men at least 50 to 1, but Ermak's troops were homogeneous and were armed with flint rifles. Kuchum's horde was composed of representatives of many tribes, some of whom hated the Tartars, and they had no firearms at all—just bows and arrows.

In the spring of 1582, Ermak led his men into the West Siberian plain. After several light skirmishes with Kuchum's advance patrols, the Russians reached the Tura River, built primitive boats there, and sailed up the river toward Kuchum's new capital of Kashlyk.

Kuchum sent a strong detachment of his warriors against them. In a sharp pitched battle, Ermak's men defeated them.

At this point some Siberian tribal princes started to desert Kuchum who fled to his capital of Kashlyk (which was also known as Sib-ir, or "the sleeping land"). As Ermak and his men approached the town, many of Kuchum's allies deserted, and Kuchum fled with the remnants of his Tartars into the frozen wilderness.

On October 26, 1582, the Cossacks occupied Kashlyk. Thus Ermak became the conquerer of Sib-ir, or Siberia.

After spending the winter in Kashlyk, Ermak started another campaign in the spring of 1583, and cleared large territories along the Irtysh and Ob Rivers, turning them over to the local tribes who swore their loyalty to the Tsar. He then sent a report to the Strogonovs, with a copy to Tsar Ivan the Terrible, informing them that Siberia was now theirs.

The new "Siberian Land" was immediately incorporated into the Russian state, and the Tsar sent two of his own administrators, Bolkhovsky and Glukhov, with 500 Russian regulars who joined Ermak in the autumn of 1583.

But Kuchum was not finished.

In August 1584, he ambushed Ermak: the weight of his armor proved Ermak's undoing, and in trying to swim to safety, he drowned.

With Ermak's death, the Russian cause suffered a setback. The Russians were forced to leave Kashlyk and depart beyond the Urals. But soon they returned, to stay.

Who was Ermak, and who were his men that played such an outstanding part in Siberian history?

Some historians describe him as a Cossack *ataman*, or "headman." The word Cossack should not be confused with the Kazakhs, the Central Asian people. Cossack simply means a free man in Tartar, and describes the free Russian peasants, usually ex-soldiers, who were settled with their families in some border region. They were given land and freed from all taxes in exchange for being forever "on call" by the Tsars. Such armed men were settled along the borders and served as a covering force against all intrusions. In time Cossackhood became hereditary— the armed peasantry retained their privilege. Organized on a paramilitary basis they formed the praetorian guard for the Tsars, both in time of war and in peace. As a privileged class they were presumed to have a large stake in the Tsarist regime, and, in fact, even during the last revolution all the Cossack regions were the last to submit to the Soviet rule.

Most historians think that Ermak was a Don Cossack by birth; others claim that he was born in the Urals, as Vasily Timofeyevich Alenin. The exact truth will never be known. The Strogonovs, as a rule, hired all those who wanted to work for them without question, and kept no records.

But whoever he was, he must have been a very talented chieftain. One of his cardinal rules was the decent treatment of all the natives—including the families of the Tartar soldiers who fell into his hands. This went a long way toward winning the sympathies of the native Siberians to the Russian cause. This explains why, when the Russians appeared again, the Siberian tribes welcomed them as deliverers from the harsh Tartar yoke, and made the subsequent conquest of Siberia so incredibly easy for very small bands of the Russians. Tribe after tribe went over to the Russians who started to build the *ostrogs*, or "forts," which later grew into the present Russian cities in Western Siberia. Tyumen was founded in 1586, Tobolsk in 1587, Pelim in 1593, Berezovo in 1593, Surgut in 1594, Verkhoturye in 1598, Narym in 1598, Mangazeya in 1601, Tomsk in 1604.

The speed with which the Russians moved across the trackless taiga and tundra, often in groups of thirty to fifty men, covering hundreds and thousands of miles, is astounding. Obviously this could not have been done without the help of the local tribes. There is not a single record of any serious clash after the collapse of the flimsy Tartar state.

From this point on, the movement into Siberia assumed a chaotic and disorganized character. Individual adventurers and small groups of soldiers, acting on their own, claimed great territories for the Tsar. It is interesting to note that wherever the Russians met with any kind of organized opposition, as they did from the feudal Turki lords further south, they just bypassed these regions and went further. Looking at the map one would get the impression of some tremendous vacuum sucking them in. Never in history has any nation achieved a "conquest" of this magnitude by such meager means. It is doubtful that there were more than two thousand armed Russians in Siberia at any time during this whole period.

Scores of local tribal chiefs fell over each other recognizing the "conquerors" and swearing their loyalty to the Tsar, hoping to preserve their privileged positions in the new Russian state.

By the early 1640s, the Russians reached the Sea of Okhotsk and the Pacific—only Chukchi had remained unclaimed. Further south the Russians reached the Amur basin with the Transbaikalian Buryat tribes going over to them to escape the barbarous exploitation of their Mongol overlords.

In the south, things were not proceeding according to the Russian plan.

In the middle of the seventeenth century, a small band of Russian Cossacks reached the majestic Amur River, founded a fort there called Albazin, and claimed the entire territory to the Pacific for Russia. But they met with resistance. The Manchurian feudal lords had established their power over China, and claimed the entire seaboard as their domain. Chinese troops, led by the Manchus, laid siege to Albazin.

The Russian government, which by now had acquired more territories than it knew what to do with, and which needed trade with China to supply its new Siberian empire, started peace negotiations. In the Nerchinsk Peace Treaty of 1689, the Chinese abandoned their claims to the Okhotsk seaboard, but the territories south of the Amur River were returned to them. Albazin surrendered, its garrison was imprisoned, and the fortress itself was dismantled.

(As a little sidelight it is interesting to consider the fate of the Cossacks taken from Albazin into China. They never returned home, and their descendants are still living in Peking. By now they are unrecognizable from any other Chinese, but miraculously they have preserved their Orthodox religion and some typically Russian names. Before the Chinese revolution there was a large Russian Orthodox church in Peking supported by these people. As a child I attended a service there, conducted in Chinese, and was impressed by the crowd of worshipers, all Chinese. Those were the descendants of the Albazin Cossacks bearing such names as Ivan, Vasily, Piotr, Nikita, Olga, Tamara,

Nina, etc.—but they no longer spoke a word of Russian. It would be interesting to know what has happened to them since the Chinese Communist revolution.)

The Nerchinsk treaty opened a trade route to China from Siberia, but the huge Amur region lay fallow and empty. There were no Chinese settlers there, and the few Russian squatters were driven out. Also the treaty denied Russia access to the Pacific Ocean through the Amur.

The Russian penetration into Siberia produced a number of brilliant adventurers and empire-builders. These men were moved both by their adventurous spirit and by greed. Furs, "the soft gold," were all-important in the economy of that time, and in addition to sable, ermine, kolinsky, silver fox, and squirrel, northern otter was added to the list of the treasures to be obtained from Siberia.

It was the quest for otter skins that dominated the Russian drive in the north. After the easternmost parts of Siberia were subjugated, the drive moved onto the continent of America—to Alaska and the Aleutian Islands, since no one then claimed these territories. The credit for the Russian penetration into America goes not to a soldier, but to a merchant, one Gregori Shelekhov, who had his base in the newly built Russian stronghold of Irkutsk. He is fondly known in Siberia today as "the Russian Columbus," and a large new industrial city near Irkutsk bears his name. Shelekhov, a man of tremendous energy and vision, had a far-reaching plan of adding the entire Pacific coast of America all the way to then-Spanish California to the Russian empire. He almost succeeded, too. He, his associate, Baranov, and a small band of adventurous Cossacks, after enduring incredible hardships in Alaska, succeeded in building a few Russian *ostrogs*. The capital was Novo-Arkhangelsk, the present-day Sitka. They built a number of seaworthy craft for further exploration. After Shelekhov's death, Baranov took over, sailed south, and on April 4, 1806, the Russian ships dropped anchor in San Francisco Bay. The Spanish governor of California, Arguello, welcomed the visitors—this looked to him like a good opportunity of establishing a valuable fur trade in exchange for California grain. After consulting his government, he granted the Russians the right to establish trading posts in California.

Accordingly the Russians leased some land near Bodega Bay along the present Russian River, and in 1812 the Russian *ostrog,* Fort Ross, was officially open for business. It still stands there, and is one of the tourist attractions of California.

Meanwhile other Russian ships reached the Hawaiian Islands, and the Russian captains concluded a deal with the royal family there, by which the islands joined the Russian empire. This was never approved by the Russian government; it is even doubtful whether the news of this new acquisition reached St. Petersburg.

But a much more tangible and much more romantic adventure took place in San Francisco as one of Baranov's young officers, Rezanov, became engaged to the daughter of the local governor, Señorita Consuella Concepcion Arguello. It is believed that Rezanov's prospective father-in-law conspired with the young man to form an independent state of California under the protection of the Russian Tsars. According to this legend, which is very much alive in Siberia to this day, Rezanov left for St. Petersburg to present the plan to the Tsar, but never reached his destination; he contracted pneumonia in Siberia and died there. A reminder of this romantic story is the Consuella Rock in San Francisco, which presumably was the place where the poor girl kept watch for the return of her beloved.

By the middle of the nineteenth century the Russian Tsars were becoming tired of the activities of their discoverers, and decided to liquidate their American holdings as bothersome and unprofitable. On March 30, 1867, all such holdings were sold to the United States for the sum of 7,200,000 gold dollars. This transaction was negotiated for the United States by William H. Seward, Secretary of State under President Andrew Johnson, and was labeled then as "Seward's Folly." Undoubtedly the Tsarist government considered the deal extremely profitable, and for a small additional sum would have sold a goodly slice of Siberia as well: the immense new territory was bringing more expense than profit to the Russian treasury.

Indeed, the new empire presented a monumental administrative headache. After some mature consideration, the St. Petersburg government decided to treat the whole of Siberia as a single province divided into nineteen districts, or *uyezds,* with a *voyevoda,* or military governor, administering each, while the *voyevoda* in Tobolsk had the added responsibility for the entire province. Each *voyevoda* was provided with a small garrison, and had practically unlimited and uncontrolled power to run his domain in any manner he wanted. A special "Siberian Department" was created in Moscow, but its authority was only nominal; the *voyevodas* ran their districts as their private preserves. Quite naturally this led to monstrous abuse of power— the military governors grew rich ruthlessly exploiting the local population.

This system of legalized robbery became so flagrant that it was not long before the Moscow government discovered that it was getting less from its new territories than it was putting into them. The garrisons had to be supplied, salaries had to be paid, while much of the taxes (collected almost entirely in sable furs) were simply stolen by the *voyevodas* and their staffs. The total number of salaried administrators in Siberia reached 10,000 toward the end of the seventeenth century.

To create an economic base for feeding this horde, the government started to encourage peasant immigration into Siberia. Since the situation of the peasants in Russia was becoming more and more desperate because of serfdom, which had been introduced there in the beginning of the century, many peasants responded, especially since serfdom was forbidden in Siberia, and it was the only part of Russia that never had this degrading practice. It was even forbidden in relation to the "natives"— not so much as a humanitarian measure, but because the government was trying to protect the Siberian tribes since tax was collected on a per capita basis.

The new migrants to Siberia, which was declared to be "the Tsar's field," had no right to own the land, but worked it on a sharecropper basis. But even that was better than remaining virtual slaves of the landlords in Russia. The government publicized Siberia by appealing to "lovers of free life" to go there— and this played a considerable part in molding a specific Siberian character. Besides the peasants, many commercially-minded adventurers went to the new territory, and settled around the administrative *ostrogs*, thus creating the first Siberian towns. The census of 1678 gave Siberia 10,289 peasant and semi-urban "households": there was no per capita count.

These Russian colonists undid much of the evil work of the Tsar's administration in their relations with the native tribes. The Russians adopted many of the local customs and ways, while the native Siberians learned agriculture and other facets of the comparatively advanced Russian culture. Throughout subsequent Siberian history, the Russian immigrants always made common cause with the native tribes against administrative corruption.

(There were numerous outbreaks against this corruption, and also against the local tribal chiefs, who quickly found a way of working hand-in-glove with the Tsar's administrators. Such outbreaks occurred in Western Siberia in 1605, 1607, 1611–1612, and 1662; in Yakutia in 1633, 1636, 1642, 1647, 1667, and 1681; and among the Evens and the Evenks in 1662. These outbreaks had a limited scope and usually were aimed at the local tax collectors. But the Siberian administrators blamed all of them on the influence brought into Siberia by the "rotten people" who were coming there from Russia. There were also outbreaks among the Buryats in Transbaikalia and some of them even moved over to Mongolia, only to find still more cruel exploitation there, whereupon they returned to the Baikal shores.)

Meanwhile the Russians were extending and consolidating their Siberian hold. In the eighteenth and the first half of the nineteenth century, Russian rule was extended to the Chukchi and the islands of the Arctic Ocean, to the southeastern parts of Siberia and to the Amur basin. In 1711 the Kurile Islands were discovered, and then the Aleutian and Commander Islands, and added to the Russian realm. A fortified line was created across the southern border of Siberia based on Yamishevsk, Omsk, Zhelezinka, Semipalatinsk, and Ust-Kamenogorsk. To man this line, the Siberian Cossack *Voysko* (or "troop") was created, and later, around 1850, the Transbaikalian and Amur Cossack troops, and still later, the Ussuri troop. The Amur, Ussuri, and the island of Sakhalin were acquired from China on the basis of diplomatic negotiations formulated in the Aygun Treaty of 1858. Siberia became Russian, more or less within its present borders.

In 1708 the old administration was abolished, and Siberia was divided into three provinces, the Tobol, Yenisei, and Irtysh, and still later, in 1822, it was further reorganized into Western

Siberia, Eastern Siberia, the Okhotsk and Kamchatka departments, and three new provinces, Transbaikalia, Amur, and the Maritime. The geographical designation "Siberia" also included then what is now known as the Far East.

In the eighteenth century, Siberia was becoming a mining country, with three main mining regions: the eastern Urals, the Altai, and Nerchinsk in Transbaikalia. Copper, lead, and silver were produced as well as iron ores. The first gold strikes were made in Eastern Siberia, and within fifty years there were 207 gold workings.

A number of trading companies were formed, many of which quickly prospered as Siberia became a trade route between Europe and Asia.

Along with the economic and industrial growth, the population was increasing. In 1727 there were 169,868 males (women and children were not included in the census), in 1763 this grew to 306,246; in 1833 to 826,080; and in 1850 to 918,355. Altogether, counting women, children, and the "natives," the population of Siberia in 1850 stood at 2,174,000—about 2,000,000 of them Russians. This growth was due primarily to the enforced migration of peasants from the poorer regions of Russia (those who were serfs of the state, and not of private landlords) and of runaway serfs from the private estates. Although, officially, serfdom was not legal in Siberia, the workers in the mines and the peasants working on church lands were often permanently assigned to their places. But this practice never took deep root in Siberia.

The fact that there was no serfdom in Siberia, and the policy of the Tsar's government of sending political exiles to Siberia as well as common criminals, played a very important part in the further development of the Siberian character. They were becoming an independent, strong breed of people. Many of those peasants who stayed and adapted to the conditions became prosperous by European Russia's standards, forming a class of so-called *kulaks,* small-time landowners who started to hire workers to work their fields.

Revolutionary outbreaks, even though sporadic and unorganized, were becoming more and more common in Siberia. The government mining centers were especially affected. There were serious disturbances in 1833, 1837, 1840, and 1842, but they were all crushed fairly easily. However, this situation worried the government which now attempted to dilute the "hard-core" Russian Siberians with masses of inert "unspoiled" peasants from Russia.

By this time, because of the orgy of extermination of fur-bearing animals, the fur trade was becoming less and less important, and the Russian authorities were losing all interest in the welfare of the native tribes. In 1822 a new law was promulgated by which the native Siberians were divided into two categories. Those who were settled acquired equal rights with the Russians, but those who still led a nomadic life were turned over to local chieftains and left more or less to their tender mercies; they had no recourse to law. Left to themselves and isolated from the rest of the population, the far northern tribes were dying out from disease, hunger, utter neglect, and brutal exploitation by their own tribal aristocracy, which acted as government deputies and were a law unto themselves.

Meanwhile a whole succession of talented and courageous explorers kept studying Siberia. The Arctic Ocean seaboard was charted and mapped, and such names as Bering, Laptev, Chelyuskin, Nevelsky, Krusenstern, Wrangell, and many others left their mark on the geography of Siberia.

Toward the end of the nineteenth century, mining in the Altai regions greatly declined, while gold mining was developing in Transbaikalia and the Irkutsk and Amur Provinces. Toward the end of the nineteenth century, Siberia produced seventy-five precent of all the gold mined in Russia, and some coal mining was developing as well in the Kuznetsk Basin and near Irkutsk. However, the economic development of Siberia was badly hampered by the huge distances and the lack of communication. This was what prompted the government to start building the Trans-Siberian Railway.

This railroad was begun in 1891 and was completed in 1905, and it was a brilliant engineering feat of the era. It was a single-track line running for some 4,650 miles, laid over some of the most difficult terrain in the world. It marked a new page in the economic development of Siberia, but led to political events which all but overthrew the Tsar's government.

Since the building of this railroad involved reaching not only Vladivostok through Manchuria but also two ports leased from China, Port Arthur and Dairen, it led to conflict with Japan. On January 25, 1904, Japan attacked Russia without a declaration of war and laid siege to Port Arthur. Russia mobilized a huge army, but because its only line of supply ran for 5,000 miles, over a one-track railway which was constantly under repair, and because of the inherent inefficiency and corruption of the Tsarist government, the war was won by Japan, and Russia lost half of the Sakhalin island, the Kuriles, and more important, its dream of obtaining an ice-free outlet to the Pacific through the two Chinese ports.

This humiliating defeat at the hands of a small Asian nation, coupled with the general decay of the Tsarist power and sharp economic crisis, led to a powerful revolutionary movement that gripped the whole of Russia, as well as Siberia, which had borne the brunt of the costly and unsuccessful war. The first all-Siberia political strike paralyzed the industry of Siberia and the railway, and in two cities, Krasnoyarsk and Chita, there were armed rebellions with the participation of the army. The Krasnoyarsk and Chita "Republics" were proclaimed. There were also peasant uprisings in most of the southern regions of Siberia.

The Tsarist government acted with determination and ferocity. Two large punitive expeditions, led by Generals Meller-Zakamelsky and Rennenkampf, were sent to Siberia and succeeded in crushing the rebellion. In 1906, the "Chita Republic" was crushed, but Siberia continued to seethe with revolt for several years longer, with some of the native peoples, notably the Buryats and the Yakuts, taking an active part.

It was then that the Tsar's government decided to send masses of peasant migrants to Siberia to neutralize the old-time Siberians and native tribes. In three years alone, from 1907 to 1910, no less than 2,516,075 new migrants arrived in Siberia. Most of these newcomers proved to be the wrong people for the hard Siberian conditions, and as many as 36 percent of the migrants of 1910, and fully 60 percent of those who went to Siberia in 1911, eventually migrated back to Russia. However, this mass population movement played an important part in the development of Siberia, especially agriculturally, and by 1910 Siberia became not only self-sufficient agriculturally, but produced a considerable export surplus.

Industrial development, however, was lagging. The census of 1908 listed 1,049 small industrial establishments in Siberia which amounted to only 3.5 percent of the entire Russian industrial production. The richest potential industrial regions were not even touched, and it seems that foreign capital was more conscious of the Siberian potential in this respect than the St. Petersburg government.

Much of the industry and trade were foreign-controlled. The International Harvester Co. of Russia, an American firm, had a near-monopoly in that field, and all large gold-mining companies were foreign-financed. Out of the entire gold-mining investments in Siberia, which amounted to 35,850,000 rubles, only 4,500,000 rubles were subscribed in Russia. England contributed 26,350,000 rubles, and the rest represented French, Belgian, and German investments. The Russian government continued to treat Siberia as a wasteland usable only as a dumping place for undesirables. In the Tsarist government's eyes it was an unprofitable and bothersome collection of dangerously unstable, potential troublemakers.

In 1912 Siberia almost succeeded in starting another revolution. Six thousand workers of the Lena gold fields went on strike, and the government, remembering the events of 1906–1907, acted with utmost brutality. Troops were sent in to break the strike and on April 4, 1912, several hundred workers were killed or wounded when the troops were ordered to open fire. The news of the Lena massacre caused a new revolutionary wave all over Russia, particularly in Siberia, where mass strikes were called in all the industrial regions.

The outbreak of war with Germany and Austria in 1914 served as a safety valve, giving the government a short reprieve: in the wave of patriotism, internal problems were temporarily forgotten. Several hundred thousand Siberians were mobilized into the army, and Siberian riflemen, as they were called, proved to be among the best Russian troops, and several times saved the Tsar's armies from the threat of disaster. (Later they were to play a very important part in the defense of Moscow in 1941.)

The February revolution of 1917, and then the October revolution that followed, found immediate and strong echoes all across Siberia, but due to a combination of historical factors, Siberia was used by the counterrevolutionary forces as the main springboard for their attack against the new Soviet state.

The October revolution, despite its name, took place in Petrograd (now Leningrad) on November 7, 1917. (This discrepancy of dates is explained by the fact that, at that time, Russia used a Julian church calendar which was thirteen days behind the Gregorian calendar: the date in Russia was October 25.)

The Soviet rule spread quickly all over the country despite some local opposition. It reached Siberia: on October 29, the union of the Siberian Soviets (councils of workers, peasants, and soldiers) in Irkutsk declared its loyalty to the new revolution. On November 10, Soviet rule was proclaimed in Krasnoyarsk, and shortly thereafter in Omsk, Yeniseisk, and Vladivostok; Tomsk, Novosibirsk (then Novonikolayevsk), and Khabarovsk followed in December; and in January 1918, Verkhneudinsk (now Ulan-Ude), Semipalatinsk, Blagoveshchensk, and Petropavlovsk followed suit. There were local clashes with anti-Communist forces in all those places, but by the middle of February Soviet rule had spread all across Siberia.

Since one of the declared aims of the Communist government was the immediate termination of the war, the governments allied with Russia in the war, England, France, and the United States, were greatly disturbed, and they decided to use the local anti-Communist forces in Russia to block the Communists, overthrow the new Soviet government, and rebuild the Russian front against Germany and Austria. Since all these countries were heavily engaged, they could not spare any considerable forces for this project. But Japan, who was also nominally in the war, had troops available, and so it was decided that Siberia was to become the springboard for the intervention.

Accordingly the Japanese troops landed in Vladivostok on April 5, 1918, and they were followed by detachments of American, French, Italian, and token English forces. It was agreed that the Japanese and the Americans were to carry the brunt of the operation in Siberia.

It was expected that this intervention would cause the rise of counterrevolutionary forces in Siberia, where the local middle class, and the more prosperous peasantry and the Cossacks had already demonstrated their anti-Soviet sentiments.

The interventionists also had an ace in the hole—the Russian admiral Alexander V. Kolchak who was to head this movement.

Kolchak, who was born in 1873, was the youngest admiral of the Tsar's navy and a brilliant naval commander. His last command was the Black Sea fleet, but he was expelled from this post by mutinous sailors. Then the Kerensky government dispatched him to the United States as the head of a military naval mission, and the October revolution caught him there. It is believed that the entire plan of the intervention through Siberia was proposed by him to the Allies.

For a while, however, no open rebellion against the Soviets materialized in Siberia, but then on May 25, 1918, every key point on the Trans-Siberian railway was seized by troops of the Czechoslovak Corps which were spread across Siberia in eighty-odd echelons. This was a highly disciplined body of perhaps 40,000 men—former prisoners-of-war who had volunteered to fight against Austria with the Russians. They were on their way to Vladivostok. From there they were supposed to be shipped to France to continue the war. They were given permission to leave Russia by the Soviet government, but they were now technically under French command.

It is almost certain that the signal for this rebellion was given by the Allies, and that the soldiers were told that the Soviets were preparing to disarm and intern them as part of their peace treaty with Germany.

They were immediately joined by local Russian counter-revolutionary forces and by June the Soviet rule was overthrown from the Urals to Vladivostok. The Provisional Siberian Government was formed in June in Omsk, and another body, the so-called Ufa Directorate, was set up in Ufa. Both these bodies included moderate socialists. The Siberian Government, in addition, entertained some separatist intentions of setting up an independent Siberian state.*

Kolchak is believed to have advised the Allies that for inter-

* In fact the Siberian flag was designed—the white and blue: "the snow covering the forests."

vention to succeed it was necessary to do away with separatism
or even nominal socialism. He argued that since Kerensky was
not accepted by the Russian people, would another socialist
government be accepted? No, he said, it was necessary to appeal
to the elements sympathetic to the Tsar's regime. Unfortunately
for the Allies, they accepted this argument, and Kolchak was
brought to Omsk in the private car of the head of the British
military Mission, General Knox. Kolchak was more or less forced
upon the Siberian Government by the Allies as the War Minister in charge of organizing and leading the "Siberian army"
from Siberia against Russia.

On November 18, 1918, Kolchak staged a military coup
d'état, disbanded the Siberian government, and proclaimed himself "the Supreme Ruler and the Commander-in-Chief of all
the Armed Forces of Russia," with the tacit help of the Allies,
who were now in virtual control of Siberia. He was a convinced
and dedicated monarchist, and he miscalculated the mood of
some of his original supporters among the peasant classes and
the Cossacks. Few of them had any sympathies with the defunct
Tsarist regime, even though they might originally have been
hostile to the Soviets. Mistakenly Kolchak attempted to crush
all opposition with force, and proceeded to reestablish the old
Tsarist institutions.

Supported by military and financial help from the Allies—in
exchange for raw goods shipped out from Siberia by them as
well as promises of future concessions there—and assisted by the
Czech troops who were led to believe that by fighting the Soviets
they were helping the Allied cause against the German-Austrian
coalition, Kolchak was successful in creating a well-equipped
army of some 300,000 troops. He invaded European Russia, eventually reaching the Volga and directly threatening Moscow. For
a while it looked as though the young Soviet state, assaulted by
the "white" armies from the south, east, and north, would not be
able to survive. But a near-miracle was beginning to take shape.
The Communist party of Russia, led by Lenin, succeeded in
rallying the people at the most critical time.

The "whites" in Russia, and their foreign Allies, completely
misunderstood the social forces which had been released by the
revolution—the forces which Lenin understood with phenom-

enal clarity. Besides, the presence of foreign troops was especially damaging to the "white" cause; the Russians always united in the face of foreign intervention.

More, Kolchak and his supporters did not realize the extent of the latent revolutionary spirit of the Siberians. As the new Soviets were crushed, the leaders fled into the taiga. There they built guerilla detachments. Within one year in Western Siberia alone over 40,000 well-armed, well-trained men were making havoc of the "white" armies' communications—and the more repressive measures that were applied, the more this guerilla force grew.

Kolchak's armies, after almost achieving their goal of a break-through into the central regions of European Russia, were defeated and pushed back to the Urals. At this point, Germany was defeated and out of the war whereupon the Czechoslovaks, the backbone of the "white" cause in Siberia, refused to fight any longer. All they wanted to do was to go home and start rebuilding their liberated homeland.

This was the beginning of the end. Kolchak's armies started to fall apart, and the Red armies poured over the Urals. Rebellions flared up all over Siberia, and Kolchak, abandoning his troops, tried to escape in a Czech troop train which carried the entire gold reserve held by his government, gold pledged to foreign powers in exchange for their help. He reached Irkutsk, which was already in the hands of the local Soviet rebels. The Czech troop train was stopped, and the Czechs were ordered to deliver the gold—and Kolchak. The admiral's free passage was guaranteed by the Allied command in Siberia, but the Czechs refused to fight and their commanders had to comply with the local Soviet's request. They left Kolchak, his prime minister Pepeliaev, and the gold, and were then allowed to proceed east.

Kolchak was shot by the Soviet soldiers.

The "white cause" was now lost. The Red armies poured into Transbaikalia, and the local *ataman*, Semenov, was defeated. One of Semenov's henchmen, Ungern von Sternberg, was a man possessed by a maniacal dream of recreating the Mongolian Empire of Ghengis Khan from India to Vienna. He retreated into

Mongolia, and he rallied the Mongols around him and drove the Chinese out of the area.

(This very little-known episode is worth recounting briefly. Ungern, a Baltic German baron by birth, was a converted Buddhist and a perverted "idealist." He was also an accomplished sadist, and his savagery knew no bounds—in this he tried to match his idol, Ghengis Khan. For a while it looked as though he would be able to perform a tremendous historical coup. After clearing all of the much-hated local Chinese from Mongolia, he married an obscure princess of the long-since-defunct Chinese imperial house and declared himself the heir to the Chinese throne, and the living Buddha. For a while the Red armies, busy cleaning up the remnants of the "white" armies in the Far East, left Ungern alone, and if it had not been for his inhuman cruelty, he might have consolidated his position. But his savagery appalled even his closest Mongol followers, and when, after completing the Far Eastern campaign, the Red armies went after him, his Mongol troops mutinied, overpowered him, tied him up, and left him in the desert to be picked up by the Red soldiers. He was later shot for his crimes. Mongolia never went back to China—it became an independent Soviet-type People's Republic. So in point of historical fact, Mongolia owes its independence to a Baltic German baron possessed with a mad dream of turning back the clock of history seven centuries.)

After the end of World War I, the Allies tried to intensify their armed intervention in Russia, but found that their troops were in no mood to fight. There was an open mutiny in the French fleet sent into the Black Sea. To protect their men from "Communist contamination," the Allied commands started hastily evacuating their troops from Russia. The American and other European troops were evacuated from Siberia, but the Japanese stayed: they had their own designs here.

To prevent an open clash with Japan, the Soviet government formed a nominally-independent Far Eastern Republic with its "capital" in Vladivostok. But while the regular red armies "respected" the borders of the new "republic," the Communist guerillas had no such scruples. They continued to operate and in two battles at Valochaievsk in August, 1922, and at Spassk in October, 1922, they defeated the remnants of the "white" troops taking cover in the new "republic" and their Japanese allies. The city of Nikolayevsk-on-Amur was seized by a detachment of an anarchistic adventurer Triapitzin, and the Japanese garrison there and much of the civilian population were exterminated. (Later the Soviet authorities shot Triapitzin for his criminal excesses.) Now the Japanese government realized that their position in Siberia was becoming untenable: they were faced with a large-scale war for which they were not ready, and they hastily evacuated their troops. On October 25, 1928 the regular Soviet troops entered Vladivostok.

The civil war in Siberia left much of the country shattered and economically prostrate. The Soviet state, still continuing the civil war on many fronts in European Russia, now faced a truly gigantic job of reconstruction in the huge, underdeveloped land of Siberia which never in its age-long history had known anything but chaos and utter neglect. After forty centuries of uninterrupted sleep, "the Sleeping Land" was finally to be awakened.

4.

God's Unfinished Work

CROSSING the beautiful and highly industrialized Ural mountain chain (the word *ural* means "belt" in the Tartar language), one enters the so-called West Siberian geological platform, one of the largest and flattest depressions on earth, the gateway into Siberia. It stretches from the Arctic Ocean down to the northern Kazakhstan for some 1,300 miles, and from the Urals to the Yenisei River for almost 1,000 miles.

This immense plain, its land area some 800,000 square miles, three times as large as Texas, is drained by the Irtysh and Ob Rivers and their numerous tributaries, all running toward the Arctic Ocean. It is drained very unevenly: while the southern steppes have seasonal droughts, the largest part of the area suffers from an excess of water, especially toward the north where huge areas are hardly drained at all. Frozen during winters, they turn into endless marshlands during each short summer. The water, resting upon the permanently frozen subsoil, has nowhere to run and fills all the depressions in the ground and forms innumerable little marshy and slimy lakes, many of them salty and devoid of any aquatic life, which stagnate there until frozen again, year after year.

It is hard to believe that water—just water!—can become a plague, but it is certainly a plague here. Monstrous spring floods of slow meandering rivers cover enormous areas of lifeless plain, receding very slowly and leaving countless slimy pools of muddy water.

The annual precipitation, which may reach twenty inches

here, replenishes the water lost by evaporation during the short summer in the areas not reached by the floods, and so the land never dries—a condition that has persisted here for millions of years. The few settlements here are located along the banks of the rivers while the rest of the huge area is marked on physical maps by a single chilling word, "swamp."

It is desolate and it is a lonely place. The Mongols during their sweep across Siberia had never reached this far north, and when it came under Russian domination almost 400 years ago, it was largely left untouched by the Russians. They built a few trading settlements along the rivers, leaving the rest of the inhospitable land to the mosquitoes and to the few nomadic tribesmen who herded reindeer, hunted sable and blue fox, and were slowly dying of hunger, disease, and neglect.

It is this part of Siberia—the Great Wet Northwest which old Siberians called *Bozhia nedodelka,* or "God's unfinished work," because here the Creator failed to separate the earth from the water—something that he was supposed to have done on the third day of his memorable work-week.

While the southern areas of the great West Siberian plain have been known since Tsarist times to contain some very important natural resources, the Wet Northwest had been thought to be absolutely worthless from any economic or political standpoint. Even though towards the south the marshy tundra gave way to the forested taiga, the lack of all communications made exploitation of timber resources difficult and unprofitable. No useful mineral deposits of any kind were expected to lie under these endless frozen marshlands. And even if they were there, how could they be found and brought out? So it was considered totally unsuitable for colonization.

It is a cold country, too. It remains frozen from 200 to 270 days each year, but the few brave souls living there dread the coming of the spring, because the land becomes an impassable mosquito-infested quagmire. It is easily the most bleak and cheerless part of Siberia. "God's unfinished work" indeed.

The entire West Siberian depression lies between 75° and 50° North latitude, or roughly, its southern rim almost reaches the United States-Canada border and its northern extremity stretches up to the northernmost point of Alaska.

Though Western Siberia is the most settled part of the country—its present population estimated at about 12,200,000—this population is found almost entirely in the southern regions along or below the Trans-Siberian Railway running through Chelyabinsk—Kurgan—Omsk—Novosibirsk—Tomsk—Krasnoyarsk. Fully 90 percent of all Western Siberians live and work there. The only sizeable city lying to the north of this line is the provincial capital of Tyumen which grew during Soviet times from the sleepy town of perhaps 20,000 people to an industrial center of 256,000 hardy souls, and a much smaller, ancient town of Tobolsk farther north. Still farther north, the country is a virtual frozen wilderness and its entire population is probably less than 350,000, spread thinly along the Ob River and its tributaries. The largest of the tributaries is the Irtysh River, rising in the mountains of the Mongolian Altai (in China) and falling into the Ob near the town of Khanty-Mansisk, the capital of the Khanty-Mansi National District, in the very heart of the northern swamp. It is the only "highway" connecting southwestern Siberia with the Great Wet Northwest.

Many Siberians consider Tobolsk the most beautiful and charming old town of Siberia. Founded in 1587, it is the second oldest Russian town east of the Urals (Tyumen was founded one year earlier), and it has retained its early Siberian, almost feudal character. Situated on a high shore of the Irtysh River near the place where its large tributary, the Tobol, joins it, Tobolsk is the only town in Siberia that has the traditional Russian Kremlin (*kreml* in Russian: literary, "citadel"). It is a beautiful ensemble of delicate lace-like architecture including walls, battlements, guard towers, cathedrals, monasteries, bishops' residences, treasury—all the trappings of a traditional Russian stronghold. Tobolsk was for many years the capital of Siberia. Many of these charming old buildings had fallen into disrepair, but they are being restored at present to all their pristine splendor.

Near the Tobolsk Kremlin there stands a high obelisk monument dedicated to "Ermak, the Conqueror of Siberia" with the date of his first arrival here in 1581, and the date of his death, 1584. It is here that he is supposed to have perished, attempting to swim across the Irtysh wearing his coat of mail which proved to be his undoing. It was also near here that the Siberian Khan Kuchum had his capital called Kashlyk, or Sib-ir, which gave its name to the entire immense country. Nothing remains of this Tartar stronghold, and the very hill upon which it was supposed to have stood has been washed away by the turbulent Irtysh long ago.

Tobolsk knew its days of glory, but also many years of almost total oblivion since the Trans-Siberian Railway, which opened the doors into Siberia at the turn of the century, passed it by and left it sitting in the taiga as almost a museum reminder of early Siberian history: a picturesque little town rich in tradition, but poor in almost anything else, the gateway into the huge northwest of Siberia which no one, it seemed, wanted to enter.

Tobolsk is the home of the earliest Russian colonists, the voluntary and involuntary exiles, "seekers after truth," and "old believers" (the members of the Orthodox sect who refused to accept the church reformation and chose persecution instead). They were sturdy, sober, God-fearing folk. It was also a land of self-styled "monks" and "holy men," "spirit-wrestlers," *khlysty* or "flagellants," who practiced their weird rites in the taiga where they were reasonably safe from the Tsar's priests and policemen. The infamous Gregori Rasputin came from here to play his tragic and unsavory part in the last years of the Romanovs' empire, and it was also here that the mysterious hermit, one "Fedor Kuzmich," created a legend and a historical riddle that still remains unsolved. Was he in fact the Tsar, Alexander I, who quit the throne to spend forty years in meditation and prayer in the Siberian wilderness? Even today many historians are inclined to believe so.

Alexander I, the conqueror of Napoleon, was a man given to mysticism, and he often spoke to his closest associates about his desire to retire from the throne and spend his life in solitude and prayer. In 1825 he traveled to the small Azov Sea town of Taganrog accompanied only by a few of his closest associates. A few days later, the news of his sudden death reached the capital. His body was brought back in a sealed coffin, in accordance with his dying wish, and rested in the St. Petersburg Kazan Cathedral for seven days. It was opened only once, at night, so that the body could be viewed by his mother who noted in her diary her son's unusual appearance in the coffin. No one else was permitted to view it, and this breach of tradition gave rise to the rumors that the body in the sealed coffin was not that of the late Tsar, but of someone else.

Much later, historians discovered that the day before the Tsar's death, one of his servants, a gamewarden by the name of Maskov, who had a striking physical resemblance to the Tsar, had died in Taganrog and was presumably buried there. However, his grave has never been found.

One year later, a new "holy man" appeared among the Russian colonists in the Tobolsk region. He called himself "Fedor Kuzmich." By all accounts he was a very unusual "holy man." He was tall, had distinctly military bearing, and despite his beard, somewhat resembled the dead Tsar. According to some political exiles who met him, he spoke several foreign languages fluently and showed an intimate knowledge of St. Petersburg society. He did not deny that his origin was unusual, and he promised to reveal his true identity in the notes which he would leave after his death. He died in 1865, and some cryptic notes were found in his cell. They still exist but no one has ever been able to decipher them. So the identity of "Fedor Kuzmich" is still a mystery.

There is only one portrait of him, drawn by some unknown Siberian artist. It shows a tall, erect, dignified man with the traditional white beard, but it provides no definite clue as to the hermit's identity.

It is interesting to note that Alexander's brother, Nicholas I, who succeeded him to the throne, discouraged all attempts to investigate the identity of the mysterious Siberian recluse, and, in fact, serious investigation of this fascinating mystery was started only after the revolution. In 1923, a Russian historian, K. Kudryashov, advanced the theory that "Fedor Kuzmich" was not the late Tsar, but one of his courtiers, Count Fedor Uvarov, who disappeared after Alexander's death. Kudryashov based his theory on the graphological study of the notes left by "Fedor Kuzmich," but up to this day the identity of the mysterious Siberian hermit remains a moot question and cryptographers are still trying to decipher the notes.

The only known portrait of the mysterious Siberian recluse known as "Fedor Kuzmich," believed by many to be the Russian Tsar Alexander I, who died under mysterious circumstances in 1825. He left notes (see next page) which he said would disclose his true identity. These notes have never been deciphered.

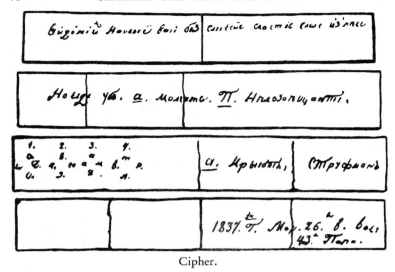

Cipher.

The story of "Fedor Kuzmich" serves as an illustration of the atmosphere of this part of the country until very recently—the mystic aura of old Holy Russia.

Now it is becoming more and more apparent that this bleak, frozen land holds the magic key to the further economic development of not only Siberia, but of the entire Soviet Union—and, perhaps, of the rest of the world.

It is still a bleak land. This is how a Soviet writer, A. Nikitin, describes it:

"Last autumn I went for a trip to the north into the land of swamps of the West Siberian plain. It is difficult for anyone living in normal surroundings even to imagine the sad grandeur of this immense land ... Under the high pale-blue sky there stretches an endless silvery moss-covered plain ... Occasional twisted birches of prehistoric appearance ... Lazy bloated rivers, small round lakes ... A rare sandy elevation, a stretch of the taiga, and then swamps again stretching in all directions ... And yet this desolate land now attracts the eyes of not only Siberia, but of the entire world."

Why?

Nikitin explains: "It so happens that this whole immense plain is one huge reservoir of high-grade oil and natural gas. The reserves here are calculated in billions of tons and trillions of cubic meters. The productivity of already existing wells is enormous. . . . Geologists also tell us that there is iron ore here, also in billions of tons. And that this whole bleak, frozen-to-the-bone land is resting on a virtual ocean of hot water!"

The discovery of oil in Siberia rates as the most important economic development in that country's recent history. Few people outside Siberia are fully familiar with this latest discovery in the long list of Siberian discoveries, and few people even in Siberia realize the magnitude and the far-reaching significance of this event for the future of their country. And no wonder: even as this is written, the Siberian geologists are still uncertain of the exact potential of this find. It is possible, just possible, that the Wet Northwest strike might be the largest in the entire history of oil and natural gas discoveries anywhere on earth. The figures are revised almost daily—and always upward.

To illustrate this situation: when natural gas was first discovered in the Berezovo district of the Siberian far northwest, the deposits there were optimistically estimated to contain 2½ trillion (a trillion is 1 followed by twelve zeros) cubic meters. (A cubic meter is 1.308 cubic yards.)

That was in 1961. Since then over 4 trillion cubic meters have been brought out, and the fields show not the slightest sign of depletion—on the contrary, many new deposits have been discovered. The longest pipeline in the world, running all the way across the Urals to Moscow and Leningrad for a distance of 2,600 miles, is now in operation.

The story of Siberia's oil is both spectacular and dramatic. Only ten years ago, the only oil in Siberia was that produced in very modest quantities on the northern tip of Sakhalin island off the Pacific coast of the country. This production was completely insufficient for the needs of swiftly developing Siberian industries, and some new oil sources had to be found if the industrialization of the country was not to be badly hampered.

In the war years of 1941–1945, when many heavy industrial plants were evacuated into Western Siberia to prevent their falling into German hands, the lack of local oil proved to be a severe handicap: while most other raw materials were found locally, oil, the lifeblood of modern industry, had to be brought in from across the Urals.

This situation had to be changed if Siberia was to be industrialized, and a large-scale search for Siberian oil started after
the end of the war. It was not a blind search. In 1932, the famous
Soviet geologist, Ivan Gubkin, studying the geological formation
of the Ural mountain chain, had expressed his belief that there
was oil in the Siberian northwest, but he could not pinpoint any
exact location. Oil slicks had been found in the rivers of Western
Siberia, especially near the Arctic Ocean, but that was a very
vague indication. Oil could be anywhere in the immense and
almost completely inaccessible territory; it was like looking for
a penny dropped into a grain elevator.

Prospecting for oil is infinitely more difficult and costly than
prospecting for any other geological deposit—it requires heavy
equipment. For almost ten years the geologists fought a terrible
battle in the marshy frozen wilderness, in an area without any
roads, and on ground where men often sank to their waists in
slimy ooze. Never in the history of geological research had nature
resisted so bitterly, so savagely; never had a task called for such
superhuman endurance, determination, and stubbornness.

And yet for over ten years it appeared that the entire colossal
expenditure of effort and money would be a dead loss. If it had
not been for the dogged perseverance of two men, the Siberian
oil might have not been found at all. These men were academician A. Trofimuk, the director of the Institute of Geology and
Geophysics of the Siberian Academy of Science, and Yuri G.
Ervye, the director of the Tyumen-Tomsk Geological Management. They staked their careers and reputations on "God's unfinished work," and they won. The first West Siberian gusher
came roaring in on June 22, 1960, near the desolate tundra
village of Shaim.

As often happens, when victory came, it came in with such
a bang that almost overnight the entire economic picture of
Siberia, and the entire Soviet Union, was drastically changed.
Within three years, oil and natural gas had been found not only
in the northwest, but all across Siberia—along the Ob River,
the Yenisei, the Lena, beyond the Arctic Circle, in Yakutia,
north of Irkutsk, and near the Siberian "capital," Novosibirsk.
But the Wet Northwest strike still remains probably the greatest
single oil strike in the entire history of geology.

How much oil is there in Siberia?

The Soviet journalist, A. Dorogin, who has followed the oil search there from its very inception, wrote two years ago:

Answering this question the Soviet newspapers often use a term which, though not strictly scientific, might be accurate in the description of the Siberian oil strike—"an ocean."

Is this an exaggeration?

Let's look at facts and figures. So far large oil fields have been discovered in the Tyumen and Tomsk provinces. In the Tyumen province, up to January 1, 1967, there had been found 35 oil and 28 natural gas fields. So far some 5,000,000 tons of oil have been brought out. In 1967, this will grow to 6,000,000 tons. New wells are being drilled all around Surgut, Igrim, Berezovo, Nefteyugansk, Urey, and many other places.

The first gusher in the Tomsk province came in during 1962, producing 500 tons daily—this is enough to fill an entire oil tank train! Recently they have announced the discovery of the thirteenth oil field there. The remarkable fact is that this new oil field was found not in the far north, but in the center of the province, less than 250 miles from the important industrial regions of Western Siberia, which had been gasping for oil for years.

And what about further east? Could it be possible that the eastern rim of the Siberian "oil ocean" rests under the Sakhalin island where they have been pumping oil for years? There is much evidence to support this theory. The recently found oil in the Irkutsk province, 1500 miles east of the Tomsk oil fields, has the same chemical characteristics as the Tomsk oil. Both are so pure that they can be used in Diesel engines without refining. . . . Yes, there are positive signs that all of Siberia from the Urals to the Sakhalin rests on a virtual oil sea. The already discovered deposits of natural gas are incredibly gigantic as well. Of course, bringing up the Siberian oil and gas is not an easy task. Most of the Siberian oil and gas fields are located in nearly inaccessible regions, in the trackless marshy taiga and tundra . . .

This was written just two years ago. Changes have occurred since then. The "one ocean" theory has been practically confirmed, and much of the Siberian oil and gas was found so close to the surface that, despite the incredible technical difficulties of bringing it out in the trackless wilderness, Siberian oil and gas are today the cheapest in the world to produce.

Many remarkable things have happened in Siberia within the

last fifteen years. Immense deposits of anthracite and brown coal have been found, gold and diamonds galore, iron ore in countless billions of tons, as well as every metal and mineral known to exist on earth, and yet the discovery of the Siberian oil, and the magnitude of this discovery, obscures everything else.

The celebrated academician A. Trofimuk, the expert on the geological resources of Siberia, has recently declared, after evaluating all the available facts and figures:

"I believe that the time is ripe to come to a far-reaching conclusion: the main factors which will dominate the entire development of Siberia and the Far East, their entire economy, will be oil and natural gas. The center of the oil industry of the country, and the world, will inevitably move here, and all science and industry of Siberia will be organically connected with the production of oil and petroleum products, their manufacture and transport."

Another expert, Y. Ervye, personally responsible for the development of the oil and gas resources in Tyumen and Tomsk provinces, calls the Northwest strike "unique," not only because of the quantity and quality of oil, but because here oil and natural gas are often found side by side and because the deposits follow such an accurate geological pattern that this practically eliminates the usual "dry hole" waste.

"We are conducting our oil and gas development with almost absolutely accurate geological prognostic approach: new wells come in whenever they are drilled—as a rule we hit our aim now with the first shot."

The Siberian oil will not put other oil producers out of business in any near future. The difficulties are still here, and they are enormous: there are no roads, nature is savage, heavy machinery sinks in the swamps, and oil rigs must be flown in by giant freight helicopters. But even today the rate of development of oil and gas production is formidable. The present production figures are impressive, but the plan, as presented recently by another celebrated Siberian oil expert, Victor Muravlenko, is truly breathtaking. If today's production may be close to 10,-000,000 tons annually, it will rise to 80,000,000 by 1975, and to 200,000,000 tons by 1980. From then on it will keep rising more spectacularly because the now inaccessible wilderness will then be connected to the rest of the country by railroads and an extensive network of pipelines. It will no longer be a wilderness, but one of the most developed oil-producing areas anywhere in the world.

This work is already going on.

Today the once-deserted frozen swampland is humming with activity. Hundreds of new wells are being drilled. At night the tundra is illuminated by the flashes of acetylene torches along the gigantic pipeline being laid across the taiga from Ust-Balyk, near Surgut, to Omsk, 400 miles as the polar owl flies. The brand-new railway has already connected the "museum" town of Tobolsk with the provincial capital of Tyumen, some 120 miles away, and eventually it will reach Surgut, in the middle of the new oil empire, 300 miles further north. It traverses some of the most difficult terrain ever tackled by railway builders anywhere. From here it will branch out toward Berezovo, the natural gas center, and north along the Ob River to Salekhard, the capital of the Yamal-Nenets National Region, which is already connected with the heartland of Russia by the northernmost railway in Siberia, skirting the Urals on the far north.

Surgut will also become the western terminus of the Northern Trans-Siberian Railway which will cut across northern Siberia all the way to the Pacific Ocean, opening immense new areas which can now be reached only by air or by the rivers. And the Siberian oil will pay for all this—and bring huge profits to the state on top of it. This is why the importance of the Northwest oil strike in the development of the "Siberian miracle" cannot be overestimated.

All the expense involved in the ten-year, incredibly difficult oil search has been fully repaid. The Siberian oil operation is already "in the black."

It is changing the entire face of the bleak land as well. Thousands of eager young men and women are working in the swamps where few humans have ever stepped before. And this is only the beginning.

Such outlandish-sounding names as Tobolsk, Surgut, Ust-Balyk, Berezovo, Salekhard, and many others will in time become as familiar to the world as Houston, Caracas, and Kuwait. The ambitious plans for finishing "God's unfinished work" are

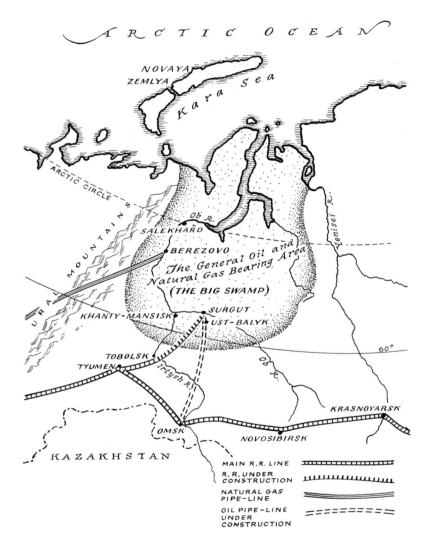

The great West Siberian oil and natural gas field.

well underway. Large areas of swamps will be drained, new roads laid, new towns built. The subterranean hot water may be brought up to heat the towns. New industries will rise, because the Northwest has been found to contain other resources besides oil and natural gas, and geological prospecting goes on incessantly.

Large-scale fish canning and seal hunting just wait to be developed. Once drained, the land will not be the horrible place people think it is. The climate is severe, but it is milder than, for instance, in Yakutia, and the fuel reserves are practically inexhaustible. Even agriculture can be developed—tomatoes and other vegetables are grown as far north as Salekhard. Eventually, thousands of acres of land will be turned into hothouses heated by natural gas and underground hot water.

The picturesque little town of Tobolsk, the gateway to the new oil empire, has suddenly become the focal point of the Siberian development, and even though this is bound to destroy some of its antique charm, other benefits will far outweigh this loss. A modern city will rise around its ancient Kremlin which is being lovingly restored today.

Gigantic oil refineries are about to be constructed here, even though there is a bitter rivalry between Tobolsk and Tyumen, which claims the honor of becoming the oil center of Siberia. But in all probability Tobolsk will win. It is the nearest town to the Northwest oil and gas fields and it can be developed into a larger river port, while Tyumen is located on the Tura River which becomes shallow during the summer. River transportation is still the best and cheapest way of moving great masses of freight in Siberia, as it has been for centuries.

At present the largest oil-refining and cracking plants are located in Omsk, the bustling industrial city of some 850,000 people, the second largest city of Siberia after Novosibirsk. At present, Siberian oil is delivered from Shaim, the place of the first oil strike in Siberia, to Tyumen, by a brand-new pipeline, and from there in river oil tankers along the Tura, Tobol, and Irtysh to Omsk in summer and by tank railway cars in winter— a difficult and costly way. But this will change shortly. The new pipeline, Ust-Balyk—Omsk, will send the Siberian oil pouring in a steady stream from the northern wilderness straight to the

Omsk refineries, and when the Tobolsk or Tyumen refineries are completed, the price of Siberian oil, even now the cheapest in the world, will again come down drastically.

All this will take time, but these days time has a different meaning in Siberia than anywhere else. Not a single map or statistical chart in existence today gives a completely accurate picture of the Siberian industrial explosion: they are out of date practically by the time they are printed.

"This is nothing" is the usual refrain of the Siberians, speaking about their country. "Come back in five years, and you will see something really interesting!" "Today is already our yesterday" is another popular maxim one hears constantly in Siberia.

With the discovery of Siberian oil in the Wet Northwest, the last remaining raw material problem standing in the way of large-scale industrialization of Siberia has been solved. For the

An oil-cracking plant in Omsk. Siberia is becoming an oil empire.

first time in history Siberia is fully independent economically in all respects; it can proceed to build a new society and a new life without turning to anyone for anything, and fully paying its way into the future.

This new life has already arrived for those small obscure native tribes who had been eking out their miserable livelihood from the frozen, marshy tundra since the dawn of history, and who were described as "dying out" in the prerevolutionary Russian encyclopedias and travel books. They will be, of course, the greatest beneficiaries of the new development: people without any hope for any future until very recently, they have been suddenly drawn into the very eye of a development tornado of an unparalleled magnitude. The new oil areas of Siberia include two National Districts of Siberia—that of the Yamal-Nenets and Khanty-Mansi. Their capitals—Salekhard, located astride the Arctic Circle, and the little town of Khanty-Mansisk, 400 miles to the south—will in time become important industrial centers. The old historic towns of Surgut and Berezovo, once known only as the places of the most dreaded exile, will blossom forth as important oil and natural gas cities. Before the revolution, the Nentsy, Khanty, and Mansi—the aboriginal inhabitants of the Wet Northwest—were counted a few hundred each, whenever they were counted at all. Occasionally old Russian hunters and trappers would come upon their settlements in the tundra only to find all inhabitants dead—destroyed either by hunger or by disease. Few even bothered to report these grisly finds, so unimportant were the tribesmen in the social structure of the Tsarist state which, after converting them to Christianity and giving them Russian names, tolerantly permitted them to live and die on their own. None of these nomads were literate, and no tribe had a written language of its own.

The revolution rescued them from biological extinction, though even today there are only a few of them in their vast, desolate, and suddenly rich domain. The census of 1959, the last one held in this region, listed less than 10,000 Nentsy, 19,400 Khanty, and 6,540 Mansi living in a territory of almost 400,000 square miles—four times the territory of the states of New York, New Jersey, and Pennsylvania, put together! One can only hope that they will fare better from the sudden wealth of their land than some of the native Indian tribes of America did when oil spurted out of their desert lands.

How do these northern people live?

Their land is still closed to all foreign travel. There are no facilities to accommodate strangers, and no conventional means of travel—only helicopter, reindeer, or dog teams. Even Soviet citizens find it difficult to go there. But one of my colleagues, the Soviet journalist M. Perevozchikov, described his visit to one of the far northern *factorias,* as the tundra trading posts are known in Siberia:

Popigai is a *factoria* located more than 400 miles north of the Arctic Circle. In the 1940 edition of the Siberia travel guide there is a short entry about the settlement: "The first wooden house was built in 1935. It housed the meterological station and the general store and warehouse. The local inhabitants are unconscious of their ethnic origin and call themselves *sahas.* They are completely illiterate. They herd reindeer, and hunt squirrel and white polar fox. In the spring, families with their deer move towards the sea where there is an abundance of grass and not too many mosquitoes. They return to the forested tundra only in the late autumn when deer can find edible moss called *yagel.*"

That was less than forty years ago. Now my guide, deer-herder Sidor Chuprin, takes me around the settlement. We visit the radio station, hospital, store, bakery, nursery, and the boarding school—children stay here while their parents go away with their herds.

"In this house lives Nikolai Katyginsky," Chuprin tells me. "Two of his daughters graduated from the pedagogical college at Igarka and both are working here: Nadya in the nursery and Fenya in the school. And here is the house of Popov, the bookkeeper. But Popov didn't like staying in the office and went into the tundra as head of the deer-herding team. And this house is the house of Bezrukikh. His elder son, Prokopi, returned last year from Omsk where he graduated from the veterinary institute . . . His sister, Albina, is studying there now . . ."

In the region where only forty years ago there was not a single person who could read or write, there are today local doctors, teachers, economic experts.

Sidor Chuprin pointed to the lighted windows of the school. "Do you think there are children studying there? No, the children's classes are over. Those are adults. There are no illiterate people in the tundra today."

The reindeer team takes us to the herd which is grazing fifty miles from the *factoria.* During the trip I learn many interesting things. The herders in Chuprin's group have a two-way radio which the herders call "the air telephone." The herders are warned about coming storms, about the movements of wild deer or wolf-packs in the tundra... Each year the herd moves 700 miles to the shores of the Arctic Ocean and then comes back in the winter... The animals must move to find food...

Chuprin takes me into his *chum*—a metal frame dwelling covered with two layers of deerskins. Skins cover the ground. These structures are ideal for the tundra—they can be taken apart in a matter of minutes, loaded in a deer sleigh and taken to a new place.

We are having tea... Sidor's father and uncles are also deer-herders, his younger brother is the radio operator. His mother, aunt, and wife keep house. The family's annual income is about 5,000 rubles.

The younger daughter of Sidor has switched on the radio and is listening to music... his son is tinkering with his radio equipment... His father is smoking a pipe... At midnight he will take his turn guarding the herd... One must be very careful—wolves are following reindeer herds all over the tundra...

This might be a slightly idealized picture, but by all accounts, the northern Siberian tribesmen, once known simply as *inorodzi* (literally, "other breeds") to the Tsarist administrators, have not only acquired their national identities, but have been largely integrated into the modern life of Siberia. Many of them have become settled in *factorias* and leave their children in boarding schools there while wandering over the tundra with their reindeer herds. Reindeer are the way of life in the far north—they provide food, clothing, housing, nourishment for dogs, everything. Once a herd is decimated by wolf-packs or disease, their owners face sure death—or rather, faced sure death, because both the herds and their herders are now protected by the state. Wolves, once a virtual plague here, were cut down by special helicopters. A radio call announcing the appearance of a wolf-pack would send the helicopters aloft with expert marksmen aboard, and this has proved to be an effective way of dealing with these predators. Few of the packs still roam even the most remote parts of Siberia.

How things have changed here during the last fifty years! I remember how, as a small child, I was traveling with my father along a taiga road, just a few miles out of Irkutsk. At one point, as we climbed upon a knoll, the horses stopped dead. Our coach-

A winter scene. Reindeer are the all-purpose animals of northern Siberia, and provide transportation, food, milk, and clothing.

man turned around, his face white with terror. All he could mutter was one word: "Animals . . ."

We looked ahead and saw a fantastic sight. The road clearing between two walls of the taiga was alive with a solid gray mass of wolves moving swiftly across it in a seemingly endless stream —there must have been thousands of them. Even from where we were we could smell them—a stench of wet fur. This, as our coachman explained to us later, surely saved us from a horrible death—had the wind blown the other way, the animals would have got our horses' scent and would have attacked us.

When the animal wave passed and disappeared into the taiga, nothing in the world could make our horses move forward—we had to return to town.

Those days are gone forever. Flying from Tobolsk to Salekhard, over the immense new oil fields of Siberia, one sees countless oil rigs brightly illuminated at night by the garlands of lights, and the taiga cut by long corridors being cleared for future oil pipelines and railways. All this will eventually complete "God's unfinished work" and bring life and wealth to a country which was once a lunar landscape of frozen wilderness.

5.

The Forge of Siberia

IN 1890, the celebrated Russian writer, Anton Chekhov, traveled across Western Siberia along the road then called the Trans-Siberian Highway. That road, also known as the Chain Track because of the convicts who walked along it into exile, ran slightly north of the present Trans-Siberian Railway, through Tyumen, and Tomsk and Krasnoyarsk.

Chekhov was shocked and depressed by what he saw. It was the most cheerless and desolate country he had even seen. He wrote:

> It is already May, in Russia forests are green and nightingales sing, in the south acacias and lilacs are in full bloom, but here, along the road from Tyumen to Tomsk there is nothing but brown earth, naked forests, dirty ice on lakes, patches of snow in ravines . . .
> . . . We are passing a convoy . . . Some thirty-forty convicts, chains clanging, are trudging along, and around them walk soldiers with rifles. Both the convicts and the soldiers are dead tired, the road is abominable, the weather raw . . . There are still ten *verstas* [*versta* = 3,500 feet] to the village where they will spend the night . . . Coming there, they will have a quick bite, some black tea and collapse into sleep, and instantly they will be covered by bedbugs, the cruelest enemy of all those who are weary and needing rest . . .

(Siberian bedbugs! Anyone who knew old Siberia knew this scourge, and Chekhov mentions them many times. Those parasites were not usual insects: They were monsters, and they learned to coexist with people in the closest proximity, and nothing, but nothing, could dislodge them from a house once they had moved in. Some old Siberians kept their houses unheated in winter—that slowed down bedbugs, but did not destroy then. In the spring they would be all over the place again and no insecticide then known had the slightest effect upon them. There was an old story in Siberia about a householder laughing hysterically watching his house burn. When asked about his strange reaction, his answer was: "I'm thinking about the bedbugs!")

Along the road there are no farms or villages, just rather large settlements with intervals of 20, 25 or even 40 *verstas* between them. There are no estates, because there are no landlords here, no factories, mills or inns . . . The only thing which reminds one of civilization is telegraph wires moaning under the icy wind . . .

This is the longest road in the world and, I think, the ugliest. At each station we, muddy, wet and sleepy, collapse from fatigue and begin to curse the road . . . And station masters and clerks tell us: "This is nothing . . . Wait till you hit the Kozoolka!" They begin to frighten one with the Kozoolka starting from Tomsk . . . One becomes so depressed that the mysterious Kozoolka begins to appear in one's dreams in a form of a bird with a long beak and green eyes . . .

Further Chekhov describes travel along the Kozoolka: the stretch of the road running between the small towns of Chernore-chensk and Kozoolsk, near Krasnoyarsk:

. . . Anyone watching us would think that we are not traveling but going insane . . . We try to avoid the elevated roadway which is impassable, and hit ditches, hummocks, ruts. . . . Now and then the coachman would pause, groan as though ready to commit some dreadful crime, and then whip the horses . . . Grrrumph!—the front wheels—grrrumph!—the back wheels, and by a miracle we would go over a ditch . . . We climb back to the roadway, our carriage moaning and groaning, our horses enveloped by clouds of steam . . . The coachman is whipping them without mercy, "come, little mothers!—come, little friends!—come, ulcers to your souls!" After dragging us for a few steps, they quit, and now no amount of whipping would make them move . . . Nothing to do, but to slide down from the road and again look for a detour . . .

. . . It is hard to travel here, terribly hard, and one becomes even sadder when one realizes that this ugly, terrible road, this black plague, is the only artery by which civilization flows into Siberia!

...If nature means anything to you, you will be terribly depressed all the way from the Urals to the Yenisei...The endless cold plain, twisted birches, pools of muddy water, slimy lakes, snow in May, and deserted gloomy slippery shores of the numerous tributaries of the Ob River, nightmarish road, monstrous floods—this is all what your memory will retain from your first two thousand *verstas* of Siberia... The nature which awes local tribesmen, which runaway convicts learn to respect and admire, and which in time will prove to be the gold mine for future Siberian poets, the original, majestic and beautiful nature of Siberia starts only after one reaches the Yenisei...Let the romantic lovers of the Volga forgive me, but in my whole life I have never seen a more majestic river than the Yenisei...

That was Western Siberia in 1890. I remember it later—after the Trans-Siberian Railway had transformed it. Traveling by train across Siberia is an unforgettable experience. It is still by far the best way to see the country. The Russian trains are among the most pleasant in the world, and the most comfortable. The daily express train *Rossya* which goes all the way from Moscow to Vladivostok is elegant and comfortable, but even in Tsarist time, the Trans-Siberian express was a good and comfortable train. But it is not the physical comfort which makes railway travel in Russia, and in Siberia, a memorable experience —it is the spirit of friendliness that goes with it. Nowhere does the gregariousness of the Russians become so evident—within an hour after the departure of the train each compartment becomes a home, and each car a friendly community with people visiting each other, eating each other's food, and sharing confidences; and within a day, this community spirit spreads thoughout the train. For some reason, the Soviet trains still have three classes, as they did under the Tsars. In first class, each car is divided into four-berth compartments, roomy and luxurious in a slightly old-fashioned, warm way, which are turned into drawing rooms in daytime. Each car has a stewardess constantly brewing tea and selling sandwiches, and at stations the local women sell fried chickens, ducks, and Siberian specialities, such as game and fish baked in dough. Of course, each train has a restaurant, but eating in one's compartment is considered quite permissible and in good taste. Almost every traveler brings food. The Soviet trains, in addition, have nursery cars attended by trained personnel where children can be deposited in the morning and taken "home" at night. The trip takes seven days and six nights.

My two brothers and myself were fanatical travelers, and our mother had a difficult time dragging us away from the car window for meals or at night—the magnificent panoramas of Siberia before our eyes held us spellbound. But every time we reached Krasnoyarsk while traveling west, or Chelyabinsk traveling east, we would abandon our window-vigil. In this part of Western Siberia there was nothing to look at.

Another traveler who went this way to his exile, Vladimir I. Lenin, wrote to his mother about Western Siberia:

"The landscape of Western Siberia which I had to cross—from Chelyabinsk to Krivoshchekovo in three days," he wrote, "is astonishingly monotonous: the naked, deserted steppe. No towns. Rarely one sees a village, now and then, a forest, and then nothing but the plain. The snow and the sky . . ."

Even in my time it was generally believed that Western Siberia had important mineral resources, but there was no attempt made to exploit them, or even to explore them. It was only after the end of the civil war in Siberia, in the early 1920s, that Siberian geologists remembered that as early as 1721 a Siberian peasant by the name of Volkov had found coal on the surface of his field near the Tom River—much to his chagrin, no doubt, for at first he mistook it for the immensely fertile "black soil" or *chernozem*. Coal was a nuisance to him. But in the '20s when Russian industry lay in shambles after the civil war, which destroyed almost all the coal fields and mines of the Donets Basin, this was worth looking into.

Exploration began, and what the geologists found in and around Kuznetsk and Kemerovo was a new coal basin so rich that it dwarfed everything else in Russia. More, the coal lay so close to the surface that all miners had to do was remove the thin upper layer of soil and get coal. This was a timely discovery because complicated mining machinery was just not available in Russia, and had to be purchased abroad.

The development of the so-called Kuznetsk Coal Basin started in earnest in the late 1920s, and within a few years it completely changed the entire economic picture of this dreary part of Western Siberia. A number of large metallurgical plants were built here while coal was brought up in incredible masses in open pits. And what coal! It was pure anthracite that burned leaving almost no residue. In the Donets Basin, veins of five to six feet were considered excellent, here veins of thirty-five to fifty feet were common, and some reached one hundred and fifty feet or more. Mining them was child's play—a steam shovel could simply bite into a coal wall and load coal into waiting trucks.

Of course it was inevitable that all of southwestern Siberia would be affected by this find, but the first planners and builders did not even imagine to what extent this change would alter the face of the land. At first the iron ore for the Kuznetz industries was brought in from the Urals, but then some enormous deposits of iron ore were discovered near the coal, and the boom was on.

During World War II, when the Donets basin fell into German hands, the Kuznetsk Basin of Siberia, affectionately known as the Kuzbas to the Siberians, become the enormous forge in which steel was produced for Soviet weapons. The nearby cities of Omsk and Novosibirsk (near Krivoshchekovo, then called Novonikolayevsk) started to blossom forth as large industrial cities.

Let us look at this part of Siberia as it is today, the same country which so depressed Chekhov.

Omsk today is a modern industrial giant, with a population of 801,000 (as of January 1, 1968) and still growing rapidly. It is a city of enormous industrial plants and handsome streets. Metallurgical, machine-building, and chemical industries are centered here, and Omsk products can be found today in every town and city of the Soviet Union and are exported abroad. In the last few years, a tremendous oil refinery was built here after the discovery of the Tyumen and Tomsk oil, in a series of plants which occupy almost 39 square miles. More are being built.

Omsk, like all Siberian cities, has a chronic housing shortage despite intensive building, and many of the old houses still remain only because their inhabitants have no other place to move, despite the fact that more than 15,000 new apartments are constructed each year. A peculiar method of urban reconstruction is used in Siberia. An old district of small wooden houses is selected, and several massive new apartment houses are built nearby. The occupants of the old houses are moved there. Once this evacuation is completed the old houses are just put to the torch and burned down. This method was found to be faster and cheaper than demolishing them. And one can imagine the jubilation of the people watching the hated bedbugs go up in flames!

Omsk has become one of the most important cultural and educational centers of Siberia as well, and also the center of a vast new agricultural region. The soil of southwestern Siberia proved to be excellent for grain farming, and because this was practically virgin soil, cultivation was organized on a large-scale basis rather than by the smaller farming communes set up in the European part of the country. The climate is a drawback, and the growing season is short, but the conditions are not much different from those of central Canada which produces excellent harvests. This region contains more than 120 *sovhozes,* or huge grain factories operated by the state, and in a good year Omsk produces more than two million tons of wheat. The grain elevator at Omsk is the largest in Europe and Asia. The large-scale reclamation and irrigation of the Baraba and Kulunda Steppes will greatly improve the agricultural picture in this part of Siberia which is rather uneven at this point, since some of the large areas are subject to periodic droughts while others suffer from an excess of moisture. This problem is now being attacked scientifically by special teams at the famous Akademgorodok, the "science city" of Siberia, and it is expected that eventually Omsk will be developed into one of the foremost granaries of Siberia.

But if the changes which occurred in the once-sleepy provincial town of Omsk are dramatic, Novosibirsk, the unofficial capital of Siberia, has had the most incredible reincarnation. A small railway town only forty years ago, it is now the largest and richest city in Siberia, and the only city east of the Urals with a population of over a million—1,080,000 as of January 1, 1968, and growing at a prodigous rate. It is the greatest industrial, cultural, and educational center of Siberia. Its virtual explosion was so swift that it suffers from the usual malaise of all swiftly growing urban centers—uniformity and a lack of color. And color in Siberia is not merely a matter of esthetics; it is an

absolute necessity in a region where the climate renders everything utterly colorless for seven months each year.

Novosibirsk is huge, bustling, and powerful, but not beautiful. Because it burst out chaotically, its urban planning is
defective: utility was the main requisite; square feet of living
space were more important than architectural effects. This is
the Siberian Chicago, the city of "the big shoulders." It is the
home of the machine-tool building industry, of heavy metallurgy: hydraulic presses, hydroelectric turbines, and gigantic
pumps are made here, along with hundreds of other products.
The turbines for the famous hydroelectric plant at Bratsk, each
developing 225,000 kilowatts, were produced at Novosibirsk,
and there are others being built here which will double and triple
this capacity. Novosibirsk is a large power producer as well—
its hydroelectric plant on the Ob produces two and a half times
more electric energy than all of Tsarist Russia produced fifty
years ago. This is the city of planners, engineers, technicians,
builders; the city that plans and thinks big. It occupies a land
area of 125,000 acres, more than Paris or Berlin, and almost as
much as Moscow with its 6,600,000 people. There is a lot of
room for expansion.

Like most Siberian cities, this is a city of young people with
one of the highest birth rates in Russia. (The new Siberian city
of Bratsk has the highest.) It is also a city of students—everyone seems to be studying. And, of course, it is the science city
of Siberia—Akademgorodok, with its cluster of scientific institutions, is administratively a part of Novosibirsk even though
separated from it geographically by some sixteen miles.

This is also a cultural center—the Novosibirsk theaters are
famous all over the Soviet Union, and some of their troupes have
had successful foreign tours. It has its own opera, its own ballet,
and eight dramatic theaters. It also has more than 500 libraries
and a publishing house that publishes some 4,000,000 books per
year.

Novosibirsk is building at a brisk tempo—more than 40 new
apartments are finished every 24 hours—but still the housing
shortage is here, what with 25,000 babies born each year and
some 50,000 new people arriving to live and to work every year.
The building tempo is accelerating constantly, but it cannot

keep up with demand for new apartments. This is by far the biggest headache of the city's Soviet, or local City Hall, which suddenly found itself with a metropolis on its hands. A huge combine of factories producing building materials is in around-the-clock operation near Novosibirsk, but it cannot satisfy all the needs of city builders.

Of course the fact that this is a bleak country still remains—it is flat, monotonous, and cold. The climate here is continental and therefore winters can be even colder than in the far north. The mean temperature for January is $-20°F$, and in July $+68°F$. The summers are short, and the snow may not disappear until late April, and it may snow again at the end of September. But the cold is dry, and there is usually no wind at all, so it is less uncomfortable than some places in more temperate zones, such as Moscow or Leningrad. For some days the thermometer may plunge down to $-40°F$, but such severe cold snaps are infrequent and do not last long. Generally the climate may be likened to that of Saskatchewan or Alberta, and the Siberians insist that Siberian winters make for vigor and good health.

But not for color! The winter sun is pale and the even mantle of snow stretching for hundreds of miles in all directions has a depressing effect. This is why the Siberians are probably the greatest plant and flower lovers in the world, and why Siberian cities spend untold millions for planting flowers in every available stretch of ground in summer. This may appear as an awesome waste of municipal funds until one takes into consideration the salutary psychological effect on the population. Potted plants can be found in every Siberian home and in every Siberian factory—again this is necessity and not luxury—and the first rays of the spring sun send Siberians out digging and planting in their backyards.

In this respect Novosibirsk is a typical Siberian town—it is a delight in summer as far as flowers and greenery are concerned. There are special flower hybrids being developed in Siberia that resist cold—some seeds are brought from as far as the Andes in South America—and, again, this is not waste, but the fulfillment of an urgent need. Many new Siberian towns are planned and built with this need in mind. Care is taken not to destroy trees, but to incorporate the forests into the cities, thus breaking up the monotony of the uniform rows of identical gray buildings which are the plague of all modern mushrooming urban communities throughout the world.

The history of Novosibirsk is an amusing one, and it is a monument to one man's incorruptibility. During the construction of the Trans-Siberian Railway, which was a formidable engineering achievement of the era, there was a bitter rivalry between Siberian towns, each wanting to become a part of this great artery. It was rumored that huge sums were collected and offered to the railway planners by various towns—somehow railroading and corruption often went hand-in-hand throughout the world! The bridging of the Ob River, known for its tremendous spring floods, was a particularly difficult problem, and coming to it, the planners were temporarily stumped. Two commercial towns, Kalyvan and Tomsk, tried to bring the utmost pressure upon the man in charge of the construction here, a well-known Russian writer, Garin-Mikhailovsky, to have the bridge across the Ob constructed at their towns. Huge sums were collected and offered. But Garin, surveying the river, selected the spot that promised him no monetary gain but was the most suitable for the purpose: the present site of Novosibirsk. This was in 1896, and this is the official birth date of what is today the greatest Siberian city. The station built here, near the tiny taiga village of Krivoshchekovo, was named Novonikolayevsk in honor of Tsar Nicholas II who had been crowned two years previously. Both the name of the town and its destiny have been changed by the revolution, but the name of the incorruptible engineer-writer is still immortalized by Garin Square facing the railway station of Novosibirsk.

But the spectacular rise of both giants, Omsk and Novosibirsk, would have not been possible without the Kuznetsk Basin.

Here, east and south of Novosibirsk, lies probably the largest concentration of industrial raw materials in the world—coal, high-grade iron ore, the largest talc deposits in the Soviet Union, the largest potassium deposits, and the second largest of sodium sulphate. Phosphorites and nephelines (the raw material for aluminum) are also abundant as well as manganese and polymetallic ores. With the new oil and natural gas deposits found in the Northwest, Western Siberia has now become the richest part of this fabulously rich land.

The development of the Kuznetsk Coal Basin has been one of the brightest pages of Russia's industrialization of the last forty years. Tiny dusty villages have turned into bustling industrial cities with blast furnaces illuminating the night for miles and miles in the once deserted wasteland.

Speak of the population explosion! The little town of Scheglovsk, which had a population of 22,000 thirty-five years ago, is a city of 400,000 today, has been renamed Kemerovo, and is the capital of this province which is known today as the Siberian Ruhr. The village of Novokuznetsk (called Stalinsk for a number of years) grew from 4,000 to 500,000; the village of Prokopyevsk from 11,000 to 300,000; the city of Belovo which now has a population of 150,000 did not even exist then, as well as Anzhero-Sudzhensk which is of an equal size. The villages of Kiselevsk, Leninsk-Kuznetski, and Mezhdureshchensk each with a population of over 100,000 today cannot be found on any pre-revolutionary map. Today, the Kemerovo Province, territorially the smallest in Siberia, has the densest population, and it is growing fast.

Fortunately, the Kuzbas, the forge in which the future of Siberia is being shaped, has escaped the usual dreariness of the coal and steel regions. Most of its new cities are neat, immaculately clean, spacious, and well-planned, and some of them, like Novokuznetsk, can be justly called garden cities. The first metallurgical complex was built with the help of American technicians. It was started in what was practically wilderness as a result of a Communist Party decree of 1927 about "the building of new metallurigcal plants," and the work was carried out under appalling conditions. I remember speaking in 1932 to a young American engineer in San Francisco who had just completed a two-year tour of duty in Siberia.

"It is mad," he told me. "They are building a tremendous metallurgical *combinat*, as they call it, with their bare hands, with nobody around but savage Mongolian nomads." (The Kuznetsk Basin was then a part of Kazakhstan.) "And the workers ... dispossessed rich peasants who hate the Soviets, local tribesmen who have never seen a screwdriver, and young 'enthusiasts,' as they call themselves, who never have held any tool in their hands. They are sleeping in old army tents and lean-tos in the bitter cold which makes you gasp. It's a fantastic waste of time and labor. My colleagues and myself often felt like quitting and going home, pay or no pay, contract or no contract, just not to be a party to this horror. Do you want a bet that they will never be able to operate these plants on their own, not in a hundred years?"

Unfortunately I did not take the bet. The *combinat* was finished, and has been operating ever since, and scores of other metallurgical and chemical plants rose in what was once a wilderness. Stalinsk (as Novokuznetsk was known then) has grown into a large, bustling, and surprisingly attractive city.

Physically, the Kuznetsk Basin is a more attractive country than the plain further north and west. There are gently undulating wooded hills, and the city builders included as many wooded areas as possible. They were extremely careful to destroy few trees, so that today this region has a park-like appearance.

Novokuznetsk is primarily a city of metallurgy. Gone are the dispossessed *kulaks* and peasants who built it; today it is a city of young specialists who work here and continue to study in the large metallurgical institute and several scientific establishments devoted to iron and steel. The city itself is built around an enormous park—a piece of virgin forest occupying over 500 acres, and were it not for factory chimneys and the open-hearth and blast furnaces illuminating the sky at night, one would think that one was on a large university campus. It is the largest and busiest of the whole cluster of new cities in the Kemerovo region, but it has an almost suburban charm.

At present another and even larger metallurgical combine of mills is being built here, and when fully completed, Novokuznetsk will become the largest steel producer in the Soviet Union, and the real backbone of the "Siberian miracle." There is great stress on automation here. The new mills will employ few men when completed, but with the chronic shortage of manpower in Siberia, this does not seem to worry anyone. The drive, all across Siberia, is on eliminating jobs rather than creating them.

Prokopyevsk, once a desolate little village, is the largest coal-mining city in Siberia. It does not look like a coal-mining city at all. It is on what is probably the largest concentration of high-grade anthracite in the world, certainly the largest in Siberia. It is here that coal veins reach 150 and more feet in thickness and are almost on the surface. Open pit mining is practiced here on the largest possible scale with steam-shovels loading coal into the waiting trucks to be taken away. The cost of mining, I was told, is practically that of its transportation. Once the surface layer of soil is removed, the coal is there for the taking, and in an almost inexhaustible quantity.

There are several underground pits as well, and it is here that the hydraulic method of coal mining was first tried and is widely used. Instead of removing the upper layer of earth by hand or by machine, a powerful jet of water slices it off as though by knife. This amazing machine was developed at Akademgorodok by the Hydrodynamics Institute of Professor Lavrentiev. It is now used in several mining operations in Siberia, but this practice was begun here at Prokopyevsk. I was told that its use saves 7,000 man-days every hour the machine is in operation: this is a powerful job eliminator. A much more powerful model is now being designed, and will be in use in a year or two. In many places in Siberia, coal lies in thick veins along the high river-banks, glistening in the sun. The new machine will simply remove all the earth in which veins are embedded, leaving the coal to be broken off and carried away in river barges.

There is also another way in which coal is being used in the Prokopyevsk region: by burning it underground. Huge underground fires are ignited and then fed by streams of air piped there. The resulting gas is piped out and harnessed as it emerges. It has extensive use in the chemical industries which are burgeoning throughout Siberia.

Generally, coal is found all over Siberia. In many places, even in my day, women went down into the cellars of their houses and broke coal off the walls as they needed it, but in most cases this was the low-quality or brown coal. The coal of Kuznetsk, however, is almost unique. It is so low in sulphur that it burns leaving almost no ash and it releases tremendous amounts of heat.

The Kuzbas coal will not only supply the swiftly developing industries of Western Siberia, but will be used to feed the "garland" of powerful thermal-electric stations being constructed at present around the town of Tomusinsk. When completed, this will be the greatest thermal power production center of Siberia, if not of the world. This is in line with the preoccupation of the present-day builders of Siberia with the production of electric power.

In Novosibirsk, I asked a young electrical engineer about this, and got the standard answer—a quotation of Lenin's words: "Communism is the Soviet Power plus the electrification of the whole country." This is probably the most widely used quotation in the Soviet Union. But then my friend became more specific: "The need for electric power in future Siberia is absolutely limitless. First of all, climatic conditions make it imperative to automate much of the industry here—no matter what we say, our far north is not an attractive place to live in, and never will be, and we must let electricity do our work there. Then, Communism presupposes generally the elimination of manpower as far as possible to create the absolute abundance of everything needed by man and release man's creative energies into more worthwhile channels—culture, education, science, arts, self-betterment. And then—why not use excess electricity to heat Siberia? This may sound far-fetched, but it isn't—already fruit and vegetables are grown experimentally on electrically-heated soil in many places in Siberia, and this practice in time may become tremendously enlarged and be developed on a million-acre basis. Electric power is our bread here, literally, until a way is found of harnessing atomic energy to replace it. Then, of course, we will heat Siberia by this energy, but this is still our tomorrow. Our today is production of electric power by every means at our disposal, and the Kuzbas will do its share."

The Kuzbas is a prosperous place, even by Western standards. Its industrial cities smell of prosperity—people are dressed better here than elsewhere in Siberia, or in Moscow; there are more consumer goods in the stores, and more private automobiles than anywhere else in the Soviet Union. In the city of Novokuznetsk there are more private cars than in Novosibirsk, which has twice as many people. The reason for the prosperity is that the wages of miners and steel workers are among the highest in the Soviet Union; a miner here may earn twice as much as a qualified worker in Moscow, and he has the same privileges as all Soviet workers: low rent, which cannot absorb more than 5 percent of his income, absolutely free medical help, free education for his children, an early, pensioned retirement, practically free public services. On vacations, his trade union pays 70 percent of the very nominal holiday cost. There is practically no income tax. As a rule his wife works as well. Few women in Siberia are housewives: for some reason that occupation is not considered worthy of a young Siberian woman. So the combined income of a family in the Kuznetsk Basin is more than ample, and the Kuzbas worker justly considers himself extremely well off.

The description of Western Siberia would not be complete without visiting its southernmost region, Altai, often called the Switzerland of Siberia. It is here that the unbroken bleak land is relieved by picturesque mountain chains: the Kuznetsk Ala-Tau (not to be confused with Altai); the Salair Ridge, and further south, the high Altai mountain system. It is here that the rivers Biya and Katun merge to form the Ob, one of the three main Siberian rivers.

The main city of Altai Province is Barnaul, a picturesque little town that has become a handsome industrial metropolis. By the latest count Barnaul has a population of 418,000 (as of January 1, 1968) and may have grown considerably since then because it is being developed into the principal center of the chemical and synthetic textile industry of Siberia. The largest combine of new factories producing synthetics, such as capron and cellophane, is located here. The production of plastics and synthetic materials is a young industry in the Soviet Union, and this is the first place in Siberia where production has been undertaken on a large scale.

Barnaul is also a city of heavy industry. Agricultural machinery, trucks, diesel engines, machine tools, and boilers are made here, as well as a wide assortment of consumer goods such as radio receivers, shoes, clothing, and cigarettes. But what is even more important, it is the center of Western Siberia's vast agricultural region. In good years the Altain region produces up to 5,000,000 tons of wheat, and large tracts of virgin land are constantly put under cultivation. When the steppe, now subject to periodic droughts, is properly reclaimed and irrigated—a work that is underway—the Altai will become the granary of Siberia. Animal husbandry is very important here as well. Fully 40 percent of the sheep of Western Siberia are here, and almost 30 percent of all its cattle, and it is the center of the cheese production of Siberia. The Altai has almost 500 varieties of feed grass, some 250 varieties of honey plants, more than 750 varieties of medical plants, as well as 100 varieties of edible plants, and more than 250 varieties of decorative plants. Barnaul is the Siberian center of hybrid plant experimentation—it is here that cold-resistant varieties of plants and vegetables are developed, and then introduced to other Siberian regions.

It is also a mining region. Zinc, marble, mercury, tin, gypsum, salt, iron, and silver are all mined here. Uranium, too, is found here.

Barnaul is a surprisingly handsome young city. Its streets are wide and lined with trees, its new buildings are elegant. Most of the factories, wisely enough, are well outside the residential zone, on a special "factory street" which stretches for several miles outside the city limits.

The city has a long and well-kept river beach which is a delight in summer—winters, alas, are as cold here as in the rest of Siberia. But many Siberians consider the Altai region the most pleasant place in Siberia to live and work in, and the influx of new arrivals makes housing here an ever-present and acute problem despite intensive building.

Another remarkable Altai city is Rubtsovsk. Before the revolution it was a dusty and totally unimportant little town of perhaps 5,000 souls. Today it is a city of 150,000 people and a center of truck building and electric motor production, as well as of farm-machinery manufacture. Some of the best heavy trucks in the Soviet Union are manufactured at Rubtsovsk, and it is also the center for a very important local agricultural area.

The third important town is Bisk, and like the rest of the Altai, it is going through a rapid transformation into an industrial center. It possesses, among other industries, the largest sugar refinery in Siberia.

Further south and higher into the mountains there lies the wildly picturesque Gorno-Altai Autonomous Region which was known as the Airot Autonomous Region until 1948 when it was

given the present Russian name. (The name means "mountain-
ous-Altai" in Russian.) Before the revolution, this was probably
the most neglected corner of Siberia, the home of the nomadic
mountain tribes. This is the country of wooded mountains,
mountain streams, and alpine meadows. It is one of the favorite
vacation areas of the Siberians, and its two mountain lakes,
a very picturesque Altyn-Kol and Teletskoye, are located in
settings of scenic grandeur which equal some of the most
picturesque mountain lakes of Switzerland. The capital of the
region is a delightful little town, Gorno-Altaisk, and the entire
region is sparsely populated—it has about 200,000 people by
the latest estimate. It is primarily a pastoral country, but it possesses some important mineral resources and enormous timber
resources. This is the home of the famous mountain deer, the
maral, whose young antlers, while they are still "in the velvet,"
contain an extremely powerful rejuvenating tonic known as
pantakrin. The pantakrin is now produced commercially, and
is used in Siberian medical practice. But the really choice pantakrin is produced not by the maral, but by a variety of deer
known as the noble spotted deer (scientifically the *Cervus
dybovskii*), found only in the Sikhote-Alin mountain range
north of Vladivostok. (It is not wise, however, to say this in
the presence of any old-time Altaians who consider their marals
the best pantakrin producers in the world. The regional patriotism of Siberians is fierce.)

The Altai Mountains have several famous curative springs;
among them the Chemal and Belokurikha.

The creation of the Gorno-Altai Autonomous Region was
an attempt to save the native mountain tribes of the high Altai
from biological extinction: they were fast disappearing during
the last years of the Tsarist regime. This attempt has been successful, and the native population has been growing. The census
of 1959 listed 45,000 native Altaians, a people of Turki origin.
Before the revolution they were dying out at a rate which
would have made their extinction final by 1935, according to
Siberian ethnologists.

In order to achieve a more efficient economic planning and
management, Siberia is divided into three Economic Areas, each
with its own "general staff" of technical and economic experts.

The West Siberian area includes six provinces: Tyumen, Tomsk, Omsk, Novosibirsk, Kemerovo, and Altai. It has a land area of 852,280 square miles, and a population of about 13,000,000— more than half the population of Siberia. It is the smallest but the most industrially developed economic area of the country.

Since Siberia's economy has always been based on three main rivers, it is important to mention the Ob, along with its main tributary, the Irtysh. The Ob is one of the longest rivers of the world, running for 3,480 miles and draining a tremendous area, the entire Western Siberia and northern Kazakhstan. It is a slow-flowing, often sluggish river with a very slight gradient, given to enormous periodic floods, particularly in its lower reaches where the width of the river in full flood may reach twenty or even thirty miles.

It is the third greatest Siberian river (after the Yenisei and the Lena) and its average discharge is 1,390 cubic feet of water per second, and the total yearly discharge, 186 cubic miles, falling into the very long inlet of the Arctic Ocean called the Obskaya Guba which stretches for about 600 miles. The Ob was for centuries the main line of communication of Western Siberia, and all important West Siberian towns and cities are located on the Ob or one of its tributaries. On the Ob proper are Bisk, Barnaul, Novosibirsk, Kolpashevo, Surgut, Khanty-Mansisk, and Salekhard; on the Irtysh are Omsk, Tara, and Tobolsk; and on the Tom are Novokuznetsk, Kemerovo, and Tomsk.

The Ob is frozen from 170 days (near Barnaul) to 225 days (near Salekhard) each year. Frozen, of course, it can be used as a surface artery. The freeze-up begins in the middle of October near Salekhard and in the beginning of November near Barnaul; the river becomes free from ice near Barnaul on about April 20, and near Salekhard at the end of May or even the beginning of June. The Ob and its tributaries contain 50 varieties of fish, but commercial fishing is practiced only in the upper and lower reaches of the river; in its middle course, the Ob provides no good fishing grounds.

Because of its slow flow and slight gradient, the Ob has less hydroelectric potential than other great Siberian rivers. The dam at Novosibirsk, which created the artificial Ob Sea, is the only important present hydroelectric development. Some Altai mountain rivers and streams can be used for the production of power, but only on a limited scale. Therefore the construction of a thermal-electric power unit in the Kuznetsk Basin has begun. Besides the tremendous deposits of cheap coal, there are even larger deposits of even cheaper peat here which can be burned into electric power.

It is estimated that the population of southwestern Siberia will grow to 60 to 100 million within the next 25 to 35 years. Then food production will become all-important. Agriculture has been called the least successful of all Soviet ventures. Critics, however, rarely take into consideration the peculiarity of the Russian climate and geography, and this is particularly true of Siberia.

Siberia has an excess of water, but not where it is needed. All Siberian rivers, with the sole exception of the Amur, flow north. They discharge countless cubic miles of fresh water every year into the Arctic Ocean, while the southern fertile regions, both in Siberia and northern Kazakhstan, suffer from periodic droughts which, in certain years, reach catastrophic proportions. This happened a few years ago, and the Soviet Union had to buy wheat in Canada.

Obviously this situation must be corrected in some way. The colossal waste of priceless fresh water must be curbed.

The map showing the principal river system of Siberia spells disaster to a geographer or an economist.

The colossal waste of masses of fresh water into the frozen Arctic Ocean represents a tragic waste not only to Siberia, but to the entire planet which is slowly but surely drying up. All over the world once fertile acres are turning into arid deserts. The catastrophe which befell the Dust Bowl of Oklahoma is still alive in many people's minds.

Water is life. Man can live without gold, diamonds, oil, coal, and iron ore, but he can't survive without water: the production of all food eaten by man depends on water. Nature uses 71,000 gallons of it to produce one ton of wheat, and 66 gallons to produce a single ear of corn. A single apple tree "drinks" 10 gallons a day.

The drainage system of Siberia, often called "The Siberian Tragedy." Note that all Siberian river systems discharge into the Arctic Ocean, leaving the fertile southern regions subject to periodic droughts.

In addition to agriculture, modern industry is a gigantic polluter of water. Aquatic industrial wastes may be a greater danger for the future than the population explosion. And a human being, after all, is also made primarily of water.

The fresh-water supply of the planet is shrinking, while the demand for it is growing astronomically. So, in the last analysis, fresh water may prove to be the most valuable natural resource for the future of humanity.

Generally, Siberia is rich in water as it is rich in everything else. Lake Baikal alone contains about 18 percent of all the surface fresh water on the earth, but unlike all other natural resources of Siberia, water is being wasted there at a prodigious rate. The artificial "seas" created by dams help to conserve some water, but they do not solve the problem: once these "seas" are filled, the water continues to escape north, into the Arctic Ocean.

But this is true of all great rivers of the world—the Amazon, the Nile, the Mississippi, and the African giants. All of them discharge their water into the seas and oceans. What is so special about the Siberian rivers?

The answer is that almost all great rivers of the world flow through fertile regions and their water is used by agriculture and industry, and only the surplus is allowed to escape. This is not so in Siberia. Here the rivers flow through frozen wastelands, unsuitable for agriculture or for industry, while the southern parts of the country, Siberia's industrial and agricultural heartland, suffer from chronic water shortage. The steppes of southern Siberia and northern Kazakhstan, potentially enormously fertile, cannot be developed fully until the water situation is altered. Planting crops there is a risky and costly gamble. In certain years there may be bumper crops, in others practically all crops are lost. Developing these regions for agriculture is playing a sort of Russian roulette.

The Siberian water "future" has been worrying Siberian planners for years. This question has been under constant study at the "brain complex" of Siberia, Akademgorodok, a unique

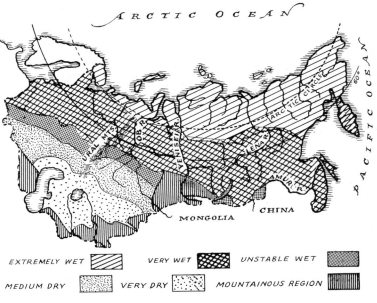

Siberia's water story: the hydrological zones.

city built for and devoted to practical science. Here the cerebral "general staff" directs the total development of Siberia.

A number of far-reaching projects have been suggested, carefully studied, and most of them rejected for various reasons.

They have ranged all the way from the construction of a vast network of canals and pumping stations that would "milk" the great rivers of Siberia as they flow north; cutting off the Ob and the Yenisei Rivers completely from the Arctic Ocean by a gigantic earth dam stretching for 300 miles across the Siberian far north; flooding all of central Siberia by a huge inland sea, and then blasting new river channels through the southern mountains, thus sending the water flowing south to irrigate the vast tracks of arid central Asia and eventually feed the fast-receding Caspian Sea.

This last fantastic project was rejected, but not because of technical difficulties, enormous as they are. It meant sacrificing all the mineral and timber resources of Western Siberia, and it was calculated that this loss would greatly outweigh the gain.

Another plan calls for the construction of a huge earth dam below the town of Salekhard on the Ob. This dam, although quite wide, would not require much height because of the very slight gradient of the Ob. The cost of the construction, though high, is by no means prohibitive: it will be paid off speedily by the electric power produced.

Instead of flooding almost the whole of Western Siberia as called for by the "Siberian Sea" project (the "sea," incidentally, would require 150 years to fill up and would obliterate such towns and cities as Omsk, Kurgan, Petropavlovsk, Tyumen, Tomsk, Tobolsk, and even Novosibirsk), the artificial reservoir created by the Salekhard dam would flood a part of the Big Swamp and considerably raise the level of the Ob, the Irtysh, and some of its other tributaries and would create a new "sea." This "Big Water," as it is called, would be tapped and sent south through a single "anti-river" over the so-called Turgai Gate into the arid wastes of Kazakhstan. Twelve gigantic pumping stations will raise this water to the level where it can start a free flow across northern and central Kazakhstan and eventually into the Aral Sea.

This "anti-river" will have a length of some 1,600 miles and a bottom width of 2,000 feet. The pumping stations will deliver 70,000 cubic feet of water per second into it—enough to irrigate tremendous stretches of land on the way, and to deliver a surplus into the Aral Sea.

The whole work would take about 10 years to complete.

This small "Siberian Sea" will cover much of the northern Big Swamp, destroying the breeding grounds of mosquitoes and affecting the climate of the region. The winters will become slightly warmer, and the summers cooler and more humid.

But what about the natural gas and oil deposits which will be flooded? Will they be lost?

No. Since the inland sea will be fairly shallow, the drilling will continue underwater: this technique is well developed throughout the world. What is more, it might prove to be more economical than drilling operations in the trackless marshlands. Some timber resources will be lost, but this loss will be insignificant compared with the general timber reserves of Siberia, and the quality of the swamp timber is rather low.

The inland sea will greatly facilitate all communications, by water in summer, and over the ice in winter.

A number of populated points will have to be relocated. Fortunately none of the large cities will be affected: they are all built on high ground as a protection against the periodic floods.

The additional food produced in Kazakhstan under controlled conditions with sufficient irrigation is expected to solve all the future food problems of Siberia for at least 100 years, and perhaps even longer. And the fishing industries that will spring up around the artificial sea will provide an additional food supply.

And after 100 years? By that time, the Siberian planners tell us, atomic energy will solve all problems, even those which today appear insoluble.

6.

The Brain of Siberia

OUR taxi, hired in Novosibirsk, was going along a very well-graded macadam road cut through a forest of pines mixed with birch. A brand-new bus and quite a few passenger automobiles passed us going to Novosibirsk. On one side of the road ran the *elektrichka*—the electrified suburban train line. Everything looked brand-new, well-painted, well cared-for. If it had not been for patches of snow on the ground here and there, this could have been a highway in northern California or southern Oregon. It certainly did not look like Siberia, neither the way I remembered it nor the way I imagined it to be now. It looked like America.

The road turned rather sharply to the left and went under a railway overpass just as a sleek passenger train went gliding over it, looking very much like an American train. There was no smoke. All railways in Siberia are electrified as far as Lake Baikal. Electricity is the cheapest power in this part of the world.

And here we saw the first sign by the roadside. It was an unusual billboard—it had no political significance. "The power of Russia will grow with Siberia. M. V. Lomonosov." Lomonosov, a celebrated Russian scientist, had said this 200 years ago. I had not known.

We were entering Akademgorodok, the jewel of Siberia, the little town with probably the biggest I.Q. anywhere—the home of "the big science," as the Siberians call it, the very brain of the country, and its pride. William Benton, the editor of the *Encyclopaedia Britannica*, called it "a symbol of the Soviet in-

tellectual challenge to the West." Perhaps. But I think it must
also be an inspiration for all future builders of new towns.

Akademgorodok was built from scratch, and it was designed
and created by three of Russia's outstanding, internationally
famous scientists, who conceived the idea of building a modern
scientific community in the heart of Siberia. They knew exactly
what they wanted. This is a town built by scientists for scientists,
and it shows it.

Akademgorodok, where every member of the community is carefully
selected. To be a gifted scientist is not enough, says the director of the
city. "The person must also be intelligent."

Every architect worth his salt has his own idea of what the
cities of the future should look like. I think they should look
like Akademgorodok. They should be intelligently conceived.
I just don't know how else to express it. Perhaps the words of
the academician Michail Lavrentiev, one of the original planners
and builders of the town, and its present guiding light, can
express it better:

"We are very careful about the people we let in here. Being
a brilliant scientist is not enough; the man or the woman must

also be intelligent. The country let us have 40,000 square miles of virgin forest around here. We must protect it from fire, harmful animals, and, in our case, learned fools."

Yes, Akademgorodok looks both pleasant and intelligent. Even its color scheme is intelligent. Many Siberian towns tend to be utterly lacking in color. Akademgorodok has color; it vibrates with it. It is color that fits the country, blends with it, marvelously matching the forest. Akademgorodok is built *in* the forest. Forest is everywhere, between the houses, in backyards, flanking the boulevards. The forest was not cleared to build the town; the town was set *into* it, became an integral part of it. "I have a balcony on the fifth floor of a new apartment building," one of the local citizens told me, "and squirrels jump from the trees right onto it, and eat breakfast with us in summer." Pastel greens, blues, creams, and pinks predominate in the color scheme, and even the flowers, which are in every window, seem to be a part of this scheme, never clashing with it, and always conforming to the general good taste of the place.

I was glad to note that some new Siberian cities are following this admirable example. One of such young cities is near Irkutsk: Angarsk, an oil center, has over 100,000 inhabitants. It is built entirely *in* the forest. It was built within the last five years, without destroying the virgin natural setting around it; it has become a part of it. This is how one foreign journalist described Angarsk: "Suddenly, out of the dense forest there appeared a brand-new, gaily colored streetcar, yés, actually from the forest!"

A well-known Siberian journalist, A. Nikitin, described this love of nature which seems to be part of all real Siberians, and which sets them apart from the millions of newcomers arriving in this fabulous land:

"We are jealous and thrifty masters of our land. Turning Siberia into the industrial heart of our country, we want to preserve its nature. We don't want our magnificent cedar to share the fate of its Lebanon cousin which one can see now only on coins. We don't want the Baikal *omul* to become extinct, and we want our 'blue Altai' to stay forever blue and green. We wince when we hear that one of our new Siberian cities has 'pushed the taiga away.' We like to see cities like Angarsk and Akademgorodok, where gigantic pines still stand in backyards and squirrels and birds come into our dining rooms to share our meals; probably in every Siberian, even if he is a member of the Academy of Science, there lives a taiga wanderer—hunter, fisherman, mushroom and berry collector, and always a nature lover."

The builders of Akademgorodok understood this well. They saw the savage beauty of the country and tried not to disturb it.

M. Lavrentiev told me:

"Of course we knew that we must have an attractive place here. People told us that we wouldn't be able to get young scientists to come and stay in the taiga. We are young, you know—the average age of our scientific colony is under 33, and young people are restless. But everyone who comes here stays—and overnight we could have had a crowd here had we not been so selective. It is no exaggeration to say that it is the dream of every gifted child in Siberia to be able to come and work here one day."

Yes, this was no accident, I thought, looking at Lavrentiev, his sparse six-foot-six tweed-encased frame sprawling in a modern, comfortable chair in the lobby of the House of Scientists, his heavily-lined, fleshy face alight with an ever-present humor. All was planned: the location of the town, the type of buildings, the color scheme, even the street names, like the Sea Prospect, the Prospect of Science, the Street of the Institutes, the Street of Tourists, the Street of Pearls, the Golden Ravine. . . . Boredom and standardization, coupled with a severe climate, make for a deadly combination that no amount of promotion could have overcome, and no amount of prosperity could counteract. So he had created a fresh and exciting town and an aura of intellectual freedom.

All this must have been planned, I thought again, as Lavrentiev drove me through the streets and we came to a place called the Children's Alley; a whole complex of schools, kindergartens, playgrounds, all brightly decorated with traditional Russian fairy story themes. Probably a child would hate to leave this place at the end of the school day, and would eagerly wait for the next morning to come back here again: the whole place had happiness designed into it.

This was Sunday, but the long central alley was thronged with children and their proud, often incredibly young parents—

Budding mathematicians in a school year at Akademgorodok solving classroom arguments during a noon break. The most gifted children throughout Siberia are selected for Akademgorodok schools through a series of competitions known as "The Science Olympics."

boys and girls who could fully share the youngsters' delights, budding scientists that they were.

We watched for a while. Now and then there would be a roar of a motor as a little boy would flash by in a miniature racing car past the official timers clocking the performance amid cheering and bursts of applause of the appreciative crowd. Each child, I was told, had to build his machine himself, incorporating at least one of his own inventions in it, to qualify for this competition.

"And you see that building there?" Lavrentiev asked. "This is the school where all of the teaching is done in English from the first to the last grade. No Russian is spoken, not even during play breaks. When they teach something here, they make a thorough job of it. With the world shrinking as it is, no scientist can afford to be cut off from the international mainstream of thought by linguistic barriers."

In addition to English, Lavrentiev can consider French almost his second mother tongue: as a young man he studied for some time at the Sorbonne, and the Department of Linguistics is a part of the scientific complex of this amazingly invigorating place. Young Siberian intellectuals are extremely conscious of being a part of the world scientific community. I have been told, for instance, that "the best English in Siberia is spoken in Irkutsk, and the best French in Krasnoyarsk," but I had no opportunity to verify this. (When I was in Irkutsk the local English Institute was closed for the spring vacation.)

We drove on. Lavrentiev named the buildings as we passed them. On a little knoll there stood four matching cream-colored modern buildings. These were the chemistry research institutes, each specializing in its special branch. We passed the imposing Calculus Center and came to a broad avenue, easily 200 yards wide, with matching buildings flanking it, and a magnificent palace-like structure forming the background. That was the Institute of Nuclear Physics. Four other institutes completed this ensemble, and, if I remember correctly, they were the Institute of Geology and Geophysics, the Institute of Higher Mathematics, the Institute of Theoretical and Applied Mechanics, and the Institute of Thermophysics.... A little apart from other buildings stood Lavrentiev's Institute of Hydrodynamics.... As we drove on, we passed other halls of learning, among them the Institutes of Automation, Experimental Biology and Medicine, Cytology and Genetics, Statistics and Industrial Organization, Mining, Economics—all in all, more than twenty institutes for advanced study. In addition, there was Novosibirsk University with its many departments, and the presidium of the Siberian Academy of Science of which Lavrentiev was head. He is also the vice-president of the Central Academy of Science in Moscow.

As we drove on we came to the business center of Akademgorodok, its "downtown," also set among trees. It was modern and immaculate—shops, supermarkets, business offices, restaurants and coffee bars, the huge Communications Center, and the glass-and-chromium building of the movie theater "Moskva" which is an almost exact replica of the "Rossiya" film palace in Moscow, only smaller—it has only 800 seats. There were sumptuous offices of the "Aeroflot" here as well. The residents of Akademgorodok, Lavrentiev told me, are great travelers, often flying to Moscow and Leningrad for weekends, and abroad during vacations. There was another movie theater called "Youth," and a legitimate theater where regular amateur musical and dramatic performances were given, with a doctor of nuclear physics perhaps playing Hamlet or a young geology professor singing the role of Traviata.

There was also a youth club here called "Under the Integral." It was the haunt of young mathematicians, where one wall in the central hall was covered by a huge blackboard on which any argument could be settled, with juke-box jazz rendering an accompaniment, and dancing couples pausing momentarily to watch the equations. There was also a lecture hall and a restau-

Young scientists dancing at the club called "Under the Integral."

rant. Apparently some of the arguments continued outside when the place closed at midnight, because the sidewalk near the exit door was covered with chalked algebra formulas. These were being now unceremoniously washed off by two young cleaning women.

The city hotel was the tallest building in sight, and was brand-new and tastefully modern. It had perhaps ten stories, and the Siberians consider it to be the best hotel in the country. Birches, pines, and larch trees form a background. Many tourists come here in summer, attracted by the broad sandy beaches of the beautiful Ob Sea and the swimming, fishing, and water skiing, forest hikes and hunting, and winter sports in winter. Scientists, too, from all over the world come here for conferences and symposiums, or just to familiarize themselves with this unique scientific setup.

We turned into the broad Pearl Street, a very unusual street. It had apartment houses on one side, and untouched virgin taiga on another. The colors of the buildings were subtly brighter here, with warm colors predominating—deep red, pink, yellow, light cream, and combinations of all these. Probably this was done in order to offset the melancholy monotony of the coniferous forest.

We drove to the shore of the Ob Sea, which was still frozen. Boys and girls were skating on it. There was a large wooded island in the far distance. This, I was told, was the private preserve of the local scientists and their families, an exclusive beach club with cabanas, cafes, restaurants, bars, a playground for children, and a mooring pier for speedboats and sail craft. (Foreign words are becoming more and more a part of modern Russian, and the word "pier" is one of them, even though it's no newcomer—it came into usage with other naval terms years ago. It is written "pirs" and pronounced "pearce.") These facilities were closed now, and the local marina, which held over 500 private boats, was frozen in, with some of the craft dragged ashore and covered with tarpaulin.

Akademgorodok must be a pleasant place to work, and a prosperous one. Many science workers draw double salaries here, one from their institutes, the other from the University, and, of course, the usual "far north" hardship bonus. Even though

Akademgorodok lies on the same parallel with southern Denmark, climatically it is classed as "far north."

As we drove into the Golden Ravine we entered a park-like area studded with two-story villas, all new and all smug-looking among the trees of the partly cleared taiga. Each had a garage and a private driveway leading to it. Here, I was told, lived the senior science workers, the academicians, professors, and doctors of science, who were the elite of Akademgorodok. Lavrentiev's own residence was here, and because it had been the first villa built here, it was more modest than the rest.

What particularly impressed me about Akademgorodok, besides its excellent planning, was the condition of the buildings. I had seen recently-built apartment houses in other new Siberian towns, and they looked dull and drab in comparison. That was no fault of the designers and builders (apart from the deadening lack of color): Siberian weather plays nasty tricks with building materials—paint peels off, cement crumbles, stones crack. How could Akademgorodok be maintained in this pristine glory?

There was an explanation, of course. Not only was all the construction here done with materials specially produced, but chemists and physicists were creating new building materials which could stand up to the Siberian climate. All of them were tried out locally before being released for general use. Those destined for subpolar and polar regions had to have special qualities because the intense cold changes the molecular structure to such an extent that the most unexpected manifestations may occur: iron bars snap like matchsticks and rubber shatters like glass. Once, as a child, I heard the story of a man coming into a warm house, removing his gloves and happily clapping his hands together, whereupon several of his fingers flew off. Frankly, I had always thought this story to be apocryphal—Siberians like telling horror tales about their weather—but I was assured that this *could* happen. In polar regions, wolves caught in steel traps often simply break off their trapped legs and escape, apparently feeling no particular pain.

Obviously, before a country like this could be made habitable, something had to be done, and something is being done at Akademgorodok, I was told. Chemistry, physics, mathematics, and mechanics are interconnected in this task. As yet they could not change the climate (although even this is planned for the far future), but they could design materials and build things which could give man and his dwellings a degree of protection against the devilish cold.

Not all Siberia is such a frozen hell, of course. But cities are being built in Siberia near and beyond the Arctic Circle, while such areas of Canada, for instance, are utterly deserted. But in Siberia they *had* to be made habitable since vast deposits of natural riches were located there.

Since Siberia in general, and its far north in particular, presented a whole array of very specific scientific problems, it was decided to build a science center here. It was no good trying to tackle those problems from far away: each had to be studied and dealt with on the spot.

Akademgorodok was the first beneficiary of all these new materials and techniques.

To maintain it, and to continue building it, a shock labor force of 5,000 highly qualified specialists was permanently settled in town. This was and is an elite group. Each man and woman is studying as well: only talented, imaginative, ambitious young workers could hope to be accepted into this community as permanent members. Akademgorodok has been a sort of practical university for city builders.

Administratively, Akademgorodok is a part of the city of Novosibirsk and is theoretically run by the Novosibirsk City Soviet, but I had the impression that in practice the presidium of the Siberian branch of the Academy, headed by Lavrentiev, runs it. Lavrentiev enjoys a unique reputation all over Siberia as a top-notch organizer and leader, in addition to being one of the world's most celebrated mathematicians. He guides not only Akademgorodok but a whole network of scientific and research institutions all over Siberia, some fifty-five science establishments in all, a virtual science empire. Only after meeting him and discussing his work with him did I understand a phrase which I had heard several times: "Well, this is not fully perfected yet, but Lavrentiev must be working on it." In Siberia, Lavrentiev had become a symbol for science in general.

Such an immense operation must be extremely costly, and

I asked Lavrentiev whether his work had ever suffered from lack of funds. His answer was quick:

"Never. Whatever we ask for, we get—immediately and without question. After all, we've already paid off the initial investment several times over, and are now showing a constant and increasing profit to the state."

This I had heard before, and now I wanted to know the details.

The new science library, reputed to be the best in the Soviet Union.

"Our work here is not merely theoretical. We are organically connected with the development of Siberia. With every phase of it. We develop new methods, new techniques, new theories— and they are instantly put into practice. Industries throw their problems over to us, and we solve them. That's why young people like to work here: they see the fruit of their work. It doesn't just go into scientific papers and magazines, and die there. They can conceive and develop theories which go into practice before their eyes—they can follow them through. Some of the things and methods developed here have revolutionized whole industries, saving countless millions, and years of time. Take our hydrodynamic cannon, for instance. It slices off whole layers of hard earth and opens coal deposits in a matter of hours—work which would have taken months otherwise. Our plasmatron cuts the hardest ore ten times faster than any conventional machine.

Our geological theories led geologists to enormous deposits of oil and coal which no one suspected existed. And we're just in our infancy here—just trying out our wings. In time Siberia will become the science center not only of the Soviet Union, but of the world—this is the only way to accomplish the job we have on hand here."

Siberia, Lavrentiev said, could use several science centers like Akademgorodok, and plans for setting them up were ready, and only waiting for sufficient cadres of young scientists to be trained to man them.

"But surely," I said, "you must have had some disappointments and failures as well as successes."

"Surely. Quite a few, but that never stops us. You see, we are encouraging our young people here to develop new theories, no matter how audacious, and try them out. If they work—fine, if not, it's never held against the authors. They are encouraged to try again and again. Some people fail through the natural tendency to invade fields they are not familiar with. That's why we stress collaboration here between different branches of science. Here mathematicians work with engineers, chemists with physicists, economists with geologists, and sometimes all of them attack the same problem. Don't try to do everything on your own, we tell our people, call for outside help whenever you need it—call again and again. The volume of knowledge has grown so vast and different branches of science so interwoven, that science has become a collective work. Some old-time science fogies warned us that this massive concentration would never work—that it would lead to clashes, conflicts, jealousies. Utter nonsense. It has worked beautifully."

"And this is why you place such an accent on youth here?"

"Precisely. We don't want people with old-time prejudices and notions, lone geniuses or sacred cows. In fact we're developing here a completely new type of scientist—not working for himself, but for humanity, and for the future. Would it offend you if I'd call it a Communist type of scientist?"

There was a quick smile, so typical of this big man with a colossal dream on his hands.

"No," I said. "But doesn't that mean changing human nature somewhat?"

"There's been a tendency to attribute every bad trait in man to nature. Cannibalism was nature, slavery was nature, violence was nature. Greed and egotism are nature. But humanity has been getting itself rid of that kind of nature; this is not only possible, but inevitable. Egotism and vanity can be eliminated by intelligence. Man can and must be made better, and we're trying to do it. A utopian dream? Well, dreams are our business; we've turned quite a few of them into reality, and we're working on many, many more. We are tackling right now ninety-six diverse problems which have long been and still are considered insoluble."

Indeed, the range of problems on which the Akademgorodok scientists are working is extremely wide. The Institute of Mines is developing radically new methods of extracting mineral resources, while the Institute of Geology is guiding geological teams to new deposits. The team of academician Trofimuk is specializing in oil and gas resources, and is largely responsible for the discovery of the gigantic oil fields in the far north. The team of the woman academician, Pelegeya Kochina, is working on the problem of turning the arid steppes of southern Siberia into an irrigated agricultural region large enough to provide food for the future large population of Siberia. Another team of biologists is working on developing special frost-resistant plants—corn, wheat, rye, vegetables. Nuclear physicists led by academician Gersch Boodker are experimenting with controlled nuclear reactions producing temperatures which will melt permafrost and "heat" Siberia: this, I was told, is nearer practical realization than is generally suspected. Not long ago, local experts achieved a controlled temperature of 100,000,000°C—the highest ever achieved under laboratory conditions; greatly exceeding the highest previously reported temperature of 40,000,000°C achieved at the Kurchatov Atomic Energy Institute, also in the U.S.S.R. It was sustained for a whole minute. But that is only a first step toward achieving the controlled temperature of thermonuclear explosion that is "hotter than millions of suns," and may reach 400,000,000°C. Once harnessed, such energy can indeed change the climate of the entire globe and turn frozen wastes into tropical jungles. In fact there are practical projects of "central heating" whole large areas of northern Siberia and illuminating Arctic towns with "artificial sunlight" during long Arctic nights. Vast deposits of boiling water found miles deep under the permanently frozen soil near the Taimyr Peninsula might be brought up for this purpose.

Siberia is not going to remain as we know it today: several scientists with whom I spoke in Siberia assured me that within the next twenty-five years dramatic changes there will astound the world, changes that will make Siberia ideally suitable for human habitation. Siberia's forbidding isolation will become a memory, and it will become a mighty base to sustain life on this planet. Even now, all the practical plans for bridging the Bering Strait and connecting Siberia with Alaska are ready: this work can commence just as soon as the cooperation of the U.S. government can be secured. There is also a project for turning the Ob and other Siberian rivers around, to irrigate vast arid regions of Central Asia on the way. Once irrigated, these areas can produce enough food for a population of many millions. This work can be started as soon as the predicted effects of this project upon the country are clearly evaluated.

Akademgorodok was largely responsible for the success of the Soviet space exploration program, and, of course, for the development of nuclear power for defense. But its main aims are for converting Siberia into a peaceful and prosperous country.

Not all the achievements of the Akademgorodok scientists are mechanical or technical. The Department of Humanistics of the Novosibirsk University works on the problems of psychology, sociology, and human behavior. The Department of Linguistics is studying Siberian languages, compiling dictionaries, and publishing them along with school textbooks in all those languages. The Institute of Mathematics, under academician Sobolev, one of the cofounders of Akademgorodok, and the team of academician Kantorovich of the Calculus Center, are working on mathematical problems which are being incorporated into computers. A team of cyberneticists, working under Professor Lebedev, have constructed an electronic computer capable of performing 100,000 mathematical operations per second. The Department of History is preparing a multivolume History of Siberia, the most exhaustive work on this subject ever attempted.

Recently a team of three young scientists, Evreinov, Kossarev, and Ustinov, using special electronic computers, broke the mystery of the ancient Mayan writings which have long been considered indecipherable.

The Institute of Automation is designing fully automated plants that eliminate all human labor. One such plant, in operation already, reduces huge logs of wood into matches with a single operator controlling the entire process. All new factories and plants built in Siberia are designed with a view to maximum possible automation.

I asked one of the young engineers, as I had asked several people in Siberia before, whether such mass elimination of labor would not create a problem of unemployment. The answer was:

"We hope so. That's the difference between our systems— you try to create jobs, we try to eliminate them. Fifty years ago, a twelve—or fourteen-hour work day was the rule in Russia. Today we cut this down to seven. If we can cut this down to five, four, three—so much the better. Communism will eventually free people from the Biblical curse of earning bread by the sweat of your brow."

"And what would people do with so much free time?"

"That's exactly the question which was asked by our serf-holders and your slave-owners. There are serious economic works written before the revolution proving that cutting the work week to mere seventy hours would lead to the general degeneration of man. Let's not worry about that! In fifty years people will consider a forty-hour work week barbaric—even here in Siberia. That's what we're working for. It's here in Siberia that the first perfect base for Communism will be created."

This man, in his late 20s, was one of the original builders of Akademgorodok. He came from the Caucasus, had no profession, and his first job was carrying bricks. He enrolled at the university here, the building he had helped to build, and was now working at the Institute of Mechanics. His wife was a doctor, and they had two children. According to him, many workers working here now are attending special evening classes at the University.

The university is an unusual one. Starting with the third year, each student is assigned to one of the institutes, according to his specialty, where he does some practical work under the supervision of experts in addition to his classes. Only the most gifted boys and girls, my young friend told me, can survive this exacting routine.

Did he like living at Akademgorodok?

Yes. Skiing in winter was magnificent. Also the so-called youth cafes: they had the latest in music—the Beatles, the Rolling Stones. He himself played the saxophone, but getting modern sheet music was a bit of a problem. He also liked the science library, a magnificent glass-encased building with over three million volumes.

How did one join the Akademgorodok staff?

It was Lavrentiev who explained this.

Periodically, the Academy publishes science themes and invites dissertations in writing from university graduates all over Siberia. They are studied, and the most interesting selected. Then a special Academy team visits the successful applicants in their towns for preliminary screening to determine their qualifications as possible future Akademgorodok staff members. Not only is their scholastic standing investigated, but also their character, personality, and potential ability to adjust to the conditions of work at Akademgorodok. Their political outlook is also important even though Lavrentiev insisted that Party pull is not a dominant factor, although recommendation by the local Party organizations is considered. Only after this preliminary screening are those chosen invited to come to Akademgorodok, with all expenses paid, to defend their dissertations before the Academy panel. Then they are sent home; and as vacancies occur in various institutes they are invited to join the Akademgorodok staff. The percentage of successful aspirants? Lavrentiev could not answer this off-hand, but obviously this is an exclusive club. However, even being invited here for examinations adds greatly to a person's prestige, whether he is finally chosen or not.

"Not passing here is no disgrace—some of the most famous scientists in the world wouldn't pass," he added with a quick sly smile. His sense of humor made him a truly delightful conversationalist. Before parting I decided to ask him a final question, making it clear that I would not be offended by his refusal to answer it:

"Do you find it conducive to work to be located so far away from all the administrative centers?"

The answer was quick and unequivocal:

"Very much so. Our freedom here is complete. No one interferes with us, or asks questions or explanations. We are not subject to academic pressures, to personal envy or vanity which, alas, are very much alive in the science community all over the world. After all, we are all human even though often we don't act that way."

This was easily one of the most pleasant afternoons I have ever spent. Meeting Michail Alexandrovich Lavrentiev was worth the cost of the trip to Siberia which, I must add for the benefit of prospective tourists, is considerable. (We shall discuss costs and prices in a special chapter.)

At the time of my visit the population of Akademgorodok stood at about 40,000. Out of this number some 15,000 are actively working at the Academy, the university, or one of the institutes. There are about 6,000 builders and building maintenance people. All others, directly or indirectly, are also connected with the life of the town.

The jurisdiction of Akademgorodok spreads over the West Siberian, East Siberian, Far Eastern, and the Yakutian science centers, with all their branches and research institutes all over Siberia.

Some specific scientific work done by these special branches is worth mentioning:

The Krasnoyarsk Institute of Physics is conducting some unique work in the spheres of magnetic physics and biophysics. The Institute of Forestry, also in Krasnoyarsk, studies all problems connected with the most effective exploitation of the timber resources of Siberia and their preservation from fires, animals, and insects.

The Irkutsk Institute of Energetics with its own cybernetics center is working on the most effective methods for the utilization of thermal- and hydroelectric resources of Siberia. Some interesting work is done also at the Irkutsk Institute of Geochemistry, Geography, Biology, and Mineralogy, and at the Institute of Organic Chemistry.

The Buryat section of the Academy at Ulan-Ude is conducting a special study of the influence of microelements on increased productivity of plants and animals.

The Yakutsk branch of the Academy is doing some remarkable work on the theory of distribution of diamond, gold, oil, gas, and mineral deposits throughout Siberia. The Yakutsk Permafrost Institute is conducting a unique study of permafrost conditions all over Siberia and the Far East, developing specific building techniques and water conservation methods in permanently frozen regions.

Volcanology students at work in the Kamchatka.

The Khabarovsk Institute specializes in the problems of land reclamation in the southern marshlands of the Far East and the all-around exploitation of natural resources of the region.

The Sakhalin Institute has developed a method for predicting underwater earthquakes.

The Magadan Institute conducts a thorough study of the enormous natural resources of the Siberian northeast, and the most effective methods to use in their development. Its Volcanology Section is studying the volcanic activity of the Kamchatka peninsula and the possible utilization of the volcanic and geothermal energy. This work has already led to the electrification and thermalization of the city of Petropavlovsk-Kamchatsky through the use of this energy.

The Vladivostok section of the Academy is studying the geology and biology of the Far East, and the biology of some local rare plants such as the famous ginseng.

All these activities are coordinated and correlated from Akademgorodok, and all findings are studied and collated there.

What is the story of this amazing town?

On May 28, 1957, the Council of Ministers passed a resolution about "the creation of the Siberian department of the Academy of Science of the U.S.S.R." appointing M. A. Lavrentiev as its head, and placing all then existing scientific organizations beyond the Urals under his management. This was the official birthday of Akademgorodok, and the "crowning" of Lavrentiev as head of Siberian science.

From this point on development was very fast. In one week a special commission headed by Lavrentiev chose the site, from several proposed ones, which fully answered all the requirements. It was a virgin forest sixteen miles south of Novosibirsk on the shores of the newly created Ob Sea. First of all, this was more or less the geographical center of Siberia, the country was beautiful, the selected spot lay astride a railway line and a highway connecting it with other parts of Siberia, and the proximity of an already highly developed and rapidly growing industrial city could both fulfill the technical needs of fast construction and create attractive working and living conditions for the future population of the town.

But planning a brand-new town is one thing, and actually building it is another, especially because this had to be a model place built in the most modern way using the most advanced industrial techniques. It was not long before the special organization created for this project, called *Sibakademstroi*, discovered that the Novosibirsk area possessed no construction facilities that could undertake a task of such magnitude.

But Akademgorodok and Siberia could not wait. Therefore in December, 1957, the regional Novosibirsk Economic Council started building near Novosibirsk a brand-new complex of plants wholly devoted to the production of building materials of the most modern type and most suitable for the local climatic conditions. It was not a temporary enterprise. Upon completion of the Akademgorodok construction, this complex was to supply swiftly growing Novosibirsk with desperately needed building materials.

Obtaining the necessary labor force came next. The Komsomol, the Young Communist League, declared Akademgorodok to be a "shock All-Union Komsomol construction" and asked its members to volunteer. The romantic aura of far-away Siberia and the unusual character of the project must have caught the youthful imagination because applications started to pour in often addressed simply, "Science, Novosibirsk" or "Lavrentiev, Siberia."

The would-be builders started to arrive in droves and were housed in frame barracks, 8,000 people in all, the vast majority of them boys and girls in their teens. Only about twenty-five percent of them had any previous building experience and now these "veterans" had to lead enthusiastic but green youngsters. In addition some special instructors were dispatched to Siberia to teach the building trades to boys and girls who had never worked before in their lives. And this was not an ordinary project, but one which had to be constructed according to the most exact specifications.

The trains bearing building equipment—excavators, cranes, bulldozers, compressors, cement mixers, graders, and various tools—started to roll into Novosibirsk from all over the country before the people to handle them could be trained. The initial allocation of 60,000,000 rubles was quickly exhausted, and by the end of the year the cost had risen to 290,000,000 rubles, or $319,000,000 at the official exchange rate. (The final cost was to rise much, much higher, of course, but no official figure is available.)

It is a remarkable achievement that the entire town was built within seven years—some Institutes started to function within a year of the day when the first ground was broken. This could not have been accomplished without the closest cooperation of the scientists who were on the spot, working side by side with the designers, engineers, and builders, advising, designing new methods, instructing young workers on the building sites. Parallel with this, special classes were held at night devoted to both general education and specific skills. All in all over 11,500 workers went through this educational mill with some 6,100 boys and girls acquiring new professions, and 5,400 improving their professional qualifications. Many of these went to the University when it was opened, and were graduated, and some stayed in Akademgorodok as permanent staff members.

On November 2, 1957, the general session of the Academy of Science in Moscow approved the establishment of the Academy branch in Siberia, and asked its members to volunteer for work in Siberia. Many scientists expressed their willingness.

On March 28, 1958, the first group was elected for the Siberian Academy. Altogether 35 members were chosen, and M. A. Lavrentiev presented his plan for the seven-year development of the new organization. Special committees were elected for various future branches.

All in all, it took seven years to create this place in what was once a virgin forest, and building continues. New apartment houses rise on the edge of the taiga. A special electric train line and a wide highway connect Akademgorodok with the center of Novosibirsk. But as soon as one leaves Akademgorodok, one finds oneself driving through dense virgin forest on both sides. There are no suburbs. The town ends just as abruptly as it starts, like a beautiful island lost in the endless green ocean.

My advice to all future tourists going to Russia: after you have seen Moscow and Leningrad, the Kremlin, the Lenin mausoleum, the Bolshoi Ballet, the museums, and all the usual tourist attractions, make a small extra effort to see Akademgorodok—even if your schedule leaves you no time for the rest of Siberia. You will not regret it.

7.

The Heart of Siberia

THE Yenisei.

Anton Chekhov was startled by the first sight of this mightiest of all Siberian rivers. This is what he wrote about it in his travel notes in 1890:

Never in my life have I seen a river more magnificent than the Yenisei. . . . While the Volga is a dressy, modest, pensive beauty, the Yenisei is a powerful, turbulent giant which does not know what to do with its enormous power and its youth . . . Man of the Volga started out with daring, and ended up with a moan, which he calls a song; his bright golden hopes have been replaced by hopelessness which is popularly known as Russian pessimism; on the contrary the Yenisei has started out with a moan, and will end up with such glory which we can't even dream about. . . . This is at least what I thought standing on the bank of the wide Yenisei and eagerly looking at its water which with incredible speed and power rushed towards the severe Arctic Ocean. There is not enough room for the Yenisei in its banks. Rolling waves are chasing one another, forming mighty whirlpools, and it seems strange that this powerful giant has not yet broken its banks, and has not drilled through its rocky bed. . . . On this bank stands Krasnoyarsk, the best and most beautiful of all Siberian towns, and on the opposite, there rise mountains which remind me of the Caucasus, misty and dream-like. . . . I stood there and I thought: what a full, intelligent and brave life will some day illuminate these shores!

Chekhov was a good prophet. The full, intelligent, and brave life is coming here, and it is coming fast.

Here starts the so-called East Siberian Economic Area—the

very heart of Siberia, potentially the richest, still largely un-developed part of the country. This area includes three large provinces: Krasnoyarsk, Irkutsk, and Chita, and two Autono-mous Republics, the Buryat and the Tuva. (Some geographers tend to include the Yakut Republic in this area, but the Soviet economists do not recognize it as a part of it, and we shall deal with Yakutia separately, as it deserves.) The Eastern Economic area covers 1,950,000 square miles, and its population stood at 7,300,000 as of January 1, 1967. It is believed to be nearing 8,000,000 at the moment of writing this. (In comparison, the area of the fifty United States is 3,615,211; its population passed the 200,000,000 mark on November 20, 1967.)

Eastern Siberia is still not fully explored, and only slightly developed, but on the basis of what is known, it contains at least 70 percent of all the potential coal resources of the Soviet Union, 40 percent of all hydroelectric resources, and at least 50 percent of all the timber resources. There are also enormous, not yet fully explored, deposits of iron, copper, tin, rare and precious metals, asbestos, graphite, mica, fluorite, and a whole

The icebreaker *Moskva* escorts a ship along the Yenisei River.

list of additional minerals; every known element in nature has been found here, without a single exception.

Krasnoyarsk on the Yenisei has become a large industrial city of 592,000 (as of January 1, 1968), and like all Siberian cities, it is growing rapidly. It is a very important center of both heavy and light industry, and its new industrial plants are being built along a single street called simply "the Krasnoyarsk Worker" which stretches for some miles out of the city. The city itself is being feverishly rebuilt and modernized, with new apartment buildings replacing wooden houses, which are often simply burned down as soon as their tenants move out into new houses.

A cement-pouring team at Krasnoyarsk. Men and women work side by side for equal pay in all occupations.

The most remarkable feature about the Krasnoyarsk region (the word *krasnoyarsk* means "red" or "beautiful ravine" in Russian—the words "red" and "beautiful" being synonymous in archaic Russian usage) is the newly constructed gigantic dam and hydroelectric plant, the largest and most powerful power-producing plant in the world. It is located in a narrow gorge a short distance from the city. The dam has created an artificial lake some 250 miles long, and displaced some 48,000 people who lived in the valley that is now covered by water.

To accommodate the displaced people, a brand-new town is

being built now, the youngest in Siberia, with the poetic name of Divnogorsk, i.e., "the city of marvelous mountains." It is being laid out on the terraced mountainside overlooking the dam and the new Krasnoyarsk Sea which it created. When fully constructed this will undoubtedly be one of the most picturesque spots in Siberia. But not yet. It is now a city of cranes and roaring bulldozers, even though some streets have been already completed.

The Krasnoyarsk Dam and Power Station are the greatest talking point in this part of Siberia. Everyone here knows the facts and figures by heart, and is eager to share them with all comers. They will tell you that the Krasnoyarsk Power Plant, at full capacity, will produce up to 5,000,000 kilowatts of energy, and that its 10 gigantic turbines, each with a capacity of 500,000 kilowatts and each weighing over 200 tons, were made in Leningrad and delivered here by water—first through the White Sea-Baltic Canal, and then up the Yenisei River on special barges. And they will insist that their plant, when in full operation, will dwarf the power plant at Bratsk which is, at this point, the largest operating power station in the world. (The turbines of the Krasnoyarsk plant will be switched on one by one as the demand for power requires it.)

They will also tell you that the largest hydroelectric plant in the United States, the Grand Coulee, has a capacity of only 1,972,000 kilowatts. I am sure that this figure is much better known in and around Krasnoyarsk, and all over Siberia in fact, than in the United States.

Generally, the production of electric power is virtually an obsession with modern Siberians. They never tire of speaking about it, and schoolchildren cite all the figures with absolute facility. If you say that you are from New York, for instance, the very first question will be, "How much electric power do you produce in New York?" And if you say that you don't know, there will be a stunned silence for a moment, and then you will be given the figure: 16,942,000 kilowatts.

Then they will tell you that besides the Krasnoyarsk plant, there are three other projects already under construction. Oh yes, they will have the figures for them, too. The one at Ust-Illim on the Angara River will equal the Bratsk plant in capacity, while the other two, built on the upper Yenisei, will produce up to 6,000,000 kilowatts each. They will add that when another projected dam on the Angara, where it joins the Yenisei, is completed, "the Angara cascade" alone will produce up to one-third as much as all the electric power produced in the United States. This, of course, in addition to a whole string of power stations being constructed all over the country, the largest of which, at Belovo, will produce 6,000,000 kilowatts and will be, of course, the largest thermal-electric station in the world.

A unified Siberian power system is already in operation, controlled from a modest-looking building in Kemerovo. This is the electric brain of Siberia, its power solar plexus. The whole operation looks deceptively simple. In the control hall one entire wall is occupied by a panel with multicolored electric lights representing power stations, both thermal- and hydroelectric, all interconnected with colored lines. Those are power lines, and each color represents a certain voltage. The control engineer on duty who sits facing this panel commands the entire huge system. At his side there are telephones connected with other control engineers of various power circuits throughout Siberia, and one word from him can change the power picture of the country. Obviously this is a highly responsible post and only highly experienced specialists work at this control table.

This unified network not only allows the most rational utilization of energy over the huge territory spanning several time zones, but permits the maintenance and repair of the equipment. At any given moment, any regional circuit can be switched off and its load switched over to another circuit while the necessary repairs or servicing are being done.

This is how the chief engineer of the control service, Moisei D. Shefkind, explains it:

"Power consumption is not steady—it falls off at night, then rises in the morning, then falls off again. Then between 9 and 10 P.M. there is a peak hour. At this point night shifts are working in industrial plants, the street lights are switched on in towns, cities, and villages, as well as the lights in millions of homes. Fortunately for us, Siberia has five time zones, and therefore the peak hour travels from east to west, from Vladivostok and Magadan to the Urals, and we can follow it across the country directing the necessary power to the region when the consumption is at its highest. This gives us an enormous economy as we draw this power from the regions where the consumption has fallen off. Also, it gives us an opportunity to keep every turbine and every piece of equipment throughout Siberia in top mechanical condition by periodically switching them off for inspection and possible repair. We have a department of specialists constantly studying power consumption curves throughout the country, and working out the most economical methods of power distribution. All regional circuits make detailed reports to us three times every twenty-four hours, and, of course, in case of any emergency. This is a complicated and rapidly growing operation as new stations are built and new power lines are connected to the system."

In time this single control system will cover the entire Soviet Union, but so far it covers only Siberia between the Urals and Lake Baikal.

In Eastern Siberia, like the rest of the country, industrial development and distribution of population primarily follows the great rivers. Here it is the Yenisei and its powerful tributary, the Angara.

Since Eastern Siberia, unlike Western, is not a plain, but rather a gigantic tableland with some mountainous regions, it is better drained. The Yenisei, its main "drainage ditch," is the mightiest of all Siberian rivers. Its average discharge into the Arctic Ocean reaches the gigantic figure of 302,000 cubic feet per second. More than one-third of this water mass is delivered to the Yenisei by the Angara.

Unlike the sluggish Ob, the Yenisei is a majestic and beautiful river.

This highway into the very heart of Siberia is now navigable for much of its almost 2,600-mile course even though in some places in its upper and middle parts there are numerous rapids and shallows. Those, I was told, will in time be eliminated by series of dams that will be constructed along the river, and a unique way of getting river craft over the dams has been designed for the Krasnoyarsk Dam, and will be used for all future dams of "the Yenisei cascade." Instead of the usual series of locks, a ship is moved into an enormous tank which is then sealed and raised on rollers along an inclined railway to the top of the dam and then released there. Ships sailing up the river are lowered over the dam in the same way. This "ship elevator" saves both time and money: each operation takes only one-fifth of the time that it would take a ship to pass through locks, and the power, of course, is supplied by the power plant on the spot.

Unfortunately, the navigation season on the Yenisei is short. The river is frozen from 140 to 170 days each year in its upper and middle course, and from 200 to 230 days near the Arctic Ocean.

However, despite all the coal and other mineral and non-mineral deposits in Siberia, its real heart is green: the famous taiga. Trees are also Siberia's greatest potential wealth because they are inexhaustible; within seventy to eighty years after one crop of trees is cut, a fresh crop is ready.

The Siberians have almost a mystic attitude toward their enormous forest. And for a good reason: it is like no other forest in the world; it is enormous and starkly beautiful. It is also mysterious. There are many spots in it never yet reached by man, and it has a strange fascination despite its seeming monotony. Let us once again return to Chekhov who wrote in his travel notes:

Soon beyond the Yenisei there starts the celebrated taiga. They have spoken and written so much about it, that one expects more from it than one finds. On both sides of the road there stretches the usual forest of cedar, pine, larch, birch and spruce. . . . The power and the enchantment of the taiga is not in its gigantic trees or its silence, but in the fact that only migrating birds perhaps know where it ends. For the first day one pays no attention to it, for the second and third, one begins to wonder, and on the fourth and fifth one begins to feel that one will never get away from this green monster. . . . You come to the top of a hill, you look ahead, and all you see is another wooded hill, and another and still another, and so on, without end. . . . You repeat this on the fifth day, and you see the same thing. You know nonetheless that somewhere ahead will be the Angara and Irkutsk, but for how long the taiga stretches north and south of the road, even coachmen and peasants born here do not know . . . and to your question they answer simply, "There is no end. . . ."

. . . And how many mysteries does the taiga hide in its enormity!

Here is a little pathway branching off the road and disappearing among the trees. Where does it lead to? To a secret forest distillery, to a forest village about which the local administration knows nothing, or a gold digging worked by a gang of runaway convicts? And what wild alluring freedom does this little pathway suggest!

The Siberians love their taiga. There are fantastic, marvelous stories about it and they all stress one point—its freedom. Man is alone in the taiga, no one is there to watch over him, to tell him what to do and what not to do.

The taiga is not for amateur hikers. There are many hidden dangers—bottomless bogs, wild animals, and poisonous insects, particularly a kind of tick which is the carrier of encephalitis. There are sudden violent storms and forest fires which can engulf a man before he has a chance to escape. Often fires are caused by lightning in summer, and in olden times they would rage for days and weeks, consuming enormous tracts of the forest. I remember going in a train through the taiga for hours and hours between two walls of swirling flames. Now, of course, these fires are fought by chemical-spraying helicopters and planes, but forty years ago no one cared how many thousands of acres of valuable forest were consumed each summer.

Old taiga hands, the so-called *taiozhniki*, swear by the taiga. No really experienced man could ever perish there, they claim; the taiga would feed him, and cure all his ills. Anyone contemplating a taiga exploration should study a little book called *The Taiga Secrets* by Boris Koshkin, the Irkutsk naturalist who lived his whole life in the taiga. It is fascinating reading. He lists all the equipment that man must carry with him, the most important of which are an axe, a knife, and a saw. Then matches, flint, and a magnifying glass, to make a fire, an aluminum kettle, and a frying pan. He needs special taiga clothing in winter, including fur socks, fur boots, and a mosquito net in summer. This, plus a good rifle, Koshkin claims, would allow a man to survive in the taiga for any number of years because the taiga is full of food—animals, fish, edible roots of plants and trees, and berries and mushrooms in summer, but one must know how to prepare and conserve this food. There is a whole list of medicinal plants for every complaint, to be collected in summer, dried and frozen, which cure anything from a heart attack to toothache. One cedar tree can feed a man throughout a year, with its marvelously nourishing nuts which can be preserved for a whole year. The nuts are full of oil, and they can also be dried and ground into flour. The same can be done with the bark of many taiga trees and their roots. The building of a taiga shelter is a specialized task: one must select a proper spot, use only special wood, and special moss to caulk all cracks, and this, Koshkin tells us, protects a man from the bitterest cold. The book lists thousands of useful hints on how to deal with every emergency, including wild animals, each one of whom, it seems, has its own idiosyncrasies, and must be approached and dealt with differently.

Finding one's way in the taiga is a special art because Siberia is full of magnetic anomalies which often make the compass useless, and compasses may freeze in winter. Every tree, every plant, every berry, it seems, can be read for direction by an experienced taiga hand, and even fox holes and ant hills can guide him.

Predicting the weather is all-important. A sudden snowstorm can cut off man's way back to his shelter, and kill him; flash floods can be deadly, as well. There is a whole set of taiga signs which the taiozhnik must know and read. Here are some of them: a clear night without dew means rain the next day; fog over the water means good weather; rising fog means rain. Rings around the sun mean rain or snow within twelve hours. Wood crackling while dry means severe frost. Ants hiding means an approaching thunderstorm. The flight of the swallows is also a taiga barometer; the higher they fly, the better the weather ahead. Frogs croaking in daytime means approaching rain. Fish breaking water in quest of insects means some stormy weather ahead. A thick layer of fat under rabbits' skins signifies a long and bitter winter ahead. Campfire smoke can also be read. If it rises straight up, that indicates frosty clear weather; if it rises in round clouds, stormy weather ahead; if it keeps close to the ground, an approaching thaw.

Bitter cold is a healer as well as a killer, according to old Siberians: inhaling frozen air can cure respiratory and pulmonary diseases, even arrest tuberculosis, and cure spotted typhus.

Thousands and thousands of runaway convicts have perished in the taiga because they did not know how to live in it, and it is interesting to note that modern geologists are given thorough survival training. Much of it is based on age-old notions which may appear superstitious, but which are based on the experience of centuries.

The most bothersome large animal in the taiga is the wolf; the least dangerous the bear. Wolves are now being destroyed mercilessly wherever they are found, and the government pays a premium for each killed wolf. It is interesting to note that Koshkin, while advocating the destruction of wolves, warns all taiga hunters against killing wolf pups near their lair, even after their parents have been destroyed: other wolves will avenge this sooner or later. The wolf, it seems, has a long memory, and a communal spirit prevails in each pack.

The native inhabitants of the Siberian taiga are the Evenks. They wander all over the taiga with their reindeer, hunting, trapping, fishing, often going for years without approaching inhabited places. The Soviet government makes a determined effort to make them settle down and bring them into the orbit of the economic life of the country, and is slowly succeeding, but still no one knows for certain how many of them roam the taiga on their own.

In some regions the policy of the Soviet government to involve the taiga aborigines in the economic life of the country has begun to bear fruit. In some instances, the Soviet ethnographers have performed meticulous work, such as in the case of the Tofolars who live in the southwestern part of Eastern Siberia. This ancient people had only 45 surviving members in 1922 when they were first "discovered." Today it is estimated that the Tofolar "nation" has passed the 1,000-member mark.

Every taiga native wishing to settle down gets a government grant for building a house and buying all the equipment for a settled life. More and more Evenks take advantage of this offer, usually leaving their oldsters and children in settlements while roaming the taiga with their deer herds. The taiga is the Evenk's way of life, economically and emotionally, and it would probably take generations to fully absorb him into the new

Siberian industrial society. An old Evenk whom I met in Irkutsk told me in his almost incomprehensible Russian:

"Taiga—big home. Sky—big ceiling. House—small; ceiling small. Evenk like big home, big air."

The Evenks, known as the Tunguses before the revolution (this term is no longer used outside of geology and geography, and has a slightly derogatory connotation), are probably the oldest surviving Siberians, its true natives, and lived in the taiga from time immemorial. They are peaceful, retiring people, never known to engage in any intertribal warfare: they shunned contact and withdrew deeper into the taiga whenever they met strangers. The Mongol domination had never touched them, and the Tsarist government left them alone, though nominally Christianizing them: many of them bear typical Russian names like Ivanov, Petrov, Sidorov, etc. They speak their own language of Tungus origin, unrelated to any other. This language was first seriously studied after the revolution, and written Evenk was created on the basis of the Russian alphabet by Soviet philologists.

The Soviet government, with its super-conscientious national policies, has created the Evenk National District in the very heart of the taiga, with the small taiga settlement of Tura as its capital. The district has a huge area of over 300,000 square miles, more than six times that of the state of New York, but it had a population of only 12,000 in 1967, many of whom were Russians. All in all, the Soviet census of 1959 listed 24,700 Evenks in the whole of Siberia, but this figure should be accepted with a grain of salt—much of the taiga is still unexplored, or only partly explored, and the Evenks have an instinctive faculty of getting out of strangers' way.

There is a medical school in Tura with an enrollment of 120, and there were 2,300 children of all grades in the district, 48 doctors, and 300 hospital beds—fantastic progress considering the fact that not a single Evenk was literate before 1930, or had anyone but the local shamans or witch doctors to treat him in the event of sickness or injury.

Paradoxically, the Evenk National District is probably potentially the richest single undeveloped region of Siberia, if not the world. Not only are its timber resources enormous, but the entire district is located in the center of the great Tungus coal "sea."

Coal can be "mined" here with a crowbar and a shovel, since most of it lies practically on the surface. There are other mineral deposits here: iron ore, copper, and tin, and probably natural gas and oil. And, of course, the taiga is teaming with valuable fur animals.

Undoubtedly some day this will be a highly industrialized region, but that day is still distant: there are too many other regions in Siberia which can be reached more easily and exploited more efficiently. At this point in Siberia's development, the so-called "complex" exploitation of natural resources is the rule: that is, only those regions are developed where all the necessary elements can be found together, since transportation and communication are still paramount problems.

So, for some time at least, the Evenks, these "children of the forest," will be left undisturbed in their green wilderness.

At present the only practical way to reach their forest capital of Tura is by air. Regular flights connect it with Krasnoyarsk and Novosibirsk, the largest air hub of Siberia. But during the winter when snowstorms rage, the town may be isolated for weeks on end. The winters are long and severe here, even though not as severe as in neighboring Yakutia, but then, there is little difference between —50° and —70° frost! But the Evenks, over the millennia that they have lived here, have learned to live with the cold.

The Yenisei (the word is Evenk, and it means "the big river") has three principal tributaries, as well as hundreds of smaller ones. The largest by far is the Angara, flowing from Lake Baikal. It was once called the Upper Tunguska, much to the annoyance of many Siberians who consider it a more important river than the Yenisei, and for a good reason: at the point when it joins the Yenisei it carries more water than the latter—so why not consider the Upper Yenisei a tributary of the Angara? Two other important tributaries are the Podkamennaya (Stony or Middle) Tunguska and the Lower Tunguska on which Tura is located.

It is here, in the basin of Podkamennaya Tunguska, in what probably is the most deserted part of the taiga, that there once occurred a phenomenon that still baffles scientists throughout the world.

At 17 minutes 11 seconds past midnight G.M.T. of July 30,

1908, some seventy miles north of the small taiga *factoria,* or trading post, of Vanavara, there occurred a gigantic explosion of still undetermined origin which, according to a few eye witnesses, illuminated the sky "like millions of suns." The flash was seen at Krasnoyarsk, 400 miles to the south, and some say, even at Irkutsk, 800 miles away, and shock was felt for a radius of at least 500 miles. In an area of almost 1,500 square miles, trees were found singed, and many were felled. Signs of this devastation can still be plainly seen. For many years it was believed that an enormous meteorite fell in the taiga, but oddly enough, no crater or any indentation has ever been found in the ground, and not the slightest sign of any explosion residue.

Many scientific expeditions have studied the Tunguska explosion, the most recent one being that of the Academy of Science of the U.S.S.R. under Professor Florensky in 1958. Their findings seemed to deepen the mystery rather than clarify it. The phenomenon has every earmark of a nuclear explosion in the 35-megaton range releasing about 10^{24} ergs of energy. It was found that whatever exploded had traveled over the taiga in an erratic course; behavior inconsistent with that of meteorites, which always travel in a straight line. The only known meteorite of comparable size struck the earth about 25,000 B.C. in Arizona near the present town of Winslow, and left a crater 4,130 feet in diameter and 575 feet deep with the parapet rising 130 to 150 feet above the surrounding plain even today. Examination of still remaining residue there showed that the crater was caused by an iron-nickel mass with a diameter of 200 to 260 feet and weighing about 2,000,000 tons. But nothing like this has been discovered about the Tunguska explosion.

The latest hypothesis, accepted by some astrophysicists, is that the body which struck the taiga was a small ice comet which exploded before reaching the ground, and the fragments simply melted and disappeared without trace. This explains the lack of residue, but not the erratic course in which it traveled, or the force of the explosion itself. A theory of an "anti-matter explosion" has been advanced as well, but this would be the first and the only case of such a natural phenomenon, and the very existence of anti-matter as such is still a moot question in physics.

Some investigators seem to believe that whatever flashed across the taiga was intelligently directed because they feel only this explains the changing course of its flight. Was it then some sort of interplanetary vehicle in trouble, perhaps intentionally destroyed by its crew? Quite a few serious scientists seem to believe so, including some Soviet ones like Felix Zigel. Every serious UFO investigation organization throughout the world lists the Tunguska explosion in connection with possible interplanetary visitors who presumably have visited and studied our planet.

I remember this matter being discussed in our home in Chita, in Transbaikalia, probably in 1914, by my father and his friend, a doctor who claimed to have visited the site of the Tunguska explosion a few months after it had occurred. The doctor had a detailed diagram showing the zig-zag course of the falling body over some 100 miles (where the tops of trees were sheared off) before the actual explosion. He also said that some unusual glow was observed each night over the epicenter of the explosion for weeks after it had occurred, suggesting some sort of radiation. My father, who was interested in the so-called "flying saucer" lore even then, was convinced that interplanetary visitors were using some parts of the taiga as their terrestrial base. He drew this conclusion from some ancient Evenk legends. (Of course, the term "flying saucer" did not exist then; it was coined by Kenneth Arnold in 1947, but the sightings of unidentified flying objects have been reported by the Siberian tribesmen, as well as the Mongols and the Chinese, for centuries.) Unfortunately all my father's voluminous notes on the subject were lost in China where he died in a Buddhist monastery in 1928.

Whatever it was, the Tunguska explosion still remains a genuine mystery. No dangerous radiation has been found there at present, so perhaps Tunguska will in time become a familiar tourist attraction as the Arizona crater is today.

Generally the Yenisei flows north, after passing the town of Yeniseisk, some 150 miles north of Krasnoyarsk. It goes through virgin taiga with only minor settlements on its shores until it reaches the port of Igarka, fifty miles above the Arctic Circle. Igarka is a center of extensive lumber industries. Its products are exported to a number of foreign countries in summer. Some 130 miles further north there is the important town and river port of Dudinka, the capital of the Dolgan-Nenets National District (now the Taimyr National District), and the outlet of the remarkable metallurgical region around Norilsk, the most northern industrial city not only of Siberia, but of the world.

Norilsk is well worthy of notice. Never before has man attempted to build a large modern city this far north, 69° North latitude.

Norilsk, located some 200 miles north of Fairbanks and Nome in Alaska, is a remarkably beautiful modern city of some 150,000 people. It is located amid rugged mountains near the glacier lake of Piesino, which stretches for some twenty-five miles. The city was founded by a party of geologists who, in 1922, found enormous deposits of nickel, copper, and cobalt here, and a practically inexhaustible supply of coal. This region lies in the northern rim of the Tunguska coal "sea"—an ideal spot for complex exploitation where everything necessary for metallurgical "combines" can be obtained nearby. In 1935 the Soviet government decided to build a modern metallurgical center here.

All the mining operations at Norilsk are conducted from open pits located on a high plateau over the city. The ore is delivered to smelting plants by inclined tunnels cut into the permanently frozen soil, gravity used to solve ore hauling problems. In 1937 a railway was built connecting Norilsk with the Yenisei port of Dudinka, and in 1942 a thermal-electric station was constructed. At present more than fifty large metallurgical and chemical plants are located here, as well as some food-processing and building material factories.

In 1939 Norilsk had less than 14,000 inhabitants; by 1965, 127,000, and by now probably more than 150,000.

The city has a permanent dramatic theater, a television center, and the largest Metallurgical Engineering Institute in the Soviet Union. The population of Norilsk enjoys the highest standard of living in Siberia, and probably in the whole of the Soviet Union.

The population is young—the average age is under 25—and Norilsk is primarily a city of young married couples. The birth rate is very high, only slightly lower than that of Bratsk, the city with the highest birth rate in the entire Soviet Union.

The climate of Norilsk is severe and changeable. A long cold winter is followed by a short and rainy summer with frequent fogs and sharp temperature changes. A warm day in June may be followed by a snowstorm the next day. The warmest month

A Siberian weather station during the polar night.

is July with a mean temperature of about $+55°F$. Long snow-storms are common in winter, and a complete polar night lasts for about six weeks while in summer the sun may shine for 18 to 22 hours a day.

Rainfall is high, and because the permanently frozen subsoil does not absorb the moisture, there are numerous small lakes and swamps. There is an abundance of water fowl and of fish, and both fishing and shooting are excellent. Silver fox, muskrat, wolverine, polar rabbit, and wild deer are found in the wooded tundra around the city.

During the winter, Norilsk can be reached only by air; in summer, for about 120 days, via the Arctic sea route, and the Yenisei port of Dudinka. The entire production of Norilsk goes through this port with Soviet and foreign ships crowding its piers.

The Arctic sea route communication center for all of northern Siberia is located on Dickson Island, 300 miles north of Norilsk. All ships sailing the route keep in constant radio contact with Dickson which, in turn, receives radio reports from some forty permanent polar weather stations and scores of weather planes that constantly patrol the entire 3,000-mile-long northern Siberian lifeline. The approach of storms and drifting ice is instantly reported to every ship on the route.

The Dickson station closes at the end of the summer season, and its personnel retire to the comparative comfort of Norilsk where work goes on full blast throughout the year.

A special study by a team of physiologists and psychologists was made to determine the effect that living and working this far north has on people. It was found that the average man or woman adjusts to this environment within a few months, and that children born in Norilsk enjoy more robust health than those born in milder climatic conditions. Many workers stay on at completion of their tour of duty to make Norilsk their permanent home. So the first true-polar city of Siberia is a success, and that holds bright promise for the country, since much of Siberia's development is in far northern regions. Even though swiftly progressing technology is bringing new ways and means of making living and working under polar conditions more tolerable, attracting people to Siberia has been a serious problem.

8.

Of Velvet Horns and Magic Roots

SHAMANISM is an integral and very important part of early Siberian history. Even though the practice is fast disappearing, or rather, changing, any description of Siberia, past or present, would be incomplete without mentioning it.

What is shamanism?

The answer is not simple. The word itself is of Evenk origin (often spelled *saman*) and it refers to the ancient priest-healers of Siberia. The word "witch-doctor" is often used to describe a shaman, but it is not altogether accurate. The shamans are both religious figures and healers. Shamanism is not a religion, since it is not based on any dogma, and its practice varies widely from one end of Siberia to another. Among the Buryats, who are predominantly Buddhists, shamanism may become a part of Buddhist religious practice, while among the Yakuts, who are Christians, the shamans have found ways of coexisting with Christian ritualism. Among other native tribes shamanism is usually based on primitive pantheism, and in some regions of southern Siberia it borrows its rituals from Islam, even though Siberian ritualism, as such, is more ancient than any of these religions.

Many early Russian colonists have come to regard shamans as an important part of their lives. While many shamans were undoubtedly charlatans, others were gifted healers relying in their practice not merely on rituals, but on an extensive *materia medica* based, primarily, on the use of the medicinal plants found in profusion in Siberia. In many cases, the more successful shamans, especially in the southeastern regions of Siberia, borrowed some practices from Oriental, or Tibetan, medicine, which is still widely accepted throughout Asia, and is based on some 6,000 years of meticulously recorded experiments.

Many of the shamanistic recipes and practices were borrowed by the local Russian *znakhari*, or folk healers, who were active throughout prerevolutionary Siberia, especially in far-off rural districts. Even in these enlightened days some of them can be found in Siberia, and many people swear by their ability to treat disorders sometimes held incurable by "official" medicine. But in the case of Russian *znakhari* (the word may be translated as "knowledgeable people") the practice of medicine rarely had any religious connotation, even though some of these healers were also local hermits and "holy men." Gregori Rasputin was undoubtedly a gifted shaman in addition to being an evil charlatan.

Whenever there was a very difficult case, it was not unusual for the Russian *znakhar* to call in the local shaman for consultation, and the two of them would treat the patient together, splitting the fee. However, shamanism was condemned by the Orthodox Church.

Usually, both the shamans and the village healers could not hope to collect fees until they produced results: the patient had to get well. This resembles the customary arrangement in old China where physicians were retained on permanent monthly fees which stopped every time there was sickness in the household, and were not resumed until the patients got well.

Before the Russian revolution, Oriental doctor-herbalists lived in most Siberian towns. These medical practitioners should not be confused with shamans who (in addition to their medical knowledge) were always presumed to possess some supernatural powers. They were supposed to be in intimate contact with the world of spirits, both benevolent and evil. Shamans have been known to perform extraordinary feats of mass hypnotism, putting themselves and their patients in a state of trance with the help of rituals and incantations, usually accompanied by striking a tambourine. Tambourines in the far north were as associated with shamanistic practices as stethoscopes and black bags are associated with modern doctors.

It is unfortunate that no serious and intensive study of shamanism seems to exist, and since the practice is fast disappearing with the advent of Western medicine to the most remote parts of Siberia, it is doubtful that such a study will ever be undertaken. Since shamanism, like all religious and quasi-religious practices, is presumed to be inconsistent with Marxist dogma, it is frowned upon by the Soviet state though not formally forbidden. Shamans have been stripped of the administrative authority they once enjoyed among local Siberian tribes. The few shamans who still function in Siberia are all venerable old men. Usually they are consulted only if and when no immediate medical help is available, and then only by old men and women. Their colorful magical rites, known in Siberia as *kamlanye*, are a thing of the past—or are swiftly becoming a thing of the past.

(It is curious to note the striking resemblance between the word *kamlanye*, the origin of which is uncertain, and the word *comblé*, describing the rites of quasi-religious practitioners in the Brazilian jungles, particularly among the Indians, which are strongly condemned by the Catholic Church as paganistic in nature, and akin to black magic. The two terms describe practically the same thing.)

I was told that there are two famous shamans in the Transbaikal Buryatia who still, from time to time, perform the *kamlanye* rites invoking spirits to bring rain, or to rid ripening fields of harmful insects. There are probably many of them in the deep taiga, and in the far north tundra, still practicing, but it seems as though the practice will probably disappear in a few more years.

To the credit of official medicine in Siberia, a rather thorough study of folk remedies is being made in several scientific institutions. The collection, classification, and study of innumerable medicinal herbs of Siberia are being carried out on a broad basis. Many of these age-old remedies have been found to possess considerable medicinal properties which are now incorporated in the Soviet *materia medica*.

A well-known Siberia naturalist, Alexei Smirnov, describes a botanical expedition which he led in 1966 into the upper reaches of the Khamar-Daban mountain range, south of Lake

Baikal. The expedition included a young woman doctor who joined the group in quest of medicinal plants, and an old taiga guide from a Baikal village. One of the members of the expedition was stricken with an acute intestinal disorder, and all the medications administered by the girl-physician failed to cure the young man who was becoming very seriously ill.

The doctor was worried, and felt that only a powerful modern antibiotic could save the young man. But the nearest town was seven days' trek away!

The old guide offered to get a "taiga antibiotic," an ancient remedy.

This is how Smirnov describes the event:

I had to accompany Stepanich (the guide) while Zoe, as a physician, had to stay with the patient. We walked all day through the mountainous labyrinth, and toward evening we came to a silvery mountain stream, the Utulika. We stopped there while Stepanich scanned an almost sheer cliff covered with lichens.

"Here," he said. Then, taking a knife between his teeth he started to climb the mountain wall. He reached a crack in the rocks which was covered with some yellowish, rust-like substance. He started to scrape it off with the knife.

It was growing dark when he came down bringing with him a match-box filled with a yellow powder.

Just a few granules of this "mountain oil," as the guide called it, produced such an effect that within a day our patient was up on his feet and full of life.

I brought some of this powder to Irkutsk and took it to the Medical Institute. They showed me a whole jar filled with it. They have collected it from all over Eastern Siberia. Indeed, it was a powerful natural antibiotic based on arsenic and a whole set of other elements.

And it has been used in Siberia for centuries, long before the word antibiotic was invented.

It is interesting to note that the young physician returned the favor by curing the old guide of his chronic alcoholism through the use of another ancient Siberian folk remedy, from another part of the country. The girl boiled in water a variety of club moss, known scientifically as Lycopodium. After administering this concoction to the old man, she made him drink some vodka. This caused him to vomit violently. This treatment was repeated several times, with the same effect, whereupon the girl pronounced the old man cured.

Almost two years have passed since then [Smirnov recounts]. And every time I call upon the old man he always remembers the young physician. "I'm completely cured—I don't touch the stuff since then. Not a drop. And cured by what? By the grass upon which I have been walking for many years without suspecting what a powerful medicine it was!"

Curing alcoholism was an old-time shamanistic practice, also successfully practiced by the Russian *znakhari.*

Many Siberians—people with education, and even some doctors—swear by some of the shamanistic remedies.

In the spring of 1967, in Moscow, I spoke to a friend, a man of extensive education and culture, who suffered from an acute allergy of many years' standing. He had had the best medical attention, but nothing had helped. I was surprised when he told me that he planned to visit an old Siberian *znakhar* who was practicing in the Soviet capital, no doubt unofficially, but who was reputed to be extremely successful in treating a number of disorders that resisted conventional medical treatment.

Indeed, Siberia produces not only mineral resources, but, it seems, a whole variety of natural curative agents of extraordinary potency. Two of them deserve a special note since, for thousands of years, they have been held as the most powerful remedies found in nature anywhere.

One is the so-called *panti,* or young horns "in the velvet," of a special variety of Siberian deer found in a wild state only in the Siberian Far East and northern Manchuria. The name of the animal, scientifically, is *Cervus dybovskii,* or, popularly, the "noble spotted deer." It is an attractive and timid animal, and before the revolution it was raised on a few farms near Vladivostok. Prior to the Chinese revolution of 1911, a large herd of these deer was also kept in the Imperial Forbidden City in Peking, but they were all destroyed.

The noble spotted deer sheds its antlers in autumn, after the end of the mating season, and grows a new set each spring. While these horns are still soft, filled with blood and covered with down which is called "velvet," they are presumed to have an extraordinary curative power and are eagerly sought after by pharmacists throughout Asia. The horns are either amputated and preserved in a special way, or removed with the upper part of the animal's skull which, of course, necessitates killing the deer.

The noble spotted deer are now raised in state-owned farms. These *panti* are ready for shipping.

Almost all species of deer, and particularly the "maral" of the Altai Mountains, produce *panti*, but the most valuable are produced only by the noble spotted deer. Unfortunately only a few of these valuable animals are left in the wild state at present, and they are rigidly protected by Soviet game laws.

The Soviet medical authorities have made a thorough study of the *panti*, and a preparation known as pantacrin has been developed and is available in the Soviet Union. Pantacrin is said to possess remarkable tonic qualities.

When I was in California, I met a Russian, a former lawyer from Vladivostok, who had spent his lifetime studying Oriental medicine in general, and Siberian folk medicine in particular.

My friend, in his capacity of an expert, was invited some twenty-five years ago to inspect a large flock of wild deer found on Antocosti Island in the mouth of the St. Lawrence River in Canada. These animals were the descendants of a pair of genuine spotted deer brought there some eighty years before. He found the animals in excellent shape, and he obtained some of their *panti*. However, when offered to Oriental pharmaceutical firms in San Francisco and Hong Kong, they were rejected by the buyers as devoid of any medicinal value. Apparently the feeding habits of the Far Eastern deer, and the soil conditions in their native mountains, were the determining factors in the chemical composition of their antlers.

Before the revolution, my friend told me, genuine *panti* were sold during annual auctions held at Vladivostok. Prospective buyers came from all over Asia. The value of each pair of antlers depended on a whole set of conditions: the age of the animal, the size, the color, the shape. Much of this was based on the Oriental mystique surrounding the *panti*. While some antlers would command a very high price, sometimes reaching 500 rubles (250 gold dollars at the contemporary rate of exchange), others, looking exactly alike to the untrained eye, would bring only a fraction of this price. It is amusing to note that very small *panti* had a special appeal to Chinese buyers, and were generally known as "bribe *panti*." They could be easily concealed in one's clothes and then passed on to an official who had to be bribed. It seems that the *panti* would not be rejected even by the most incorruptible Chinese functionary since they were considered to be "an honorable offering" rather than a bribe.

The farm herds of noble spotted deer were almost totally destroyed during the Russian revolution and during the subsequent occupation of part of the area by the Japanese who simply confiscated and killed the animals for their *panti*. At present the Soviet government, conscious of the high export value of this merchandise, is again building up the herds.

But if the genuine *panti* are highly valuable, the real star of the Oriental *materia medica* is the celebrated ginseng root, known to the Chinese as *pang-tsui,* and to the native tribes of Siberia as *orkhoda.* Among the Russian healers of Siberia it is known as *koren zhizni,* or "the root of life." For over 6,000 years it has been considered in Oriental medicine to be the most powerful healing substance produced by nature, the virtual cure-all. But, unlike the noble spotted deer, attempts to cultivate the root under controlled conditions have generally been unsuccessful.

It is found in its wild state in the Sikhote-Alin Mountains of the Siberian Maritime Province and in some mountainous parts of the Chinese northeast, northern Korea, and parts of North America, but the Sikhote-Alin root is presumed to have the highest medicinal properties of all.

There is so much Oriental mysticism surrounding ginseng that it is hard to obtain accurate data. For centuries almost magic properties have been ascribed to ginseng—it has been considered in China as the most potent general rejuvenating medicine, and old China hands tell stories of senile men in their eighties and nineties growing black hair, new sets of teeth, and taking young wives after undergoing ginseng treatment which, we must add, was extremely expensive.

What then is ginseng, stripped of its mythical Oriental aura?

Botanically known as *Panax schinseng*, it is an extremely rare grass-type plant of the Aralea family, found usually in the most inaccessible mountain gorges where there is constant shade and abundant moisture. It is a plant of considerable longevity— its span of life is believed to be around 15 years, or even longer. It is very difficult to spot since its appearance is not remarkable in any way. It reaches the maximum height of about 20 inches, has a single thick stem and a single crown of leaves on top of it. It blooms for a few weeks each June or July, producing small, pale green flowers, and then, small reddish berries which are the favorite food of many birds and also of field mice which, of course, makes the plant all the more rare. Almost always found growing singly, it is very rare when two plants are found together, and I have never heard of more than two being found at once. It shuns sunlight and is botanically considered to be a degenerate plant. The Siberian cedar and larch are the trees near which ginseng is usually found. Neither pine nor birch ever grow along with it.

The medicinal value of ginseng is in its root; its stem, leaves, flower, and berries are worthless. The ginseng root reaches its maturity on the seventh year of the plant's life, and over-mature roots, those ten years old or older, quickly lose their value. The root, which has the size of a young carrot or horseradish, has a delicate fleshy color, and often resembles a naked human body. The greater the resemblance, the more valuable the root, and it can also be either "male" or "female;" the "male" roots command a higher price. Besides the original four "extremities" which a good root is supposed to have, there is also a whole network of small and extremely brittle shoots known as "the beard," and to bring the top price none of them should be broken or blemished. Therefore, getting the root out of the ground is a painstaking and protracted operation.

Generally the value of each root in the eyes of the Oriental buyer does not depend on its size or weight alone, but, as in the case of *panti*, on a whole set of factors—its age, "sex," color, form, and general condition: any blemish lowers the price, as in the case of gem diamonds. Very good roots could bring almost astronomical prices, up to 2,500 gold rubles, and in exceptional cases, the price could be much higher. A Chinese pharmacist in New York's Chinatown told me three years ago that he would be prepared to pay up to 10,000 dollars for a real ginseng root—if he could find one.

For the Chinese, ginseng prospecting was surrounded by a whole set of superstitious beliefs. A ginseng prospector not only had to have skill and infinite patience, but be a pious and moral man in all respects, clean in body and spirit, a strict vegetarian and a celibate. He also had to be Chinese by birth with no mixture of any alien blood.

The Chinese ginseng prospectors, known as *va-pang-tsuis*, formed a kind of monastic order, with their own rituals based on the deification of mountain spirits, and particularly of the great *van*, or the Far Eastern tiger.

Setting off for a ginseng-prospecting expedition, the *va-pang-tsui* first went through a purification routine of fast and prayer. He could not have anything metallic on his body—even the buttons of his *kurma*, or long jacket, had to be made of bone, and his only tool was a flat bone knife. This was a dangerous rule since the mountains teem with wild animals, and the Ussuri tiger, the *van* of the ginseng prospectors, is the biggest cat in the world, and a ferocious one. However, old Siberians swear that there was never an instance of a *va-pang-tsui* falling prey to the *da-van* (literally, "the great ruler") to whom they prayed three times every day during their expeditions.

(All this was before the revolution—the Soviet border is so tightly sealed now that the Chinese ginseng prospectors cannot penetrate it, and all their activities are now centered in the Manchurian and North Korean mountains. Generally, the practice is dying out, since the Chinese revolution has largely eliminated the class of rich buyers of ginseng preparations.)

Besides wild beasts, the *va-pang-tsui* in old Siberia had other and more dangerous enemies, the so-called "white swans," the Korean taiga outlaws. They had no ability to find ginseng, but would try to find a *va-pang-tsui* who already had found one. The outlaws had no scruples about metallic objects and were usually armed with rifles, and would make short work of any *va-pang-tsui* found in the mountains. Escaped Russian convicts would hunt both *va-pang-tsuis* and the "white swans." So the *va-pang-tsui*'s life was far from secure, and only a few of them lived long enough to retire in the plush comfort which even one good root would buy them.

They usually spent winters in Manchuria, and then slipped across the Amur and the Ussuri Rivers which marked the Russian border. This was extremely easy to do before the Russian revolution, since every spring a great many seasonal Chinese workers came to the Russian side, where they could earn better wages than at home.

(I remember my father telling us an amusing story from his own experience as one of the builders of the Amur Railway. One day, a Russian railroad contractor hired 500 coolies at 50 kopeks a day. To his amazement, he found a double number of men the next day: each original worker had hired another coolie to work for him for 20 kopeks, while he sat in the shade and supervised his substitute.)

Once he crossed the border, the *va-pang-tsui* would head into the mountains. He would return in late autumn, sometimes bringing a precious root with him, but in most cases empty-handed. This did not mean that he was unsuccessful, however. Often when he found a young plant, he would leave it to mature for a year or more and then return to dig it out, hoping that another *va-pang-tsui* did not find it meanwhile, or a "white swan," following him, did not dig it out on his own.

When he found a mature plant, the *va-pang-tsui* would go through a long routine of prayer before attempting to dig up the root. Since moisture-loving ginseng usually grew near mountain brooks, the *va-pang-tsui* would use the water to slowly wash out the root in order not to break off any of its tender rootlets. If the plant contained berries, the seeds would be planted by the *va-pang-tsui* near the parent plant with the hope that the new growth would be ready for harvesting in seven years. Very few of such planted seeds would sprout because the forest mice and moles were extremely fond of them, but even if just one plant sprouted, this was worthwhile.

Meanwhile the unearthed root would be dried in the sun, wrapped in a clean linen cloth, secreted on the finder's body, and the lucky *va-pang-tsui* would start the long and dangerous trek to the market. The root would usually be sold in Vladivostok, where all great Chinese pharmaceutical firms had their representatives, and real rogues they were, always brutally short-changing the poor *va-pang-tsui* who would be fortunate to get part of the true value of his root.

In some instances, the root would be placed on the apothecary scale and its weight would be matched by gold dust. Spectacular as such procedure was, it was also absolutely dishonest, since the "gold" would be generously "cut" with ground sulphur which was known in Siberia as "Chinese gold."

The buyer who acquired the root would pack it in a few layers of tin foil, and send it to his firm by a trusted messenger. Tin foil was always used because handling the naked root could lead to the so-called "ginseng sickness." Was this caused by harmful radiation? It is possible, if the ginseng was growing in radioactive soil. Some ginseng roots have been known to cause severe burns; they were called "hot" by the Chinese buyers and were particularly valuable.

Some roots, like some diamonds, were legendary. There was one root, brought out in 1900, which was reputedly bought by the Chinese governor of Ninguta for 20,000 gold rubles, and which actually glowed in the dark. My father saw it. Its fate is unknown—it may be still hidden somewhere in China, or it may have "died," i.e., lost its radiance, and then have been used for medicinal purposes.

Once a root arrived in the hands of a Chinese pharmaceutical firm, it would be examined by experts. Some especially fine specimens were always sold intact to extremely wealthy buyers; others were turned into medicinal preparations.

Each firm had its own secret formulas. Generally, however, the root would be placed in a jar of alcohol for some short time, usually a week, and then this "first generation" infusion would be sold in small containers at an extremely high price. Then the jar would be refilled again and again until the root lost its original "strength," but it is believed that a good root could yield up to 100 gallons of the infusion. This infusion was never taken straight, but added in almost microscopic doses to alcohol or tea. The daily intake varied depending on the condition of the patient and the strength of the infusion which could be judged by its color, but excessive use of ginseng could be harmful, or even fatal.

Once the root was "milked" out, for infusion purposes, it was ground and added to various preparations usually composed of many herbs—and again every firm had its own recipes. It is difficult to estimate the terminal profit that one root could yield, but it would be safe to say that it ran into thousands or even tens of thousands of dollars.

What is the actual therapeutic value of ginseng?

Soviet scientists experimenting with cultivated ginseng have found that it possesses some important physiological substances which produce a stimulating effect upon various organs of the human body. Used in very small doses it stimulates the function of the heart, kidneys, liver, certain glands, and the respiratory system; it also enlarges blood vessels, and often decreases high blood pressure. It is prescribed by Soviet physicians as a general tonic and energy builder to be taken under medical supervision.

Since the wild root is practically unavailable, ginseng cultivation has been started recently on plantations in Eastern Siberia, but it should be noted that Oriental medical practitioners do not consider that cultivated ginseng possesses even a fraction of the medicinal value of the wild root.

Ginseng is also cultivated all over Asia and in the United States, but all these cultivated roots are sold by weight and at a very moderate price. A number of substitutes are sold by herbalists and only an expert can distinguish them for what they are. The so-called American ginseng (*Panax quinquefolius*) can be found growing wild west of the Missouri and north to the Canadian border, but according to the Oriental pharmacists it has no important medicinal value. In northern China and Korea the so-called clinging ginseng (*Panax repens*) is extensively cultivated, and in Japan and the East Indies there grows a plant called "false ginseng" (*Panax pseudoginseng*) which can easily fool unsuspecting buyers. These varieties, though used in Oriental medical preparations, are considered to be merely mild stimulants like coffee and tea; they are abundant, and sold quite cheaply.

The best cultivated ginseng came from the Sikhote-Alin Mountains and was grown in secret mountain plantations in the regions where the real ginseng was once found. It fetched a fairly high price on the Oriental market, but all such plantations were abandoned after the Russian revolution, and the only ginseng available in the Soviet Union comes from ginseng farms near Vladivostok, and it is not highly regarded by Oriental practitioners.

The only genuine root known to exist in the Soviet Union at present is the one displayed at the Permanent Agricultural Exhibition in Moscow, and it is reputed to be insured for 25,000 rubles, or 27,500 dollars at the official exchange rate.

It is interesting to note that genuine ginseng has been used in China, among other things, for the treatment of bleeding, including hemophilia. It is a general belief in Siberia that Rasputin's "magical" ability to stop the hemophilic bleeding of the Tsarevich Alexei, the only son of the last Tsar, was based on his use of some ginseng preparations, along with his prayers. As a native Siberian he was probably quite familiar with ginseng, and it is known that upon his arrival in St. Petersburg, he formed a close friendship with the celebrated Tibetan doctor Badmayev, who was in practice there. It would not have been difficult for Rasputin to obtain genuine ginseng from Badmayev.

Of course, this can never be proved, and will have to remain just a fascinating speculation.

It is generally believed that both the *panti* and the ginseng have been used in China and throughout Asia as powerful aphrodisiacs. This is incorrect. True, both have been believed to cause a spectacular improvement in male sexual potency but that, all Oriental practitioners insist, is caused by the general improvement of health. As my learned Vladivostok friend put it once, "using aphrodisiacs is like beating a tired horse while using ginseng and *panti* is like building up the horse's strength so that it can pull the load again." The main purpose of ginseng and *panti* treatment has been to overcome senility and all its unpleasant effects. It could have promoted longevity, as is often claimed, but again this was not its main aim—the main purpose was to combat the effects of old age, both physical and mental. According to Oriental medical philosophy, old age is a disease which, although incurable, can be slowed down and made bearable, if not actually pleasant. And both ginseng and *panti* are presumed to be the most effective way of doing this.

An Oriental superstition? Perhaps. But it is almost unbelievable that billions of people could have been so cruelly fooled for so many years: the ancient recipes found in Tibetan lamasteries dating back almost sixty centuries mention both these remedies.

The modern young Siberians, indoctrinated in dialectical materialism, tend to hold both shamanism and the taiga folk medicine in contempt, but serious Soviet scientists continue to study these practices, and often stumble on valuable medical discoveries.

The medical sector of the Geographical Institute of the Siberian Academy of Science, headed by Dr. Evgenyi Ignatiev, has been compiling a medical atlas of Siberia indicating "healthy" and "unhealthy" regions, and studying the reasons for such distinctions. This work is being done at Irkutsk. Local medical information is channeled there from all over Siberia. The techniques of local folk medical practitioners is taken into consideration. This study is invaluable for the development of the country, since many regions, at present deserted, are known to be dangerous to health. Research may discover ways to deal with these dangers.

Whole regions, for instance, are infested with a special kind of tick which is a carrier of encephalitis and Asiatic rachitis. The tick must be destroyed before people can be allowed to live and work there. Before the revolution, some Cossack villages in Transbaikalia were affected by a crippling local disease causing bone deformation. Only now has the cause of this condition been determined; a faulty local diet deficient in calcium and rich in strontium. By the same token, there are regions of Siberia completely free of many common diseases, usually due to the existence of some natural preventive remedies, such as certain local herbs. Those disease-free conditions are studied for possible duplication elsewhere.

Every summer dozens of medical expeditions are sent into the most remote sections of the country, and the local shamans and folk healers are questioned, their recipes recorded, and then studied.

How many of its secrets the taiga will yield to man mainly depends on this study, and Dr. Ignatiev and his staff may well be responsible for saving the future Siberians a great deal of misery, and saving innumerable lives, by studying the medical inheritance of the shamans and folk practitioners.

Mr. Paul Kourennoff, a grandson of a once celebrated Siberian folk healer of the Novosibirsk region, at present living in Los Angeles, has been collecting old Siberian medical lore for some fifty years and has incorporated some of this material into a book called *The Russian Folk Medicine Manual* published in the Russian language as an ethnographical curio. It contains some extremely interesting descriptions of simple remedies that have been used in Siberia, many undoubtedly borrowed from local shamans. While many are frankly "unscientific," to use the favorite current Soviet expression, some of them have been used for centuries by Siberians living hundreds of miles from the nearest medical help and are useful, many old Siberians swear, in alleviating suffering and even saving lives.

Just for the sake of curiosity, I would like to list some of these practices, selecting only those which obviously cannot cause harm, even if tried, though I do not recommend trying them.

Carrying a small raw potato, unpeeled, in one's pocket

throughout the winter, is supposed to prevent the wearer from getting common colds. As a child I always carried one. It should not be changed even when the potato becomes wrinkled and as hard as a stone.

Fresh cabbage leaves applied to one's throat and changed every two hours have been used to treat angina, a sort throat, and even diphtheria.

Dry blackberry leaves boiled in hot tea, or hot milk cooked with caraway seeds, have been given to alleviate intestinal pains, including appendicitis attacks.

A fistful of hops under the pillow, or some clay mixed with buttermilk and applied to forehead, have been used to cure insomnia.

Amber beads worn around one's throat were believed to prevent headaches, goiter, and malaria.

The following three treatments for migraine have been used: placing a small rag dipped in beetroot or onion juice into the patient's ear, putting a compress of homemade sauerkraut behind one's ears and against the temples; and eating salted herring.

The following methods of removing warts have been prescribed: cutting off a twig of any tree with a knot in it, rubbing the cut end against the wart and then throwing the twig away over one's shoulder—all this done during a night of the new moon; cutting a potato into twelve segments, rubbing each segment against the wart, putting them together, wrapping them in a rag and burying the whole mess in a manure pile; encircling the wart with a knot made of red thread, and burying the thread, again preferably in a manure pile. All these methods have been held infallible.

For centuries young Siberian girls have been ridding themselves of acne and freckles by rubbing them with freshly laid, warm, unwashed chicken eggs.

Suppositories made of raw potatoes have been used in the case of painful hemorrhoids, as well as grated raw apples and carrots taken internally.

High blood pressure has been treated with a strong infusion of potato peels or garlic, taken internally. Generally, garlic and onions, taken raw, have been highly recommended for a whole set of disorders such as scurvy, sclerosis, and all conditions caused by vitamin deficiency. Both can be preserved frozen.

A strong infusion of onions in vodka, or of young birch buds in vodka, has been recommended for the elimination of intestinal worms.

An infusion of pine needles or aspen buds has been used to combat scurvy and vitamin deficiency, when no onions or garlic were available.

Grated raw potato, unpeeled, and cabbage juice have both been held effective in cases of intestinal ulcers.

All rheumatic pains have been treated with hot baths with fresh birch leaves in them, or by wearing a red woolen thread on the opposite arm or leg from the afflicted limb. Carrying a raw wild chestnut in one's pocket was supposed to be extremely effective as well, as a preventive.

(There are several radical treatments for rheumatism and arthritis, such as burying the patient up to his neck in a hot compost pile, and also using a preparation of the most poisonous of all Siberian plants, the aconite, but they can be undertaken only under supervision of a very experienced shaman or a folk healer.)

Stubborn nose-bleeding could allegedly be arrested by placing a key on a string around the neck so that it would rest between the shoulder blades.

All types of neuralgia have been treated by pouring three drops of beetroot juice into the patient's ear.

Toothache has been treated in four ways: washing the tooth with an infusion of a certain herb botanically known as *acorus colamus*; packing the hollow of the tooth with a mixture of church incense and bird-cherry; placing some grated onion in a clean rag in the patient's ear on the opposite side from the aching tooth; placing crushed garlic in a rag against the patient's pulse, also on the opposite side from the aching tooth.

Many shamans and folk healers also made careers out of "talking away" the toothache—a form of hypnotism.

There were innumerable other treatments used. For centuries, for instance, willow bark and dry lilac leaves were used as a substitute for quinine, which was absolutely unobtainable in

Siberia in olden days. They have been found to possess good curative properties.

There are many books published in Siberia about medicinal plants and other natural substances; they are obtainable in public libraries and are still often used.

The foreigner is often surprised at the rather limited list of preparations offered at Soviet pharmacies. This is explained by the fact that the entire pharmeucutical industry is government controlled; there are no patent medicines, and all duplications are eliminated. Instead of having scores of preparations based on aspirin, for instance, as there are in the United States and Europe, there may only be one or two. There are no competing firms trying to outsell one another. And in Siberia, particularly, the so-called "folk remedies" are still widely used, some with the blessing of doctors.

Since medical service is offered to the population free of charge and private practice is frowned upon, medicine cannot be called a profession in our sense. There is no way for a Soviet doctor to grow rich or to be more successful than another doctor of the same category. Is this leading to the lowering of medical science standards? This is a debatable question.

There are virtually thousands of folk recipes, some of which require the use of certain herbs, and some call for such local commodities as bear and dog fat, Siberian ants, rotten earthworms, cobwebs, (to stop all external bleeding), etc., etc. Some Siberian shamans have been known to tackle such presumably incurable diseases as rabies and cancer.

Siberia abounds in curative springs, some of them still not properly studied. Many have been discovered during the last three years in the Kamchatka, and undoubtedly some of them will be developed as summer curative spas in the future.

A celebrated curative spring, which was once a medicinal Mecca for all Asia, was called Khulun-Arshan, and the use of the past tense is intentional—it is completely inaccessible at present, since it is in a remote border region between Outer Mongolia and Mao Tse-tung's China. But sooner or later this region will be open once again to health-seekers from Siberia and elsewhere.

I had heard about Khulun-Arshan since my childhood, but

for its description I shall go to Kourennoff, who visited it and described it in his book in glowing terms.

"Without any fear of exaggeration," he flatly states, "if all the health resorts of the world were put together and multiplied by a thousand, the sum would not equal the curative power of the Khulun-Arshan springs."

This hyperbolic enthusiasm is typical of many Siberians who used to visit the place, though they are all old since the place has been inaccessible for well over forty years now.

According to them, some supposedly incurable cases, such as advanced cancer, were completely arrested or even cured at Khulun-Arshan. Of course, these claims have not been scientifically proven. But some Siberian doctors to whom I have spoken recently have confirmed the fact that to the best of their knowledge the Khulun-Arshan waters possess truly remarkable qualities. None of them, however, had ever visited the place.

Khulun-Arshan, it seems, is sacred to the Buddhists, and in olden times, it was run by a team of Mongolian lamas or monks, who prescribed and supervised all treatments. The springs themselves are an oddity of nature since they form a huge natural pool having the outlines of a reclining human body. This undoubtedly endeared it to the Mongol mystics who discovered it thousands of years ago. The other oddity is that different parts of the pool have permanently different temperatures, an effect caused, no doubt, by several underwater springs. Each new patient was examined by the monks and then assigned the part of the pool fitting the region of his affliction—usually corresponding to the "anatomy" of the pool. There was also a part of the pool that was used for "diagnostic immersions" to determine the nature of the patient's affliction, whenever it could not be determined by external examination. This was located near the heart of the pool, was called "sacred Tsynkyr" by the Mongols, and had a constant temperature of just 60°F throughout the year. Immersion here was supposed to pinpoint the weak area in the patient's body, including all future danger points, whereupon a course of treatment would be prescribed.

The treatments consisted both of bathing in the pool and drinking its water—always taken from the specified spot.

According to eye-witnesses, by autumn the entire area

around the legs of the pool would be covered with discarded crutches, and they would be used for firewood by nomadic Mongols during the winter when the springs were closed. The pool itself, however, never froze. This was considered to be a miracle by the superstitious patients even though this probably resulted from the constant flow of the hot springs.

It was a pleasant place in summer. There was excellent fishing in the nearby Khalka River and the mountain valleys were carpeted with wild strawberries. The patients lived in makeshift Mongol *yourtas,* sort of wigwams covered with coarse felt, and since the desert nights could be quite cold, they were advised to bring warm clothes.

One feature of the place which might seem unpleasant was the abundance of water snakes in the pool. Those reptiles were tame and harmless. As a child, I remember seeing snapshots of some people visiting the springs; they had snakes wound around their bodies. The snakes were supposed to contribute to the curative properties of the water.

Khulun-Arshan was not, in my time, easy to reach. It is located some 200 miles from the nearest railhead at Khailar in Manchuria, and at present it is sealed off against all travelers. But as the place where shamans used to send their hopeless cases, it was part of Siberian medical lore for centuries, and one can only hope that it will again become accessible to everyone, including foreigners.

This may appear to be a strange chapter in a book describing modern Siberia, but then Siberia is a strange land full of surprises, oddities, and contradictions.

My personal encounter with Siberian shamanism was fleeting, but remarkable. As a child of perhaps eight, I traveled with my father to a large Cossack *stanitza* (as the Cossack villages were called), a few miles out of the Transbaikalian capital of Chita. What brought my father there I don't remember, but I remember our arrival at the large wooden house of the local *ataman* or village head. Unlike most peasants in Russia, the old Siberian settlers were often quite prosperous, and I distinctly remember that the large room of the house contained a very incongruous piece of furniture, a shiny grand piano. Our host was drinking vodka with a villainous-looking, huge Buryat with

piercing red-rimmed eyes. After greeting my father and offering him some vodka, they resumed their discussion. The *ataman*
was complaining about a plague of caterpillars which were
devouring his cabbages and was asking his Buryat friend for
help. The Buryat, speaking barbarously broken Russian, was
willing to help, but demanded three rubles for his services. After
some protracted bargaining, the deal was made—if I remember
correctly, for two rubles—whereupon the Buryat got up and
walked out of the room.

"Who's that?" my father asked.

"Innokentyi—an empty man, and a drunk. His father was
doing time at the Aleksandrovsk Central Prison and he got
together with a Buryat woman who brought Innokentyi up.
He's no good, but, ulcers to his soul, the power has been given
him. Let's go and watch."

We went to the cabbage field, and found Innokentyi kneeling
among the cabbages, and holding a large cabbage leaf in his
hand. Two emerald-green caterpillars were having their noon-
time meal on it. Suddenly Innokentyi gave the leaf a sharp down-
ward jerk, and the two caterpillars dropped to the ground, curl-
ing up in death. At the same moment, incredibly, there was a
soft "shush" sound as thousands of caterpillars all over the huge
field showered to the ground, dead.

Innokentyi rose to his feet and spat on the ground.

"That finishes the worm . . ."

After he collected his fee, he turned and walked away.

Our host said, "He's a thief, but a pretty good shaman, ulcers
to his soul." His voice held grudging admiration. "Once he gets
rid of them, they never come back."

That happened many years ago, and all the participants in
this scene, except myself, are long since dead. But old Siberia,
I discovered, lives on.

I told this story to a young woman in Irkutsk because she
was interested in the local lore, including fairy tales and legends.
To my surprise she did not appear to be particularly surprised
by it.

"Some old people around here seem to know something we
don't," she said. "My sister is a doctor in Bratsk. She has been
married for eleven years and had no children, despite all the

medical advice she got. Then one day she treated an old Evenk woman, who told my sister that if she wanted to have a child she should put some fresh willow branches in her bedroom . . ."

"And turn to her right side after her husband has made love to her—if she wanted it to be a boy?" I asked.

The girl blushed—sex is not a discussable subject with women in Russia. "How do you know?" she asked.

"I lived here long before you were born," I said.

"Well," the girl said, "this was ten months ago, and last week my sister had twins. Two boys."

9.

The Siberian Microcosm

AN Englishman whom I met at the Moscow Rossya hotel was quite impressed when I told him that I had just returned from Siberia.

"I say, that's a smashing idea," he said, "many of my friends have been to Moscow and Leningrad, but I don't know anyone who has been to Siberia. How does one go about it?"

"Go to the Intourist office here at the hotel, and they will take care of it. There are several places in Siberia open to foreign travel. And take your visa along with you."

From the moment you are on Soviet soil, you become the charge of Intourist, a state organization which is responsible for you. There is nothing sinister about Russian cities and towns not open to foreign tourism—it simply means that Intourist has no facilities there as yet to accommodate foreign travelers; it is a matter of bureaucratic arrangement more than anything else. Some closed cities, for instance, may have better hotel facilities than the open ones, but those hotels have no contractual agreement with Intourist.

"But," my English friend said, "my problem is that I must be back in London on Monday—all I have is six days. Can one see Siberia in six days?"

"No," I said, "but one can see enough to get a good idea what modern Siberia is all about. There is just one place where this can be done."

"What is it? Novosibirsk?"

"No," I said, "Irkutsk."

"I say," my friend said, obviously not convinced.

I don't know whether he took my advice or not. But for the benefit of those travelers whose time and means are limited, I am convinced that there is no better way of getting an impression of Siberia, both old and new, than to go to Irkutsk and, using it as a base, take few easy side trips. Only there can the "Siberian miracle" be seen in condensed form—not all of it, no, but enough to get a fairly good picture.

To me Irkutsk is Siberia, both as it was, and as it is.

It was founded in 1661 by a troop of vagabond Cossacks, led by Yakov Pokhabov. The city is situated on the right bank of the matchless Angara, the queen of all Siberian rivers, where it is joined by a smaller stream called the Irkut, for which the city is named.

Pokhabov's choice of site was good. Dozens of other "Tsar's forts" throughout Siberia have withered away and disappeared, but Irkutsk continued to live and develop steadily. And it is a fine old city.

First and foremost, Irkutsk is the gateway to Baikal, by far the most remarkable and beautiful lake of Asia, if not of the world. But this is not all.

Before the Russian revolution, Irkutsk was the capital of the immense Government General, a virtual empire which included the entire eastern half of Siberia, the present provinces of Krasnoyarsk, Irkutsk, Chita, and the Yakut Autonomous Republic, the largest one of the Soviet Union. It was from Irkutsk that the Governor General ruled this huge domain in the name of the Tsars, and Irkutsk was an imperial city with all the shabby splendor of that era. For many years the name of Irkutsk was almost synonymous with Siberia, and this is why Jules Verne selected it as a focal point of Michael Strogoff's improbable, albeit exciting adventure.

Under the Tsars, Irkutsk was a city of great contrasts and, in fact, still is. It was a prosperous commercial town and the wealthy Siberian merchants had delusions of grandeur. Even before the Trans-Siberian Railway was built, it was considered a status symbol in Irkutsk to have one's personal laundry done in London—a round trip of almost a year. It was an Irkutsk merchant who, while visiting the famous Paris Exhibition of

1867, bought the largest plate glass ever made up to then, only to discover that the only way of delivering it to his Siberian home was to carry it by hand. Relays of workers were hired who carried it all across Europe and Asia, a trek of four years. According to the legend, which might be apocryphal, he then discovered that it would not fit his home, whereupon, in a towering fit of Siberian rage, he had it shattered to pieces and dumped into the Angara. This story is very typical of old Irkutsk.

Isolated from the rest of Russia by months of travel, the Irkutsk gubernatorial "court" tried to rival St. Petersburg's splendor. The basis for this extravagance was supplied by the rich merchant class: Irkutsk stood at the tea-trade crossroads between China, Mongolia, and Russia. Some of the Siberian merchants maintained lush establishments in Hankow in the heart of China, the city which later had a "Russian concession," a miniature Russian enclave in the heart of the Celestial Empire. And no wonder: Russia was the largest tea-drinking nation of Europe and tea caravans traveled from China through Mongolia to Irkutsk, and into Russia. Also, of course, the fur and, later, the gold trade moved through Irkutsk, and huge fortunes were made there.

It was a city of great wealth and of almost unbelievable squalor and misery, because it was also the hub of the great prison empire. Stately homes of wealthy merchants and the officials of the Tsar stood side by side with wretched wooden hovels. While pigs wallowed in liquid filth in some streets, the magnificent palace designed by the celebrated Italian architect, Jacomo Queringgi, stood just a stone's throw away, facing the swift-flowing, crystal-clear Angara. Built in 1804 by the local merchant Sibiriakov, it was the symbol of the era, and it is still one of the handsomest buildings of Siberia. For many years prior to the revolution it was used by the Governor Generals of the Irkutsk empire (how else can one describe a domain larger than the whole of Europe?) but after the October revolution of 1917, it was seized by the Bolsheviks (as they were known then) and became briefly the seat of Soviet power in Eastern Siberia. A few weeks later, in December, when anti-Soviet rebellion swept the city, the palace was besieged for eight days and nights while local Communists, some of them women, defended it against waves of attackers, until they were relieved by the armed miners of the Cheremkhovo coal mining town eighty miles away.

Scarred by shell-fire and pockmarked by bullets, this building, known as "the White House" to the Irkutians, has been completely restored in all its graceful elegance. It now houses part of Irkutsk University. It is both a revolutionary shrine and a seat of the learning which the revolution has brought to this part of the country.

The main street of Irkutsk in 1917.

I honestly feel that Irkutsk is the most pleasant large city of Siberia. This is not all nostalgia. There are more spectacular cities in Siberia—Novosibirsk, Kemerovo, Novokuznetsk, and Norilsk —and some of the new towns are both beautiful and charming. But Irkutsk to me still is (and I hope my Siberian friends forgive me for saying it) an imperial city, a city steeped in tradition. It has avoided the disorganized population explosions of other Siberian cities, and it has grown without the deadening monotony of blocks of uniform apartment houses made of pre-fabricated concrete panels. Its new buildings are stately and solid, just as the city is, and they do not clash with the venerable struc-tures standing side by side with them. There is a whole portion of the town with old Siberian wooden homes covered with fret-work, handsome and elegant in their chocolate-colored decay. They will not stand there for long, but the best of them, I am told, will not be demolished but preserved in an open-air museum near Lake Baikal.

Irkutsk, like Rome, has found a way of combining the mod-ern with the old; it looks ahead, but it does not try to forget or obliterate its past. Unlike the new industrial cities of Siberia, Irkutsk has a history and is preserving it. The Museum of Regional History is the pride of the old Irkutians, and old Irku-tians are fiercely proud people. They consider themselves the only true Siberians and the keepers of Siberian tradition. This attitude is preserved in the younger generations: they are in love with their city and with its past.

They still venerate the names of the Decembrists, the aristo-crats who rose against Tsarism in Russia almost 150 years ago, who were banished here. They will show you the grave of Prin-cess Ekaterina Trubetzkaya who followed her husband into exile and was immortalized in the celebrated poem of A. N. Nekrasov, "The Russian Women." And they will show you the grave of Gregori Shelekhov, the Irkutsk merchant who "discovered" Alaska and claimed it for the Tsars. History is alive in Irkutsk, and is lovingly preserved even to the names of some villages such as Varnachya, named after *varnaks* or runaway prisoners, or Koti, named after a pair of prison shoes called *koti* found discarded here. Showing you the handsome new "House of the Soviets," they will tell you that this was the site of the old cathedral, the largest church of Siberia, which was demolished during the street fighting in 1917.

"It's a lucky day for our city," a dedicated young Communist told me in Irkutsk. "Finally we have been allocated enough gold leaf to restore the cupolas of our churches here."

That was typically Irkutsk, I thought.

A meeting in Irkutsk to celebrate the revolution of 1917. Ten months later the cathedral in the background was destroyed by artillery fire. The same square today: the House of the Soviets in the background.

Today, it is a city of almost 450,000, with a tradition of culture far in excess of its size. Irkutsk theatres are among the best in the Soviet Union, and a new education and science center, Irkutsk's own "science city," is being built near the new dam, the first one constructed on the Angara, which has created the Irkutsk Sea, stretching all the way to Lake Baikal 31 miles away. (The Irkutians like to include Baikal when speaking about the Irkutsk Sea, which would, of course, make it the largest dam "sea" in the world, but that, alas, would not be geographically correct! Whatever Baikal is, it is certainly not a man-made wonder.)

The Angara is probably the most ideal river for hydroelectrical development anywhere in the world. It is fed by Lake Baikal, and has a steady and powerful round-the-year flow with a rather sharp gradient and many narrow mountain gorges. Its name, in the Evenk language, means "breaking through the mountains." The Angara's first dam is at Irkutsk. But that is a minor project compared with the dam at Bratsk. That is built in what was once known as the Padun Gorge, wildly beautiful, savage country of mountain crags and dense forests.

Bratsk (the name means literally "brotherly" in Russian, and it alludes to the local name given to the Buryats, "the brotherly people," by early Russian settlers) is not a new town. It was first begun in 1661, the same year that Irkutsk was founded, but unlike Irkutsk, it did not flourish, but degenerated into a tiny taiga hamlet. The original village does not exist any longer; it is buried at the bottom of the Bratsk Sea which is the largest man-made body of water in the world. The only part of the original which has survived is a wooden watchtower which has been transferred intact to the new city.

Between the old town of Bratsk and the Padun Gorge, there were two other rapids, called Pianyi and Pokhmelnyi, literally the "drunk" and "hangover" ones, and both of them have ceased to exist, along with their descriptive names.

When the Padun Gorge was selected as the site of the largest hydroelectric development on the Angara, it became obvious that the project could never be accomplished without first creating a source of electric power to nourish it. This is how the

Irkutsk dam and hydroelectric project came into being: Irkutsk was to beget Bratsk.

The Irkutsk project was started in 1955, and in July, 1956, the Angara was bridged; in September, 1958, the eight units of the Irkutsk Electric Station went into operation with an aggregate capacity of 660,000 kilowatts. The dam raised the level of the Angara 98 feet, creating an artificial lake stretching for 31 miles to Lake Baikal, and raising the level of the lake itself almost three feet.

The builders of the Bratsk dam faced seemingly insurmountable obstacles from the very start. First and foremost was the remoteness of the site. Not a single road led there. Then the site itself, a gorge 2,950 feet wide through which the water was roaring at the rate of over 100,000 cubic feet per second, afforded no suitable construction site. It was absolutely impossible to bridge the river at this point using the usual pontoon bridge. For the first time in dam construction history, the river's ice cover was used as a bridging platform. From that masses of huge rocks were poured into the stream. But before this could be done a power line had to be strung for 300 miles from Irkutsk through virgin taiga, and a whole network of roads had to be cut along the almost sheer walls of the Padun Gorge.

The Bratsk reservoir began to fill on September 1, 1961, and the last units of the electric station came into service in 1964. The dam is more than three miles long, and its location makes it one of the most picturesque in the world. It has raised the level of the river at the dam site 479 feet, forming an artificial Bratsk Sea almost 350 miles long and from 3 to 12 miles wide. The Bratsk Sea has a surface area of 2,100 square miles and it is the largest, deepest, and clearest man-made lake in the world. (Lake Victoria in Uganda is slightly larger, but that includes a natural lake.)

Today Bratsk electrical energy is the cheapest in the world to consumers, and still the station operates at a healthy profit. There are 800 people employed by the project for its operation and maintenance, including 150 graduate engineers, more than 50 of whom are women. All servicing and repairs are done by the staff, but only nine people are necessary to operate the whole huge project at any given time. It has at present 18 turbines, each with a capacity of 250,000 kilowatts, and the station, at full load, has a capacity of 4,500,000 kilowatts, making it the largest operating plant in the world. (The Krasnoyarsk station, though possessing a larger potential capacity, is not expected to operate at full load for some years, not until all the energy produced can be profitably used.)

The Bratsk Dam—the largest working hydroelectric project in the world.

The city of Bratsk, an industrial beehive built in the heart of the trackless taiga, is impressive because of its youth, vigor, and headlong rush into the future. As of today the city has some 175,000 inhabitants, almost all very young. It is expected to grow to 400,000 within the next few years. It is growing at a mad rate, with rows upon rows of swinging cranes rising over blocks of uniform five-story apartment houses, and this creative activity is not all limited to concrete: Bratsk has the highest birth rate in the entire Soviet Union.

The average age of Bratsk inhabitants is under 27, with teen-agers arriving from all over Siberia, and Russia. More than seventy distinct nationalities are represented here, not counting local taiga tribesmen who occasionally come with their deer and dogs to buy supplies before going back into the taiga. What brings young people here?

First of all, the high wages which, with the usual far north bonus, are higher here than anywhere in the European part of the country. Then, good housing conditions: a brand-new apart-ment here rarely takes more than 3 to 5 percent of the family's income. The rent is computed by square meters of living space with kitchen, bathroom, corridors, and closets thrown in free, like everywhere else in the Soviet Union. Home building in Bratsk is almost keeping pace with the increasing population. Gas and electricity are included in the nominal rent, and the telephone, if one can be obtained, costs about 2.50 rubles a month without any limit on the number of calls. The climate is severe in winter, though the presence of a huge body of water nearby slightly moderates it, but the summers are delightful. The workers of Bratsk also enjoy longer annual paid vacations, and a younger retirement age than most of Russia. Winter sports are excellent, and in summer there is boating, hunting, fishing, and hiking in the taiga. The schools and nurseries are first-rate: as everywhere in Russia, children are the privileged, pampered, and often spoiled here. And Bratsk is no longer a God-forsaken and inaccessible hole. Several daily flights connect it with Irkutsk, and the new railway line joins the main Trans-Siberian Railway at Taishet.

And, of course, the romance of Siberia works like a power-ful magnet on young people of the crowded and often uncom-fortable old Russian cities. This is the Russian Far West, but without cowboys, cattle-rustlers, gunfights, and brawls because, primarily, this is a family place. There are as many young women here as young men, and early marriage is the general rule. Here, as everywhere else in Siberia, the presence of women is a most beneficial factor, for Russian women are, and have always been, superior to men in many respects and are the great moderating and ennobling influence upon their men, who tend to become unstable at times, especially under the influence of alcohol. Drink has been a dire problem in Russia for several hundred years, and still is.

Bratsk is fast developing as one of the greatest industrial centers of Siberia.

The largest wood-working and wood-processing combine of factories in Siberia turns 5,000,000 cubic yards of wood into various products here annually, including lumber, cellulose, cardboard, paper, newsprint, rosin, turpentine, etc., with hardly any industrial waste. Raw material is supplied locally by lumber camps and sawmills around the man-made lake, and this supply will never be exhausted; the standing timber will supply the factories and mills for the next 100 years, and by that time the next crop of trees will be ready for cutting.

An enormous aluminum-producing plant is another feature of Bratsk. Eventually Bratsk will become an important steel-producing center, as it is connected by rail with Zheleznogorsk, 100 miles to the northeast, one of the newest and richest deposits of almost pure iron ore in Siberia. Zheleznogorsk, meaning literally "the mountain of iron" is located amid three mountains composed entirely of iron ore. The first mountain is slowly being cut away at present, terrace after terrace, and fed into the large smelting plants which were built here very recently. Zhelezno-gorsk, a small but handsome modern city, did not exist at all ten years ago. In 1957 there were just six wooden barracks here which housed the first surveyors, and the first real construction was only begun in 1960.

The existence of immense deposits of iron here has been known for over 300 years. In 1655, the local Russian *voyevoda*, B. D. Oladyin, reported to the Tsar that the district was rich in iron and requested the necessary capital and manpower to build a smelting plant: five men and 200 rubles. But the Tsar apparently found the request unreasonable, and nothing at all was done for over 300 years. Now, besides the original iron mountains, 15 other iron deposits have been discovered in this region, making it one of the richest iron ore areas in Siberia. The ore is so close to the surface that the mining per-man productivity at Zhelez-nogorsk is the highest in the Soviet Union.

While in Bratsk, a visitor should visit one of the new rest homes for workers which are springing up around the Bratsk

Sea. Immaculately clean and functionally comfortable, they are for vacationing workers from all over Siberia, and one can see boys in cowboy shirts and dungarees, and girls in miniskirts sunning themselves and listening to jazz. A surprising number of the girls are very pretty: it seems that the Siberian climate plus ample and balanced diets have been responsible for turning out this new crop of beauties. They watch their weight: there is a scale in each rest home, with girls lining up constantly to check their kilos.

About eighty percent of the cost of transportation and expense of staying at rest homes and vacation resorts is paid by the trade unions which, of course, are not trade unions in our sense of the word. They are organizations responsible for the correct application of state laws governing each trade or profession. The average out-of-pocket cost of a small private room and four meals a day comes to about 1 ruble per day per person with no charge for children or people on pensions or those sent here for medical reasons.

After visiting Bratsk and Lake Baikal and its Limnological Institute, any visitor to Irkutsk should make an attempt to see three neighboring cities, two of them brand-new, and another so vastly transformed as to be virtually new, and at least one of the neighboring lumber camps in the deep taiga.

The new cities to see are Shelekhov and Angarsk, both of which are less than ten years old, and the great old mining center of Cheremkhovo which was once the only coal mining town of Eastern Siberia, and which has been now transformed into a mining giant.

Like every new Siberian city, Shelekhov and Angarsk have sprung up in the wave of industrialization of Siberia, and both are model cities, built from scratch.

Shelekhov, named after the "Russian Columbus," is really a satellite city of Irkutsk, located in the taiga across the Angara River from it, among wooded mountains. It is a clean, modern city with wide streets, attractive, well-stocked stores, and three- and four-story apartment houses. The city is so built that the forest is an integral part of it and some of the streets are laid out so that houses face the taiga.

Shelekhov is the aluminum city, but its enormous aluminum

plant is located two miles outside the city proper, in a wide valley between tall wooded mountains. It is an extremely picturesque location where virgin nature serves as a backdrop for one of the most modern industrial plants anywhere.

The building of the plant and the city was facilitated by the discovery in neighboring Buryatia of large deposits of perlite, also known as volcanic glass or pearl stone. Subjected to high temperature for just thirty seconds, it expands enormously, up to four times its original size, and is then used for construction. Compared with concrete or brick, perlite is much lighter, more soundproof, and more weather-resistant. It permits the construction of walls fifty percent thinner than brick walls, with the same thermophysical qualities, and it weighs four times less than brick. A brick building that would take three or four months to construct can be built in twenty-five days with the use of perlite panels, and the cost is sixty percent lower than the cost of any other building material. It is an ideal material for the Siberian climate, and should be studied by builders of other countries. It is now mass-produced here, but at this writing there is not yet enough for all Siberia's building needs, and none is available for export.

Shelekhov has about 120,000 people at present, and is growing. As in all of Siberia, young women work side by side with men, fitting panels, laying bricks, welding, plastering, painting, fitting plumbing and hardware, operating cranes. This strikes a foreigner as peculiar, especially when some young men are at the same time waiting on tables in restaurants and standing behind counters in stores, but I was told that the girls themselves insist on this equality, because of the "hardship" time bonus which leads to lower retirement age, and gives a number of other privileges. Wouldn't this affect the family life, I wondered? Surely a woman laying bricks for seven hours a day in —50°F cold would hardly have any energy left for anything else. But apparently they manage: Shelekhov, like all new Siberian cities, is teeming with children.

The archaeology-minded might be interested in visiting the neighboring village of Malita where the remains of a large settlement of prehistoric Siberians were discovered by Professor M. M. Gerasimov in 1937, and where excavations have been going on since then, with thousands upon thousands of unique relics finding their way into museums throughout Russia. Malita is to Siberia what Pompeii is to Italy—an intimate glance into the past. Some caves have been found practically undisturbed since some prehistoric catastrophe destroyed the settlement. Mark Sergeiev describes one so intact that the whole head of a mammoth lay untouched in the hearth. It was undoubtedly being cooked for a substantial family meal, and then left uneaten.

The latest hypothesis is that Malita, like Pompeii, was overwhelmed by some sudden geological cataclysm, probably a violent earthquake which buried the settlement under many feet of debris. This is the only prehistoric "town" of such size ever found in Siberia and it is a seemingly inexhaustible source of various household objects used by these earliest known Siberians.

Cheremkhovo is a city based on coke—some of the best coal to be found anywhere. To see it is to see the fabulous wealth of Siberia. Here the hills are split into deep open corridors with walls of coal on both sides, and rails laid at the bottom. Whole trains are driven in and then their open gondolas are simply loaded with coal by electric shovels.

The town of Cheremkhovo is brand-new and full of children, nurseries, and schools. Children are everywhere in Siberia, and they are both seen *and* heard, for Russians in general, and Siberians in particular, are great child-pamperers. In almost any Siberian streetcar or bus a child instantly gets a seat, even if old women and invalids have to stand up. And women or men with a child in their arms get to the head of any queue, and get served instantly in the most crowded store or restaurant.

But, back to Irkutsk.

It has several permanent theaters and concerts and a circus, which, next to the ballet, can be called the favorite art in Russia: the well-known circus artists are celebrities of the entertainment world, just as poets are stars of literature. A well-known poet, reading his works, can fill any concert hall to overflowing, and the poetic tradition is very strong in Irkutsk—fully one half of all the members of the local Writers Union are poets. Being a poet here is both honorable and lucrative: poetic works are published in astronomical printings, and the Soviet poets are among the most prosperous citizens of the Socialist society. "Our millionaires," the Siberians call them proudly, but this is an exaggeration: it is doubtful that anyone in the Soviet state has a million-ruble estate even though accruing royalties may be huge and the income tax on super-incomes does not rise over 17 percent.

A visit to Siberia is not complete without a trip to the taiga. There are several large lumber camps around Irkutsk, and a trip to one of them may easily be arranged: all of them have regular bus service connecting them with the city.

A road cut through the taiga connecting a lumber camp with a lumber mill.

I visited a lumber camp located some forty miles from the city, and because there was a thaw, getting there was a bumpy proposition: the taiga roads become all but impassable when the snow melts. We drove in a large jeep-type car belonging to the office in Irkutsk which administers the lumber camps in the region; all the arrangements were made by my good friend, Lev Nosov, the photographer of the Moscow Novosti Press Agency without whose cooperation this book would not have been possible.

We were supposed to start out at eight o'clock in the morning, but at ten we were still waiting in the lobby of our hotel. A phone call disclosed the fact that Vassya, the driver, had celebrated his 20th birthday the night before, and was still recovering. Could anyone else drive us, I asked. No, Vassya was the only one who could handle this road.

At eleven o'clock the car arrived driven by the still badly-shaken Vassya. With him came the representative of the Irkutsk lumber office, Victor G. Zverev. Ten miles out of Irkutsk it became obvious why no one but Vassya could drive us: in many spots the road was under a foot or so of water and one had to know exactly where the road was, or risk disaster, and Vassya was an expert pilot.

The lumber camp to which we were going is called Bolsherechensk and is located fifteen miles from the shore of Lake Baikal. The lumber from the camp is either floated to the lake by a small river that skirts the camp, or delivered by drag-trucks in winter. Then it is taken across the lake to a new combine of cellulose plants being built on the Buryat or eastern side of the lake. The camp has a population of 1,700. Out of this number, 630 men and 170 women are directly employed in cutting and processing lumber, and the rest are involved in administration and services. There are 350 children of all ages. There are a few non-working oldsters who are not classed as dependents since they are drawing pensions and, of course, taking care of the children.

The camp looks like a substantial Siberian village. There are well-constructed wooden houses, and all married couples have their own homes. Only unmarried boys and girls are housed in communal dormitories. There are few of those; as a rule just as

Women work along with men in Siberian lumber camps. Because of the special "far north" provision, these ladies can retire at full pension at age forty.

soon as a new home becomes available, there is a couple ready to marry and to claim it. Sex life, it seems, is closely connected with the availability of housing all over Siberia.

Each house has a plot of land used in summer for vegetable gardens, and almost every family keeps some domestic animals, mostly cows and goats, chickens, geese, and ducks. The settlement has a large club with a motion-picture theater, a dining and dance hall, a library, a hospital staffed with one physician and four nurses, schools for all grades, and a nursery for children, all staffed with professional teachers. We visited the nursery just as the children were having their afternoon nap, some asleep and some pretending to be.

The director of the camp, Anatoly A. Pankratov, met us and gave us a sumptuous Siberian dinner featuring the matchless fish from Lake Baikal, *omul*, and the inevitable *pelimeni* (the Siberian meat-stuffed ravioli) and a whole range of cold and hot hors-d'oeuvres, known as *zakuska*. There were several varieties of vodka, some excellent Georgian wine, and some sweetish Soviet champagne. A word of warning: vodka in Siberia is often spiked with pure alcohol since it is a Siberian tradition to have the percentage of pure alcohol in vodka match the latitude of the place where it is to be consumed. Fortunately our latitude was only 50°, and so our vodka was merely 100-proof. Drinking is a ritual, and an old tradition among the men. So are the endless toasts. It is absolutely useless to plead mercy: it will not be granted. However, getting sloppily drunk is not a disgrace here, and will only endear one to one's hosts.

After dinner (as the noon-time meal is called in Siberia) we had a rather unsteady tour of inspection around the camp, and were followed by a flock of taiga boys who appeared from nowhere to look at "a real American." Americans are immensely popular in Siberia, and Siberians like to compare themselves to Americans, and indeed there are many points of similarity. Generally, the hospitality in Siberia is overwhelming—so much so that a visitor must be careful not to develop delirium tremens, which, today, is a real danger there. Is drinking a problem here? I asked.

"No problem at all," Mr. Pankratov said brightly. "All the men drink in their spare time."

"Any trouble ever?"

"None. Any violence is a crime under Soviet law, even a slap on the face. We have arguments sometimes, yes, but never any trouble."

"Do you have any police here?"

"No. Women keep order, and believe me, they are tough. Look at her."

He pointed to a young woman, a handsome one, who was operating an electric saw reducing a huge log to firewood. Yes, I thought, this girl could certainly take care of herself, and anyone else too.

We discussed the economics of the camp. Activities included both cutting lumber and reforestation. New trees were constantly planted. April is officially designated as the "month of the green friends" throughout the Irkutsk province; thousands upon thousands of trees are planted then in the city and in all the towns and settlements, including Bolsherechensk. The Siberians have a passion for trees, and the *ozelenennye,* meaning "greening up," of all towns is a communal task which brings hordes of Siberians, particularly schoolchildren, out every spring.

What was the average income of a Siberian lumberjack—man or woman? For, like everywhere else, women work side by side with men in the taiga.

The working week is 41 hours, I was told, and in the taiga it is spread over five full days and a "short day" each Saturday, but soon, Pankratov told me, it will be cut to 35 hours and five days, without any reduction in pay. The pay, with the northern bonus, averages around 175 rubles a month for a qualified "specialist" woodcutter, slightly less for less "qualified" workers, with a minimum of 100 rubles. Each family averages at least two workers with an aggregate income of 250 rubles, or more. The rent for cottages varies from 4 to 7 rubles a month, electricity and water included, and each family has an allocation of free firewood for winter. Each year worked in the taiga is computed as 18 months toward retirement, which requires 25 working years. People can retire early here, at around 50, or even earlier, at eighty percent of their pay for life. Retirement is not compulsory, however, and many people continue to work. Each worker has a vacation of 24 work-days each year with full pay and his trade union pays the lion's share of his vacation transportation within 500 miles from the camp. Every three years the government pays the full cost of the worker's round trip to any place in the Soviet Union.

The main budget expense item is food, which can take up to fifty percent of income, since Siberians are hefty eaters. Next came such items as clothes, television sets, washing machines, motorcycles and, in some cases, automobiles. Saving is encouraged, but not particularly popular. Since all sense of insecurity is eliminated, especially with regard to children, people tend to spend their money freely. Women are spending more and more for clothes and on cosmetics, which are available in the local store. Men spend for sports equipment, and, of course, vodka and wine. Both are rather expensive items in the Soviet Union, but if high prices are maintained, as it is claimed, to discourage drinking, the effect is not readily noticeable. In Irkutsk I was accosted outside a store by a well-dressed young man who invited me to go into partnership with him to buy a bottle of vodka. Apparently the price of the project was prohibitive for him to handle alone. This, I was told, is a rather common procedure, and such fleeting sidewalk drinking partnerships are formed quite often between perfect strangers.

Drinking among women is not prevalent, except for special occasions, and it is considered quite unseemly for a woman to get tipsy. In this one respect the equality of sexes, I am happy to say, has not been achieved.

Anyone expecting to see any Wild West local color in the Siberian taiga will be disappointed. The taiga camps and communities are surprisingly sedate and even prudish as far as manners are concerned, and sex morals between boys and girls are old-fashioned by our standards.

Married couples have an employment preference. "We don't want loafers or skirt-chasers here," Pankratov said. "Above all, this is a family place, where people can live and raise their families. And you know something? They stay. Even if they go away, they often come back! The taiga is poison; once it gets into your blood, it stays there. They couldn't pay me to go back to Vladimir, and I'm a hereditary *bogomaz!*"

(For some reason the natives of Vladimir are called the *bogomaz's* in Russia, literally the "God-dubbers," since all the best ikons used to come from there. Old ikon-painters are still at work there, and carefully produce ikons that seem to have the patina of age. Many foreign tourists who return from Russia with "ancient ikons" are in fact bringing out these fakes.)

Our parting was warm. Pankratov threw his arms around me and kissed me on both cheeks. Men often kiss in Siberia, while kissing a woman in public is considered highly improper for a man.

The drive back to Irkutsk seemed to be much easier than driving out, since of us all, only Vassya, our driver, was dead sober. The night before he had promised his wife to stay off vodka for a while, and he kept his word.

My companions sang an old Siberian song, and I had drunken, sentimental tears in my eyes. Never, but never, should one mix Siberian vodka with Georgian wine!

The sun disappears in the clouds,
The sky is the color of rust . . .
The prisoners trudging in crowds
Are churning the thin roaside dust . . .
   Ding-a-ling, ding-a-ling . . .
Hear them clang away . . .
Ding-a-ling, ding-a-ling . . .
The old Siberian way . . .
Ding-a-ling, ding-a-ling . . .
Through forests, snow and swamps . . .
Our comrades, our comrades—
Are going to prison camps . . .

10.

"The Glorious Sea"

The sacred Baikal, the glorious Sea,
The glorious craft—a fish barrel with sail . . .
The Barguzin winds, please be gentle to me
Deliver me safely from anguish of jail . . .

THUS goes the most famous of all folk songs of Siberia. Its
origin is unknown, but to an old-time Siberian this is an unofficial national anthem, and it is sung from Chelyabinsk to
Vladivostok and from the Dickson Island to the Altaian Tuva
mountains. It describes the flight of a chain-gang prisoner from
the prison gold mines in the Nerchinsk region, and his emotion
at the sight of Lake Baikal.

If you meet a Siberian, do not refer to Baikal as a lake. That
is a fighting word. Baikal—or the Baikal (even though there
are no articles in the Russian language, there are subtle ways of
indicating this distinction) is a *sea*, never a lake. And a sacred
sea, at that. To a Siberian, the Baikal is what Mecca is to a
Sudanese dervish. It is a wonder, to top all wonders. What
wondrous things they tell you about it! Not only is it the oldest,
the clearest, the deepest, the most beautiful lake in the world,
but it is endowed with mysterious powers and qualities that are
magical and inexplicable. It is the home of some strange sea
creatures not to be found anywhere else on earth, the cliffs and
mountains around it abound in fabulous riches, and the forests
are filled with unusual animals and old shamans who can cast
mortal spells and raise the dead. There are curative springs around

it which can undo any physical damage that befalls the human body. One old Siberian told me with a straight face that one medicinal spring in the savage Khamar-Daban mountain range, flanking Baikal on the southeast, has the power to promote the regrowth of severed limbs, and swore that a Buryat friend of his had grown a brand-new leg in place of the one he lost when a tiger attacked him. It was senseless to point out to the man that this was a biological impossibility, and that there are no tigers anywhere near Baikal, but only further east. Another man, a hunter, told me that he saw two flamingoes floating by upon an ice flow in all their pink glory. (It is quite true that a flamingo was shot in the Baikal area in 1909, but that must have been a completely disoriented, lost bird, and the Baikal magic had nothing to do with it.)

But the Baikal is truly a remarkable lake, and sooner or later it is bound to become a great tourist attraction, and quite deservedly too.

There are a few things about Baikal not yet fully explained, about which there is disagreement among experts. The lake is being closely studied now by a special scientific institution set up upon its shores, the Limnological Institute of the Siberian Academy of Sciences. (The Greek word *limnos* means "lake.") The institute occupies two handsome, three-story buildings and has a permanent staff of over 100 specialists, not counting the crew of the large boat used for explorations. It is located at the small town of Listvyanka at the mouth of the Angara River, the only outlet of the lake. The Angara drains a tremendous basin of over 200,000 square miles, with some 336 rivers, streams, and brooks flowing into it.

Visiting Listvyanka was an emotional experience for me. When I was a small child, our family used to spend summer holidays there. It was, and still is, a charming lake-side village built on flat land, with larch-covered hills in the background. (The village's name means "larch town" in Russian.) Its main feature was a small ancient church set on the very shore of the lake, and I was disturbed to see this landmark gone when we approached Baikal. However, as I discovered later, the church had been simply moved further inland because the lake level had risen after the construction of the Irkutsk hydroelectric dam. I was told that the church was still "working," and that its parish priest was a war veteran who had earned several Soviet decorations on the way from Baikal to Berlin. He was also a history major at Irkutsk University.

The broad purpose of the Limnological Institute is the study of all Siberian lakes (and there are over 700,000 of them with an area of ½ square mile or larger), but so far the institute has been busy studying Baikal, and all the other lakes must wait their turn. The scientific staff of the institute annually finds and classifies an average of 200 new animal and plant forms in Lake Baikal, most of which are not found anywhere else on earth.

Boris Fillipovich Lut, one of the directors of the institute, was kind enough to answer my questions.

The sober facts about Baikal are as follows:

It is the largest fresh-water lake in Europe or Asia. Its surface area is 11,780 square miles (for comparison, the areas of the Great Lakes are: Superior: 31,800; Huron: 23,000; Michigan: 22,400; Erie: 9,910; Ontario: 7,600 square miles). Lake Baikal is about 395 miles long, and from 15½ to 50 miles wide, with an average width of about 35 miles. It lies between 55°46 and 51°29 North latitude, or roughly between Sitka in Alaska and Calgary in Canadia, i.e., well north of the northernmost point in the United States, though not counting Alaska. Its mean elevation is 1,492 feet above sea level, and the mean annual fluctuation less than two feet, so that for all practical purposes its level is considered constant.

It is the deepest lake in the world—including both salt- and fresh-water lakes. The deepest confirmed point is 5,314 feet, well over a mile, and this is now accepted as the maximum known depth. What is more important is that extremely deep water covers large areas of the lake—two-thirds of the lake bottom is under 1,600 feet of water, and a quarter under 3,280 feet, giving Baikal a mean depth of 2,395 feet—by far the deepest of any lake. (For comparison the maximum depths of the Great Lakes are: Superior: 1,333 feet; Huron: 750 feet; Michigan: 923 feet; Erie: 210 feet; Ontario: 802 feet.)

The lake most like Baikal is Lake Tanganyika in Africa, not only in its shape, the geological structure of its basin, and the chemical composition of its water, but also in its depth,—second only to Baikal.

Lake Baikal is the largest reservoir of fresh water anywhere on earth. It contains about 18 percent of all the surface fresh water in the world—about 15,500 cubic miles of it, or almost the amount of water of all five Great Lakes, and 70 times as much water as the nearest big lake in Asia, the Aral Sea, which has more than double the surface area of Baikal (25,300 to 11,780 square miles for Baikal).

Lake Baikal is the oldest known large lake in the world. It has been established that Baikal was formed during the earliest known geological era of the earth, and has been in its general present form for at least 23 million years. Measurement of the sediment on the Baikal bottom, composed of microscopic remnants of dead animals (this is one of the ways of determining the age of any body of water) even in the shallow areas of the lake show the incredible depth of over 3,000 feet, and there are indications that in some deeper spots they may be over a mile deep. No other lake in the world approaches these figures.

Lake Baikal has the clearest and cleanest water of all known lakes. This is explained by the fact that Baikal water has a very low content of salts and other minerals. One of the oldest and still most widely used ways of measuring water transparency is to dip into the lake a white-painted metal disk about one foot in diameter. Then the length of the cable is measured underwater to the point at which the disk becomes invisible. Transparency of water varies with the seasons—in Baikal it is at its clearest in May shortly after the melting of the surface ice, and then the transparency level often reaches a depth of 130 feet in the deeper areas of the lake. In comparison, the transparency of even the clear mountain lakes of Siberia, untouched by industrial wastes, rarely reaches 50 feet, and in all the lakes into which industrial wastes are dumped, 25 feet is considered exceptional.

The transparency of the Baikal water is largely the result of its depth, because even the most violent surface disturbances do not reach the bottom and do not disturb the sediment there. As the temperature of the water rises, transparency decreases. This is caused by the appearance of masses of microorganisms, but this process is considerably inhibited in Baikal where the temperature of the water is low throughout the year. At great depths the temperature stabilizes and remains constant throughout the year. At 650 feet it stays at 38°F, at 2,952 feet it is 35°F, and at the deepest places (5,000 feet or more) it is a constant 34°F.

Baikal is probably the most beautiful large lake of the world. The color of its water is peculiarly blue, regardless of the cloud cover. This is explained by the transparency of its waters which filter the light spectrum eliminating red and other colors of quick absorption until finally the blue is left, blue being the most absorption-resistant color. And although on a cloudy day (very rare here) the water may appear grey, yet when observed from even a slight elevation, such as a cliff, it appears blue or greenish-blue, depending on the season.

Baikal is surrounded on all sides by high mountain ranges which are so close to the shore that in several places they form sheer walls of many hundreds or even thousands of feet. These mountains form a magnificent unspoiled frame for the lake. There are no large towns in the vicinity of the lake, and its shores are not yet fully explored.

Because Baikal has not been part of any sea, and because of its great age, its flora and fauna have developed independently from other water basins. Of 500 distinct plant forms, and over 1,200 animal forms that live in the lake, more than two-thirds are not found anywhere else. New forms are found and classified every year. The fauna of the lake bottom at the deepest areas still has not been studied. Baikal may present science with some amazing zoological surprises, though organic life at any great depth is quite limited.

There are a few such surprises known already. Baikal is the only fresh-water lake in the world that supports a large population of Arctic seals, whose nearest relatives are found 2,000 miles further north in the Arctic Ocean. The Baikal seals, or *nerpas*, as they are locally konwn (scientifically they are *Phoca sibirica*), are no temporary zoological fluke. They have been here for a long time, and their present population in the lake is estimated at over 23,000 head. Despite the fact that some controlled hunting is allowed, the seal population is growing. They are wary animals, and until helicopters were used, any head count was difficult. But thanks to the transparency of the Baikal water, the helicopter census-takers were able to count them accurately;

at no depth to which a seal can dive in Baikal is it hidden from aerial observation.

The presence of seals in Baikal is still a zoological mystery. At first it was believed that at one point Baikal was a part of the Arctic Ocean, but this theory has been disproved. It is now thought that they migrated down the Yenisei river and then down its tributary, the Angara, into Baikal and became acclimatized there, but no seals are found anywhere in the Yenisei, not even at the point where this mightiest of all Siberian rivers empties into the Arctic Ocean. True Arctic seals are strictly salt-water animals, and do not even frequent areas close to the mouths of fresh-water rivers. So this is still an oddity, but the Baikal seals certainly seem to thrive where they are.

There are 40 varieties of food fish in Baikal; over 20 of them are indigenous, and some have no close relatives elsewhere.

By far the most celebrated of the native fish population is the famous Baikal *omul* (*Coregonus autumnalis migratorius*). A fish of the salmon family, it is the most important item of Baikal commercial fishing, and represents over two-thirds of the fish caught in the lake. It has a delicate trout-like flavor and is prepared in a great variety of ways, and no Siberian dinner is really complete without at least one *omul* dish. The average size of the adult *omul* (aged 6 to 7 years) is about twelve inches and its weight about one pound, though some older fish may weigh up to two pounds. The spawning time of the *omul* is late August or early September, when great schools of these fish collect near the mouths of the four largest rivers that flow into Baikal, and then travel upstream to the river spawning grounds. Unlike most other salmon-type fish, this occasion is not fatal to the *omul*: it returns to the lake for the winter. Ichthyologists and local fishermen distinguish at least four distinct varieties of the Baikal *omul*, each variety spawning in its own river basin. The *omul* eggs hatch in May and the baby fish are then swept back into Baikal, some of them to be eaten by their own parents: baby *omuls* seem to be the favorite food of adult fish.

(There are *omul*-like fish caught in some Siberian rivers, particularly the Lena, but the Baikal *omul* is zoologically different from its river relatives, and is a native of the lake.)

Fishing for *omul*—the "living gold of Baikal"—goes on

throughout the year. In winter holes are cut in the ice and nets are lowered to the great depths where the fish spend the winter months. The *omul* gives a sharp cry when hauled out. It is the only fish known to do so; all other fish die silently. "He cries like an *omul*" is a saying among Baikal natives when they speak about someone given to whining or complaining.

Catching the *omul* in Lake Baikal.

Since the *omul* is tremendously valuable as a commercial food fish, the lake is constantly restocked by two government-operated hatcheries which release masses of fingerlings into Baikal, when they reach the age which makes them safe from most of the predators, including their own parents. So there is no prospect of the *omul* being fished out—the fate which almost befell the most valuable food fish of the lake, the magnificent Baikal sturgeon (*Acipenser baeri baicalensis*).

For some years, fishing for sturgeon has been strictly forbidden. The sturgeon population of the lake is steadily growing now, despite the fact that the protective law is broken now and then by human predators. The adult fish sometimes grows up to seven feet long and weighs up to 500 pounds, producing not only delicious flesh but, in season, the extremely valuable black caviar. The large hatchery located on the Selenga River, the largest tributary of Lake Baikal, specializes in Baikal sturgeon, and raises the young fish in specially constructed ponds. At present the young sturgeon are flown to Bratsk, Novosibirsk, and Krasnoyarsk to stock the artificial lakes created by the construction of high dams. So there are hopes that within a short time the dwindling world supply of black caviar may be replenished. Some mature egg-laden females are shipped this way, each given a sedative injection to keep her quiet during the air voyage.

The most curious fish in Baikal, however, belongs to the zoological class of *Comaphoridae* and is locally called *golomianka*. There are two types of this fish in Baikal, and nowhere else, the large and the small *golomianka*, 6 and 8 inches long respectively at maturity. Instead of laying eggs it produces live progeny, about 2,000 of them at each "confinement." The blessed event occurs in early autumn, whereupon a certain percentage of adult fish die. When they die, most sink to the bottom and are devoured there, but the females of the large type *golomianka* float to the surface and are periodically washed ashore in great masses, probably because their bodies contain large quantities of a light oil, which makes them both buoyant and near-transparent. Left in the hot sun these females actually "melt away," leaving nothing but head and bone structures. Two small fish weighing 1½ ounces each can supply a man with a full daily requirement of vitamin A, and the oil of the dead *golomianka* is harvested and used for industrial purposes. From time immemorial it has been used by the local Buryats for their lamps, and *golomianka* oil has been and still is used medicinally as well. However, because these fish do not stay in schools and remain at a considerable depth, they are not caught commercially. The *golomianka* is a cold-water fish and water temperature above 45°F kills it. This is why it usually stays at depths of between 700 and 1,600 feet and rises to the surface only during cold autumn or spring nights when it becomes a favorite food of seals.

This is the only known viviparous fish in Baikal, and one of a very few known to exist anywhere else.

There is in Baikal a species of small shrimp-like *Amphipoda* (over 280 varieties), which is not found anywhere else, as well as a unique multisegmented water worm (*Manayukia balcalensis*) which is the only multisegmented worm known to live in fresh water anywhere. There is also a small bottom fish of the *Cottidae* species which is a part of the unique Baikal fauna.

It is interesting to note that various types of these aquatic inhabitants of Baikal keep to different sections of the lake, as though respecting imaginary borders, and that less than one-third of them are found in any other fresh-water lakes. The entire aquatic life of Baikal below the 1,500-foot level is unique to Baikal. The absence of common forms of aquatic fresh-water life is especially surprising since the large Baikal tributaries, the Selenga, the Barguzin, and the Upper Angara, continually bring in large quantities of these species which, for reasons that are still mysterious, do not survive in the lake.

There are many other valuable food fish in Baikal which should delight any sport fisherman. Three of those deserve special mention—*maxun, sazan,* and *kharius*—all of the salmon variety, which, although found in other fresh-water basins, are particularly numerous in Baikal. The so-called "black *kharius*" is so rare elsewhere that it should be considered uniquely a Baikal fish.

The plant life of Baikal is equally unique, but since only specialists can distinguish specific plant forms, they are not as noticeable as aquatic animals. However, one form should be mentioned: it is a warm-water sea sponge which is never found in any other fresh water.

The description of Lake Baikal fauna would be incomplete without mention of a special type of flightless water insect known locally as *rucheiniki.* These insects breed along the Baikal shores in such enormous numbers that they often completely cover the water for several feet off shore, as well as the neighboring rocks. They are important for the biological balance of the lake since they represent the favorite seasonal food of the *omuls* which gorge themselves on the *rucheiniki.* While they live in the larva state for three or even four years, the adult *rucheiniki*'s life-span is two to three days. After laying masses of eggs in the water, they die, but because not all *rucheiniki* hatch at the same time, their breeding season may last for several summer weeks, much to the delight of the *omuls* and other fish who feed on them.

Lake Baikal has 27 islands, all of them small except Olkhon Island which occupies an area of 280 square miles. This island and several Ushkan Islands are part of an underwater mountain chain which runs across the Baikal bottom. Olkhon Island, the top of a huge underground mountain, has no water. In fact the word *olkhon* means "waterless" in the Buryat language, and the island well lives up to its name. Not a single brooklet or spring can be found anywhere on the island, and the precipitation is extremely low. Even when the entire area is covered by clouds there is usually a "window" of clear sky over the Olkhon, the result of the air up-drift rising from the island. This is the sunniest spot in Baikal, and the whole Baikal region has more sun than any other similar area of Siberia. The lack of local water probably will not prevent building on the island, which is surrounded by masses of pure drinking water. There are now two large fishing settlements on Olkhon Island.

Around Baikal there are numerous small lakes known as *soras*, often connected with Baikal by narrow straits. They are shallow, but some of them are large enough to afford fine fishing, and they support fishing communities. Those are recommended to sport fishermen since they are not subject to the dangerous sudden storms which are frequent in Baikal proper.

For many centuries, the aborigines considered Baikal to be an area of some supernatural powers. To the Evenks it was the Holy Sea, the home of the Angry Spirit, probably because the lake lies in the seismic belt and underground volcanic activity, small earthquakes and ominous underground rumblings, are common. The new towns built around the lake are constructed with this in mind. The houses are built of wood logs, which can resist even sharp earthquake shocks. The last seismic upheaval of near-catastrophic proportion occurred in 1861, when a whole stretch of the Baikal shore covering some 70 square miles became covered with water, and formed the present Proval Bay. No serious disturbances have been recorded since then, but the ominous rumblings can still be heard.

Another phenomenon which terrified people who lived around

the lake were the cracks which appeared in the Baikal ice during severe winters. As the temperature plunges, the ice cover contracts, and cracks with a thunderous sound. Such cracks may run for many miles. They represent a serious danger for the ice traffic across the lake. Even the local inhabitants, well accustomed to these manifestations, are often unnerved by these explosion-like sounds, which occur usually during very cold nights.

The presence of an immense mass of water locked in high mountains produces other strange phenomena: sharp temperature changes often cause a low fog to rise from the water, and the lake seems to be "steaming," to use the local expression. It is a beautiful sight: the brilliant sun shining overhead and white wisps of fog rising from the mirror-like surface of the great lake.

Water spouts have been known to occur in Baikal as well, but this phenomenon is rare, and only the old fishermen still remember some of them, which reputedly flung countless tons of *omul* high into the air and deposited them on the shore.

Another peculiarity of Baikal, still baffling the scientists, is that the level of oxygenation of the water does not seem to decrease materially with the depth of the lake. Usually, at a depth of 1,000 feet, the oxygen content of water falls off at least 75 percent, and at 3,000 feet, there is only 5 percent of the normal oxygen. In Baikal, however, the oxygen content does not seem to decrease at all at 1,000-foot level, and the water remains highly oxygenated even at enormous depths, thus promoting the existence of organisms where all life usually ceases to exist. There is no logical explanation of this condition, unless Baikal is fed by underwater springs at its deepest levels. This once led limnologists to believe that Baikal has an underwater connection with the sea, but this has been disproved.

The peculiar air conditions over the lake cause frequent mirages. Lamakin, one of the explorers of the lake, witnessed a night mirage, a brightly-lit train gliding over the lake while, in fact, this train was passing some thirty miles away. Night mirages, however, are extremely rare. Daytime mirages are rather common: distant shores appear to be floating in the air over the lake, and this so impressed the Buryats in olden times that they ascribed magical qualities to the lake.

There are certain places where sudden changes of temperature make the shore sands "sing." This so baffled the aborigines that all sorts of fantastic legends were connected with the phenomenon. This has been explained now: the whistling and murmuring sounds are caused by the expansion of grains of sand, which force the air out of the sandy deposits.

Baikal is a very unusual, and, in many respects, a unique lake. However, it hasn't any monsters. Another lake in Siberia, much further north, claims this honor. It is called Lake Khaiyur, and is located in Yakutia in the Kular Mountains west of the Lena River and some 100 miles south of the Laptev Sea. It was in this thermal lake that in the summer of 1965 a biological expedition from Moscow University both heard and saw a monster. The staff members of the Yakut Academy of Science even sketched it. According to them it closely resembled a prehistoric Ichthyosaurus, and had a small head, long gleaming neck, and huge body covered with a jet-black skin. It had a vertical fin along the spine, and a long tail. Two subsequent expeditions did not see the creature, but "heard it"—or rather, heard a very loud splash which disturbed the surface of the entire lake, which has a diameter of some 600 yards. The creature presumably dived into the lake from one of the very steep shores when it heard the approaching men.

Baikal is an extremely cold lake. Even in June the water temperature rarely rises above 39°F and in the northern part of the lake some floating ice may be encountered until July, though the summer water temperature of other Siberian lakes, even those lying north of Baikal, rises to 50°F or even higher.

But if Lake Baikal absorbs warmth very slowly, it is also very slow to give it up. While other lakes in the same vicinity become ice-bound by the end of November, Baikal freezes over only at the beginning of January, and often later.

There is a very peculiar phenomenon common to all fresh water, and particularly lightly-mineralized water, such as that of Baikal: while water expands as its temperature rises, yet at approximately 39°F it develops a physical anomaly, caused by its molecular composition, and begins to contract, thus growing "heavier." Once this "magic level" is passed, it begins to sink while the colder lower layers begin to rise. This process of inversion repeats itself in the autumn and since the water at great depth remains at a constant temperature slightly above freezing point, it begins to rise and replaces the surface water which is ready to freeze. Thus the process of winter freezing is delayed.

It was once believed that Baikal annually received more water through its 336 large and small tributaries, and from precipitation, than it discharged through its single outlet, the Angara, but now it has been calculated that Baikal annually receives almost exactly the same amount of water as it discharges. That is why its surface remains almost static, with only minor fluctuations from year to year. This makes the Angara's flow constant, rendering it a remarkably good stream for hydroelectric development.

The presence of such a tremendous body of water affects the climate of the Baikal area, making the air cooler in summer and warmer in winter than that of outlying regions. When, for instance, the temperature in Irkutsk falls to −20°F, on Baikal it is only −12°F. In summer, however, when the temperature in Irkutsk may rise to 90°F it may be 70°F or even lower on Baikal. Baikal receives an average of 2,583 hours of sunshine annually, more than many famous resorts, and rains are rare and usually fall at night. This is explained by the peculiar geological conditions of the Baikal area, where the high mountain ranges keep the low clouds away.

It is interesting to note that different areas of Baikal show different air temperatures, and this difference may be considerable. For instance at the northern end of Baikal, at Nizhne-Angarsk, the mean summer temperature is considerably lower than in some regions further south such as at Babushkin. In winter this is reversed, and the winter temperature in northern Baikal is milder than that at the southern end of the lake. The moderating influence of the Baikal waters affects its mountainous shores, too: while the flora near the lake level is alpine, further up it abounds in plants common to temperate zones elsewhere, since the air temperature is considerably higher, in some regions up to 10°F higher at 500 feet, than at lake level.

The mountainous contours of the Baikal shore cause the famous Baikal winds, which can be treacherous and savage. Even when the sky is clear and the water absolutely calm, this condition may change within minutes. The most treacherous and most dangerous wind is called *sarma* which bursts into Baikal through the river gorge of the same name on the western shore of the lake. The squall winds may reach the velocity of a hurricane—100 or more miles per hour. There have been instances when the *sarma* threw houses and animals into the water. It has sunk large fishing boats by icing them over with the freezing water "dust" raised by the wind. However, the *sarma* does not cover the entire lake, only limited areas.

Another typical Baikal wind is known as the *gornyi* and though this rarely reaches the savage force of the *sarma*, it may cover the entire lake and persist for days, especially in late autumn. There are several varieties of this wind, bearing local names, and the local inhabitants can usually predict them fairly accurately. Other winds, though intense at times, are less dangerous.

The currents in Baikal also represent something of a mystery: their origin has not yet been fully explained. There is a distinct pattern of four circular currents in Baikal, moving in a counter-clockwise direction. What is even more baffling is that they persist throughout the winter when the surface of the lake is covered by three to four feet of ice. Baikal ice in some sections of the lake is a delight to see. Because of the extreme transparency of the water, the ice may be completely transparent and the sunlight penetrates through it and into the water. Then one can watch fish swimming under one's feet. This occurs in regions that freeze while the water is absolutely calm, and where the surface snow is blown off by the wind before it can become frozen to the ice surface.

The word *baikal* means "the rich lake" in the Buryat language. They should know: the Buryat have lived around the lake for at least ten centuries, and perhaps longer. They are of almost pure Mongol stock. Much of the eastern shore of the lake lies within the Buryat Autonomous Soviet Socialist Republic which, in turn, is a part of the Russian Federation.

For two centuries the mountains all around Baikal have been thought to be rich in gold, and in fact, many prospectors eked out a livelihood working the small streams that join the lake. However, the latest research has failed to find gold here in any significant quantities, outside of one fairly productive field along

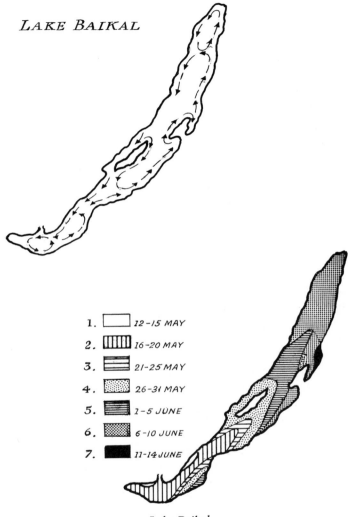

Lake Baikal.

Upper map: Water currents of Lake Baikal. These are summer surface currents, but were found to persist under the ice as well. Lower map: The dates of the disappearance of the ice cover of the lake, based on many years' observations.

the Barguzin River. The real wealth of Baikal is its enormous timber resources. Some of the taiga's most valuable timber grows around the lake, and is cut and processed at lumber camps nearby. "Plant two trees for every tree cut," is the government rule for these cutting-*cum*-reforestation permanent lumber communities. In summer, huge logs are tied together into what are locally known as "cigars," and floated down the rivers into Baikal. They are towed across the lake and into the Angara by tug boat and to the loading railhead. In winter they are dragged by specially built tow-trucks along the icy roads.

Around the southern edge of the lake in the Khamar-Daban mountain regions there are large groves of magnificent Siberian cedar, the queen of the taiga. They are annually harvested for their edible cedar-nuts, which also yield valuable oil. The cedar bark produces a clear gum which the Siberians have chewed for several centuries. This chewing habit is dying out now, because it is considered "uncultured." I remember newspaper ads in the Irkutsk papers offering employment to "non-smokers, non-drinkers, and non-chewers."

Siberian cedars are tall, stately trees, erect and trim, some of them several hundred years old. One of these patriarchs, when cut, showed 1,400 year circles in the stump. Cedars are never cut down to be used for lumber, but only cut for the pencil factories.

In recent years the cedar groves have been in dire danger of destruction from a plague of the caterpillars of a small Siberian moth known as *shelkopriad*, literally "silk weavers." Untold millions of these creatures descended upon Siberian forests, destroying them more quickly and more surely than the most disastrous forest fires. When hordes of them approached, their chomping could be heard half a mile away, or at least so Siberians told me, and nothing seemed to stop them. Cedars were killed outright. Pines, silver firs, and larch trees could recover in time after being denuded, but the precious cedars would just wither and die. Thousands of acres of forests were sprayed with insecticides, destroying much of the wild life and poisoning mushrooms and wild berries, but that did not stop the "silk weavers," who just continued their chomping rampage, and brought bark-boring insects in their wake, who finished their work.

The credit for saving the Siberian cedar forests goes to an Irkutsk biologist, Evgenyi V. Talalaev. He noticed that the *shelkopriad* caterpillars often fell victim to some mysterious and fatal disease, and after some experimentation, he was successful in isolating the previously unknown microbe causing it, the "dendrobacillus." He tested it on various animals and, as the story goes, even on himself, and discovered that it was deadly only to this particular kind of caterpillar, and better still, that it spread from one insect to another with great rapidity. Masses of the culture were grown, mixed with dry clay and spread over the *shelkopriad*-infested forests. There was no immediate result. The insects continued their feeding. It appeared that the method was a failure, but the next year young caterpillars started dying by tons. The stench of their rotting bodies drove animals away. The microbe had attacked the cocoons of the *shelkopriad* and all newly born caterpillars were infected. The battle was won, but not before countless thousands of acres of precious cedar forest had been destroyed all over Siberia. An extended campaign of cedar reforestation is being conducted now. Fortunately, the Siberian cedar is both a fast-growing and a long-living tree.

A huge cellulose-paper combine, the largest in the Soviet Union, is now being built near the lake. Building work was delayed two years by a battle between the combine designers and the Baikal locals who feared that the lake might become contaminated by industrial waste.

The lake lovers won when it was proved that even a very small amount of waste dumped into the crystal-clear Baikal water would affect the highly sensitive omul. The credit for this discovery goes to the Baikal Limnological Institute.

Now the cellulose-paper combine has new features in its construction which will eliminate all harmful wastes almost completely. Waste will be processed to extract useful industrial products, such as tars and soap, turpentine and chemical oils, while the contaminated water that remains will be run through a series of filters and sediment-collecting basins before reaching the lake.

Mr. Lut, of the Limnological Institute, seemed to be satisfied that the wastes will be purified.

"We are not going to repeat the mistake of America and other industrial nations; we won't permit the pollution of our inland waters, and especially Baikal. What has been done has increased the construction cost of the factories enormously, but it is a small price to pay for keeping Baikal the cleanest freshwater lake in the world. Baikal is our national treasure of incalculable value, and nothing, but nothing, must be permitted to destroy or even harm its unique qualities."

Now the government has decided to turn the entire Baikal area into the first national park of the Soviet Union, and to ban all further industrial construction in the area. Existing industry will not interfere with the development of the area into a tourist preserve.

Present government plans call for the eventual construction of a whole network of resorts and hotels around Baikal with an ultimate capacity of 250,000 visitors.

This development should include the Angara River, by far the most beautiful of all Siberian rivers, especially at the point where it breaks out of the lake through a wide mountain gorge. It is just as cold and almost as clear as Baikal—a small coin dropped into it can be seen settling at the bottom at a depth of twenty-five feet or more. It is almost a mile wide there and is cut in two by a jagged rock called the Shaman Rock. This name is a part of an ancient Buryat legend: It appears that Baikal was a miserly widower who doted on his only beautiful daughter, whom he kept in a virtual prison surrounded by mountains. He collected water from the many streams pouring in, and never let a drop out. His daughter, Angara, was very unhappy in her father's prison where an evil old shaman guarded her. From birds she learned that far away there was a handsome giant, the Yenisei. Angara fell in love with this hero sight unseen, and decided to escape and join him. One night, in a howling storm, she pushed aside the mountains and broke out. The evil shaman was not quick enough to stop her, but did manage to awaken old Baikal and handed him a big rock. Enraged, Baikal hurled the rock after his errant daughter, but it was too late—Angara was on her way to Yenisei, the rock landed harmlessly in the stream, and so it rests there now as a silent memorial to triumphant love.

The Angara River in winter.

This story is immortalized in countless folk songs and ballads, one of which goes like this:

> The Baikal is forever collecting
> Strains of silver from left and from right
> But his daughter, her father neglecting,
> Squanders all in her furious flight . . .

The mountains around Baikal once abounded in wild animals —bears, ermine, kolinsky, squirrel, and the famous Barguzin sable—but many years of unrestricted hunting have greatly depleted this population. The sable especially, long a virtual currency of early Siberia, has all but disappeared in many regions of the country where it was once abundant. A widespread campaign is being conducted now to restock these areas. Professional hunters are paid as much as 200 rubles for every animal brought in alive, which is at least double what they could possibly get for a skin, even on the fur black market. This is praying off. Hundreds of animals are brought in every season and then flown into the areas where they were once common, and turned loose. This, of course, is a wise investment. Unlike silver fox and mink, which now are raised on huge government farms, sable does not breed in captivity. It quickly dies if deprived of freedom.

Another Baikal region native, a diminutive deer called the *kabarga,* is still quite numerous. The bear is referred to as "the master of the taiga," and the *kabarga* is called its "spirit." It is a friendly and trusting animal and will often approach men in the forest in response to a whistle which it mistakes for a mating call. Unfortunately a sharp whistle can also bring in a bear in quest of the *kabarga,* but the Baikal bear is a timid creature and rarely attacks anyone unless it is attacked or wounded. The best way to get rid of a bear, I am told, is to walk straight toward him: he will turn tail and run. Frankly, I would not care to go through such an encounter.

The flora of the Baikal area is extremely abundant in summer, and is so varied and unusual for this northern region that the Baikal mountains are often called the cold tropics. The Khabar-Daban mountains are especially unusual, particularly in their highest reaches where the entire foliage often has a bluish rather than green cast, the result of the peculiar climatic conditions of this particular area. There is an abundance of flowers, many of them of tropical appearance, while others are alpine in character, and from time immemorial the Khabar-Daban Mountains have provided the Buryat healers and shamans with a wide variety of medicinal plants and herbs.

The peculiar character of the Khabar-Daban fauna is caused by early, sudden, and abundant snowfall which insulates the ground from the extreme cold with the result that it does not ever become fully frozen, and many plants which are usually killed by low temperatures survive under this snow cover to blossom another spring. Some of the largest and most luscious cultivated strawberries, for instance, are grown here although they require hot-house conditions elsewhere in Siberia, except in its extreme southern regions.

11.

Diamonds

WE stood at the bottom of a huge hole in the ground, the five of us, and around us there were diamonds in untold carats, no, tons.

This was "the Pipe of Peace," the largest diamond digging anywhere outside South Africa, the diamond center of Siberia at the town of Mirny (meaning "peaceful" in Russian) in Yakutia, the capital of the newest and richest "diamond province" of the Soviet Union.

We had flown from Irkutsk early that morning in a blinding snowstorm, the three of us, Lev Nosov and Stanislav Illyin, both of the Novosti Press Agency in Moscow, and myself. We were fully prepared for murderous cold, for Yakutia is the coldest place in Siberia, but we found spring-like weather instead, and as we stood in the bottom of the hole, a brilliantly blue sky was over us and the ground was muddy with an unseasonal thaw.

According to my young companions, I was the first foreigner to visit Mirny and they were surprised with what ease I had secured permission to do so. One must specify all the towns one wishes to visit in the Soviet Union and all of them have to be marked in one's visa which is a special separate document. There are cities which are open for foreign tourism, and Mirny is not one of them. However, when I mentioned Mirny as a place I wanted to visit in Siberia, no one raised any objection. Probably the fact that my trip was sponsored by Novosti was responsible for this.

Mirny is a young town, one of the youngest in Siberia. Ten

years ago there was absolutely nothing here. It was utter wilderness. Unlike some other young Siberian towns, Mirny was not planned. It came into being in a wave of the diamond rush, with thousands of people arriving before the first solid building had been put up. And it shows it: it is still a frontier town with blocks and blocks of barrack-like buildings constructed of prefabricated cement panels. Over 40,000 people live here now, but the town is unlikely to grow into a giant, for large-scale diamond mining does not require masses of miners. The whole operation is highly mechanized.

Valentin V. Vecherin, a local newspaperman, met us at the airport. A tall and husky man wearing a light overcoat of immaculate cut, he conducted us through the deep Yakutian slush to his brand-new Volga car, also surprisingly spruce-looking. Automobiles suffer from the bitter cold just as people do: two or three years is the average life-span of a car in Yakutia, I was told. When the thermometer plunges down to —70°F, something happens to metal; it becomes brittle, the paint cracks, the doors fail to close, and the motor has to be heated before

The city of Mirny, the diamond center of Yakutia.

it will turn over. Foreign tourists in Russia often comment on the fact that taxi doors, even in Moscow, do not seem to fit properly. This is not the result of neglect, as often suspected, but of climate.

But the weather in Mirny was beautiful, crystal clear and quite warm.

"Things, here are never what one expects them to be," Vecherin explained as we got into the car. "But all in all, this is a fine place. Plenty of space, plenty of fresh air, good fishing in the Vilyui River, and with luck, one may pick a diamond from the ground. We are driving over them now. They are all over here, really, but wait until we get to the pipe."

He used the Russian word *trubka*, literally "a little pipe," a word used to describe a smoking pipe.

"*Trubka?*" I asked.

"Yes, that's what they are called geologically," Vecherin explained. "Even though they can be huge. We have a real monster here at Mirny. The diamond pipe is a natural shaft going straight down to the molten core of the earth. Millions of years ago, the red-hot magma erupted through them—like bubbles through a very thick porridge. And that's where the diamonds are—the crystals of pure carbon baked by volcanic heat, the only way they can be produced."

We did not drive through the town—the road from the airport ran directly to the modern building of the Mirny Diamond Administration. Here we were met by the director, Pavel Semenovich Novoselsky, a very well-dressed man, perhaps fifty, with a handsome expressive face and well-groomed chestnut hair.

"You've come here to see diamonds, of course?" he asked after shaking hands with us. "Very well, let's go to the pipe. Would you like a little drink of cognac before we start?"

We said, no, thank you, not yet, whereupon he took his topcoat from the clothes tree and his hat. The coat of thin wool could have been made by a London Savile Row tailor. Sartorial elegance is not a characteristic trait of the Soviet Siberians, but both Novoselsky and Vecherin were exceptionally well-dressed men by any standards. Was this an English overcoat, I asked, perhaps a little tactlessly.

Novoselsky smiled. "It was made right here in Mirny. We are careful of our appearance here. After all, we live in the richest town in Russia, perhaps in the world, and we can afford to look like capitalists. But it wasn't always like this. When my wife and I—she's a geological engineer, too—first came here nine years ago, we were given a tent, with a small wooden stove in it. We took turns tending the stove at night—that was a matter of survival, because it was a particularly bad winter. We slept in fur coats and fur boots. Let's go to the pipe."

We drove to the pipe.

"Have you ever seen a diamond pipe before?" Novoselsky asked.

"No," I said.

"Well, you might be disappointed. There it is."

I looked and saw nothing, just a flat plain.

We got out of the car and walked for perhaps fifty feet, and we stood on the rim of it. It was a tremendous circular hole dug in the ground, over a mile in diameter and at least 500 feet deep. A circular terraced road led down into it. It did look disappointingly unglamorous, rather like a disused city dump. At the bottom several steam shovels were at work, scooping up huge broken pieces of rock and loading them into dump trucks. The walls of the hole were a dark brown color with occasional bluish splotches.

I asked "That blue stuff is kimberlite, isn't it?"

"No," Novoselsky said. "This is the blue clay which usually comes with kimberlite—the kimberlite clay. But the real kimberlite are those rocks there. That's where diamonds are. Shall we go down?"

We drove down, the car sliding dangerously now and then along the steep, narrow road. The ground below was even soggier than above, and it was colder there. The heaps of broken brown rock looked quite commonplace and uninteresting. This wall, Novoselsky explained, had been blasted in the morning and these broken rocks were the result of the blast. Now the rock was on its way to the "enriching plant": there were three of them in Mirny working around the clock.

So we stood at the bottom of the hole, the five of us, and just looked around.

I picked up a small piece of rock and looked at it. Novoselsky smiled.

"Looking for diamonds? The chances are against you, but some of them have been found here. One of the best was found by a driver who brought a group of Moscow journalists here. He went behind a rock to relieve nature and came back with a rock with a crystal in it. It was an excellent gem stone of nine carats." He looked at the stone in my hand. "Still, a diamond prospector would get quite excited over this."

"Why?" I asked.

"Because of this reddish speck there."

I looked and at first I saw nothing. But then I noticed a very small dull-reddish speck—no bigger than the head of a small needle.

"That's a pyrope," Novoselsky explained. "It's quite worthless in itself, but any time you come across one, start looking for diamonds. Both are found around volcanic pipes—even though pyropes might be spread for miles around. This place was found by following pyropes—I'll tell you the story later on, if you're interested."

I said that I was.

The heavily laden dump truck chug-chugged up the spiral road running up the wall of the hole—pardon me, the pipe.

"How many diamonds are here?"

I knew that the question was stupid even before I had finished the phrase. I had been warned in Irkutsk that none of the people connected with the Yakutia diamond strike were permitted to cite any figures.

But Novoselsky did not seem to be taken aback. "Quite a few," he said with a smile. "You probably mean gem stones, don't you? Most of the stones found here are industrial, but to us they are every bit as valuable as the gem ones. Without them, many industrial operations, including oil and natural gas drilling, would be difficult, if not impossible. Diamond is the hardest substance in nature, and quite unique—it just can't be replaced by any other material. But this pipe produces a very high percentage of gem stones—around twenty percent, I'd say. I can't quote exact figures, of course, but today the Soviet Union is second only to South Africa in diamond production. At this point we produce all the diamonds we need or can sell abroad, and when we need more, we'll produce more. It's that simple."

"But aren't you working at full capacity now?"

"No—we could easily double our diamond production, or triple it. There are three pipes in operation in Yakutia now, and our geologists have already discovered over 300 other pipes, some of them as rich or richer than this one. So we have probably the largest potential diamond reserve in the world. We've been working this pipe for almost ten years, and it shows absolutely no sign of depletion."

Later, we drove to the place where lunch (called dinner here) was waiting for us. It was a cosy small dining room, immaculately clean and bright with a profusion of flowers and potted plants, probably a sort of executive canteen. It was run by a couple—a neat oldish man with a small silver beard and a motherly-looking woman, probably his wife. There was a "service girl" here as well (the word "waitress" is thought undemocratic in Siberia today), a red-cheeked, snub-nosed lass. She served us with cheerful dignity and efficiency.

There were fresh cut flowers on the table, and a large bowl containing oranges, pears, and bananas. "Fresh fruit is flown daily to Mirny throughout the year," Vecherin explained, "and they grow flowers, tomatoes, and cucumbers in hot-houses here, even in winter. People eat well here. Vitamin deficiency in Siberia is our yesterday—it will never be a Siberian plague again."

The food was traditionally Siberian and traditionally good, even though a bit on the heavy side. In Siberia this midday meal is the main meal of the day, at the end of the day's work which usually lasts for seven hours with only a tea break. And since work often starts at seven, it terminates at two. To understand the ability of an average Siberian to withstand this Spartan routine, one should remember that Siberian breakfast is almost as hearty as dinner (that is, lunch) while the evening meal, called supper, may consist only of sour milk, cooked fruit, and tea. An old Siberian saying advises one to "eat breakfast alone, share dinner with a friend, and give supper to an enemy." Siberians usually retire early and rise very early.

So we shared our dinner, washing it down with vodka, wine, cognac, and champagne, in that order.

The Siberians, even more than the Russians, are traditionally heavy drinkers. Among men, drinking is almost universal and is often overdone, and getting drunk, as we have noticed before, is no disgrace. "He who is both drunk and intelligent has a double quality to him," according to an old Siberian saying. Another one asserts that "a drunk will sleep it off, but a fool, never."

My companions knew and understood diamonds, and told me about them. It is from them that I learned the full diamond story of Siberia.

Besides a gold reserve, the Soviet government possesses the so-called Diamond Fund, an immense collection of gem stones which had been accumulated by the Tsars and other aristocratic families of Russia over a period of three centuries. The fact that those treasures were not cashed in during the desperate years of the early Soviet rule does credit to V. Lenin, who declared that they were inviolate since they belonged to the people. From time to time these treasures, or some of them, are placed on display in the Kremlin, but the exact size of this collection is not public.

There are two world-famous stones in this collection, a diamond known as "Orlov," and another known as "the Shah." The "Orlov" is the most remarkable and rates as one of the best in the world; in its time it was the largest pure-water diamond in existance—189.62 carats. It was found in the beginning of the eighteenth century in Ceylon, and originally weighed over 300 carats, but some of the weight was lost in cutting. What makes it especially valuable is its pale greenish cast, next in value only to the blue and pink diamonds. (The largest blue diamond is the 44.4-carat Hope diamond, and the largest pink weighs only 24 carats and is now in the possession of the Queen of England. It is valued at 1,500,000 dollars, but would probably bring much more in an open auction.) The "Orlov" was originally part of a sacred Indian statue and was known as *Derianur,* or "the Sea of Light." Somehow it came into the possession of the Persian Shah Nadir, and in 1773 it was purchased from him by Count Gregori Orlov, one of Catherine the Great's "favorites," for the then incredible sum of 450,000 rubles. Orlov, of course, presented it to his imperial paramour. "The Shah," weighing 88.7 carats and found in the sixteenth century, came from Persia. It was presented to the Tsar by the Shah of Iran in 1829 to assuage the Tsar's anger at the killing in Teheran of the Russian ambassador, the famous Russian writer, Griboyedov, who was torn to pieces by a crowd of religious fanatics.

There are scores of famous stones in the Kremlin collection, and its entire value is truly astronomical. But not a single stone in it is of Russian origin.

The first Russian diamond, weighing a mere half-carat, was found in 1829. It was found in the Urals. In 1823, a German naturalist, Alexander Humboldt, who had studied the gold fields of Brazil which produced occasional diamonds, came to the conclusion that the gold fields of the Urals must have diamonds, too. He came to Russia in 1828, and declared that he would not leave without "at least one Russian diamond." The search was started, and on July 5, 1829, a Russian boy found a small diamond near the Krestovozdvizhensky gold fields in the Urals. He reputedly sold it to Humboldt, whereupon the German naturalist happily departed for home—in possession of the first Russian diamond.

It was only in 1898 that Count P. Shuvalov, the owner of those gold fields in the Urals, decided to look into the diamond situation in his domain. Accordingly he hired an expert, a Frenchman by the name of B. Boutan, who had had some experience in diamond mining in South Africa. However, Boutan's search was not very successful. All in all, between 1829 and 1939, only about 300 very small crystals of no particular value had been found in the whole of Russia.

In 1939, the first Russian diamond field was found in the Urals by Soviet geologists, but it was even poorer than the very poor Australian fields, and production was so expensive that it hardly justified the effort. However, by this time, industrial diamonds had become a life or death necessity for Russian industry, and the Ural field was put under exploitation, even though it yielded less than ten percent of the minimum Soviet need for industrial diamonds.

"We had to buy diamonds abroad," Novoselsky reminisced. "But then the world diamond merchants entered into a 'gentleman's agreement' not to sell any diamonds to the Communists. Our relationship with South Africa, the largest industrial diamond producer of the world, was non-existent (and it still is extremely bad), and so we had to go to private sources, the international diamond market. We were charged fabulous prices, and could get only a few stones. For a while it seemed that our industrial development, and especially oil and gas drilling, was to be curtailed, and the entire industrialization plan was in danger."

Then, in the early thirties, a young graduate of the Leningrad Mining Institute, one Vladimir Sobolev, went to investigate the so-called Central Siberian geological platform, a hilly region between the Yenisei and the Lena Rivers. He found that geologically it was almost identical to the famous South African platform where in 1871 the largest diamond strike in the world was made.

He spent several years studying the Siberian platform. Shortly before the outbreak of the war in 1941, Sobolev filed his report with the Government Planning Commission, the Gosplan, recommending a thorough investigation of the Siberian diamond potential, and particularly a survey of the Vilyui river basin in Yakutia.

The war interfered. It was not until 1947 that a fleet of hydroplanes brought a large geological party to the remote Evenk village of Erbogochan. Here the geologists split into three groups. They were encouraged by a story which they had heard from local hunters about an Evenk deerherder who, several years previously, shot a polar partridge and, cleaning it, found a small glass-like stone in its stomach. Of course, he simply threw the stone away and ate the bird. This was not much for the geologists to go on, but at least it was something.

In the winter of the same year, all three groups returned to Irkutsk with exactly nothing to show for their efforts. It seemed that all the labor and expense had been wasted.

Meanwhile the diamond hunger of the Soviet industry was growing more and more acute.

The next spring, the geologists went back to the tundra, this time equipped with a special X-ray equipment which could pinpoint even a microscopic crystal. The expedition produced nothing.

The geologists came to the conclusion that they had been looking in the wrong area, and someone remembered Sobolev's advice to investigate the Vilyui basin. But so much time and money had already been spent that it was impossible to approach Moscow for new credits; they would not be granted. Then the local Irkutsk Soviet decided to finance another expedition from local funds.

On August 7, 1949, a small stone was found. Now the search concentrated in the immediate region, and at the end of the season the geologists were in possession of 22 small crystals, a miserable diamond "strike" to be sure, but nonetheless more than any previous expedition could produce.

While analyzing the samples of the first Yakut expedition, geologists noticed the presence in some of them of small reddish crystals, the pyropes, which had no commercial or industrial value. So no one paid any attention to them—that is, no one except two women geologists working 5,000 miles away from the Vilyui wilderness.

In 1944, during the war, a Soviet science fiction writer, Efremov, wrote a story entitled "The Diamond Pipe" in which he called pyropes "the cousins of diamond." It was a completely wild guess, and no one paid any attention to it.

That is, no one except two Leningrad geologists, Natalia Sarsadskikh and Larissa Popugaieva, both avid science fiction fans who, studying the samples of the Vilyui expeditions, evolved their own pyrope-diamond theory. According to them, pyropes, looking very much like pieces of broken glass and having about the same value, were produced by the same kind of volcanic action as diamonds. They theorized that, by following pyropes, one could eventually locate a "diamond pipe."

To test this theory, Larissa Popugaieva went to the Vilyui taiga in the spring of 1954, and she and her worker-companion followed a pyrope trail and found the first diamond pipe in the whole of Siberia. They named it "the Thunder Flash." This was on August 21, 1954.

From that day on, the Popugaieva Theory, as it has become

known in geology, has been used consistently in locating Siberian diamond pipes.

The very next year, three potential diamond pipes were discovered, one of which has subsequently proved to be commercially productive. It is known now as "the Udachnaya Pipe" ("the Lucky Pipe" in Russian).

Mirny was born in December, 1955, at the height of the bitter Yakutian winter. The pipe had been located before, and now a convoy of snow trucks delivered a party of the Komsomol voluntary workers. The first winter was incredibly hard because there were no amenities of any kind, and the young men and women slept in tents, taking turns tending the stoves. One could freeze to death in a matter of minutes in one's sleep, and never notice it. Freezing, it seems, is one of the most painless ways of dying, and the freezing brain produces a series of beautiful visions. At least some people who were nursed back to life said so. But the youngsters who came here (the place still had no name) had not come to look for easy death, and so the first task of the party was building the *zimovyes*—the "winter huts" in local Siberian. There is a special technique to building these shelters, and they provide the most practical defense against Siberian cold.

The task was indescribably difficult. Constant snowstorms kept helicopters away, and some days all the supplies grew dangerously low, there were no matches or salt, and frozen bread had to be chopped with axes. But somehow the Mirny pioneers survived.

"Today Mirny has every modern convenience," Vecherin said. "In summer everything is delivered here from the Lensk anchorage—machinery, cars, refrigerators, washing machines, furniture. Because of the special northern rate of pay, people here have a good deal of money to spend, and they demand the best. And all the factories of the Soviet Union have a standing order to give priority to all orders from the Arctic areas. In winter there is a truck road to the Lena River, as well, kept open by snowplows and bulldozers. The truck caravans use the frozen river to deliver the supplies to Lensk. And, of course, there is a whole system of supplying Mirny by air from Irkutsk and Novosivirsk. We see new films here before they are released in Moscow, and we hear morning news broadcasts and telecasts seven hours before they hear them in Moscow, because of the time difference."

"Do men bring their families here?" I asked.

"Yes, or else they marry here. This is encouraged in all northern Siberian enterprises. Families get the best housing. And they try to keep husbands and wives working together: it's good for morale, and for efficiency. No one can control a man better, we discovered, than his wife, and some men need controlling; especially those who have learned to drink the Yakut alcohol straight. In the factory we are going to visit, all really responsible work is done by women."

"Because of their affinity for diamonds?" I asked.

"Because of their dependability and conscientiousness, and sobriety, too. This is exacting work requiring concentration and alertness. A man with a hangover is no good here. In a single blink of the eye one can miss a valuable stone."

The factory was an enormous, windowless wooden structure, perhaps 100 feet high. It had survived several Yakut winters and its appearance was drab, somewhat like a huge disused warehouse. But this was misleading. Inside it was neat and very impressive, and very noisy, with a dozen or so tremendous metal drums revolving at high speed with a deafening roar. Across the entire central part of the building, which was about 100 feet high, there was hung an enormous banner, "More diamonds for our Motherland!" There were smaller banners all over the place.

One entire wall of the building was glassed off, with several tiers of small cubicles mostly peopled with young women in white surgical gowns. Almost all the women were very young, some in their teens. Because of the low retirement age in Siberia (45 for women and 55 for men) there are few old or even middle-aged people working there.

The factory director led us into his private office. Cognac and cookies were brought in, and for about an hour Vasiliev described all the phases of the operation in minute detail. Roughly, the process consisted of gradually breaking up the rocks, or rather "shaking" them to pieces in the fast-rotating iron drums, with the help of cast-iron balls in each drum. Then the resulting rough sand-like mass was run through a number of "dressing processes" to eliminate all surplus material; the remaining stuff was submitted to all sorts of chemical reactions based on the peculiar molecular composition of diamonds which, for instance, would adhere to certain oily substances while all other particles would be rejected by them. Electronic equipment was used to isolate the precious crystals. But the very last phase was done by hand by highly qualified specialists—all women.

Obviously this was not a process for amateurs and freelance prospectors; some very heavy equipment was necessary to extract diamonds from kimberlite ore.

"It is possible to find a diamond without all this procedure?" I asked.

"Occasionally, but not often enough to justify private prospecting. Some exceptional stones have been found, however. There was one called 'Shiny,' for instance, 37 carats; another called "Mine Workers," 45 carats; and still another one, called 'Valentina Tereshkova' in honor of our only woman cosmonaut, 51.45 carats. The biggest one found outside was caller 'Modest' and it weighed 54.6 carats. The bulk of our production is much smaller stones, from 1 to 4 millimeters in diameter. About twenty percent are gem stones and go into the international jewelry market. This is higher than in the other two working pipes, the Udachnyi and the Aykhal."

"What is the biggest diamond ever found in Siberian history?"

"That was one called 'Maria' found in 1966 by a woman worker, Maria Konenkova. It weighed 106 carats. I did not see it, but it was by far the largest stone ever found in the Soviet Union."

"Found by another woman!" I mused.

The meaning of this remark was lost on Vasiliev. He just nodded.

"Yes, most of the large stones have been found by women; they seem to have a special eye for them. I wouldn't know how to run this place without women. Some sixty percent of all the employees here are women, they are my *otlichnitzi*—'exemplary workers.' "

He spoke to someone on the telephone on his desk and soon two young women entered the room. Both were young and pretty and both wore immaculate white gowns and white ker-

chieves over their heads. One of them brought with her a
leather container that looked like a cup for shaking dice. After
greeting us, she removed the top and rather unceremoniously
poured a mass of diamonds onto the felt-covered table.

Sorting diamonds at Mirny.

Raw, uncut diamonds are very impressive—to an inexperi-
enced eye they look just like cut diamonds, and most of them
have a symmetrical form with at least eight even facets. There
were some rather large stones in this batch, some of them, it
seemed to me, as large as dime coins. There were also some very
small ones, almost like large sand. How many carats were there?
Only a specialist could determine this, but it seemed to me that
there were at least a hundred or more large stones. One very
large stone was dark-grey, almost black.

"Is that a diamond?" I asked.

"Oh yes, and a good one," Vasiliev said, picking it up and
looking at it. "This is a first-class industrial bort—that's what

they call them in Africa, and that's the term we use here. There's no mistaking a diamond. It's a remarkable thing, at least ninety times as hard as the next hardest natural element, the corundum. But not all diamonds are of the same hardness. The hardest diamonds come from Australia, and ours at Mirny are almost as hard."

He dropped the stone into the pile, and the girls quickly collected them using tweezers for the smaller crystals. This whole operation took seconds; these were true experts. Putting them back into the cup, the girls wished us good day and walked out.

"Have you ever had any diamonds stolen here?" I asked.

"You mean do we search our workers as they leave here, as they do in South Africa? No. Our workers are extremely conscientious and honest, and then—even if a bad one were to get in—he would find it extremely hard to steal any stones. All work is done collectively, and he would have to form a syndicate of thieves, which is completely impossible. If someone finds a stone outside, he'd get a better price from us than anywhere else. No, we haven't had a single case of theft here. Not one."

"How long did it take you to get all the stones we have just seen?" I asked.

Vasiliev smiled. "Unfortunately I can't tell you. But I can tell you that our factory is the most profitable enterprise run by the state. We have days that pay for a year's operation. From here all our production goes to Moscow. I don't know how it is distributed, but I suppose the best stones go to the cutting plant in Smolensk, our Amsterdam. Ten years ago there wasn't a single diamond-cutter in the whole country, and now there are hundreds. And I've been told that Soviet diamonds are every bit as well cut as those from Holland."

Vasiliev thought that Mirny was the largest diamond producer in Yakutia at present, but another place, called Aykhal, located 350 miles north of Mirny, had all the earmarks of a first-class diamond producer. But it was located in the coldest weather belt in the northern hemisphere, and attracting technicians there was a difficult task.

"Compared to them, we are in the tropics here," Vecherin confirmed. "We rarely get more than minus 50° here, but at

Aykhal they hit 80° below now and then, and there is a whole set of special problems whenever it gets that cold. That's why they are building the first fully enclosed town there—with controlled microclimate throughout the year."

The diamond center of Aykhal, where the first fully enclosed town is being built.

Vasiliev produced some pictures and diagrams. The "enclosed town" was a poetic exaggeration, but it was a remarkable idea. Not that a fully enclosed town would be impossible to construct, but there were other problems—the stickiest one was the permafrost which in certain parts of Yakutia reaches a depth of 1,000 feet and even more. The heat of such a town would gradually melt it, and the town would sink—this happened to many of the first buildings in Yakutia. So the Aykhal project has plans to build apartment houses on steel piles raised about ten feet from the ground, and then connect them with plastic-enclosed galleries. There would be a series of "gardens" also raised from the ground to provide insulation from the permafrost, where plants could be grown. The heating would be provided by natural gas, plentiful in the region, and later, by electricity, if the gigantic Lena project was built. Another problem in Aykhal was the heat in summer: during July and August the temperature in Yakutia often rises to 100° or even higher, and the sun may shine for twenty-two hours a day. Obviously a powerful air-cooling plant would have to be constructed to ventilate this "enclosed town." This would be easier to do with electric power, but it was not yet available in that part of the country in sufficient quantity. The Aykhal project was going to supply the planners with the first practical experience in this entirely new field.

Our visit was coming to a close—we had to catch a plane for Yakutsk that evening.

I asked a last question:

"Won't the unlimited diamond production in Siberia depress the world price of diamonds?"

"It certainly could," Vasiliev said with a smile. "This is why we are not in too much of a hurry to develop diamond mining here to its full potential. We are in the international diamond market, so we might as well support the prices. It would be unfair to the ladies of the world if all their diamonds became practically worthless, wouldn't it?"

On this note we parted.

12.

"The Possessed"

WE flew from Mirny to Yakutsk, the capital of the Yakut republic, in a rather small but extremely serviceable AN–2, the passenger plane which connects numberless little airstrips in northern Siberia.

Flying over northern Siberia at night is like flying over the dark side of the moon. For miles and miles and miles there are no signs of life. It is just one snowy immensity in winter and a dark green nothingness in summer, crisscrossed by innumerable erosion ravines, and laced by sluggish streams, many of them running nowhere. Since the permanently frozen subsoil affords no natural water drainage, evaporation is the only way for the moisture to escape during each brief summer, and therefore much of northern Siberia turns in summer into endless marshlands in which mosquitoes and other bloodsucking insects breed by cubic miles. In summer these insects often envelop the ground in a sort of thin haze, blurring all natural landmarks. Anyone who has lived in Siberia is familiar with this haze phenomenon, known by the collective appellation of the *g'nuss*, a morbidly descriptive word derived from the Russian adjective *g'nusnyi*, or "vile." In some portions of Siberia this is a bigger problem than marauding packs of wolves or the murderous frost in winter. It is a true plague. All experienced *taiozhniki*, or taiga hands, and the construction workers of the projects rising all over Siberia, tell bloodcurdling stories about the *g'nuss* which has been known to stop building projects dead in their tracks until workers were provided with special clothes and nets to protect them from these often almost microscopic piranhas of the air. For in addition to the familiar and sufficiently unpleasant mosquitoes, there are three other kinds of creatures that compose the *g'nuss,* each more vile than the other, and each ready to descend upon any human being with nightmarish ferocity. A man, unless properly protected, can actually be eaten alive by these little monsters.

But since men are really quite rare in the northern taiga, for a long time I could not understand what the insects generally fed on. Then a Siberian entomologist explained to me that they fed on nothing: they hatched, lived for a few days, laid eggs and perished, often without having a single meal in their short lives. Some species are even born with undeveloped digestive tracts, but apparently they don't know this, and heaven help a man who meets them unprepared!

But now it was April and the ground was hard-frozen. There was no *g'nuss,* there was nothing in fact, but the incredibly bright frozen stars in the black sky and the unbroken black below with occasional splotches of dull white that were snow-covered small lakes or clearings in the forest.

Then gradually I saw, out of the plane's window, some very small flickering lights that appeared at infrequent intervals.

"What are those?" I asked.

The plane stewardess looked through the window and shrugged.

"Oh, campfires . . . the possessed are all over the place . . ."

She used the Russian word *oderzhimye.*

When I was a child, it used to describe the taiga gold prospectors, a special breed of maniacs possessed with the dream of finding gold. Year after year, they would strike out into the taiga, singly or in small groups, in a usually fruitless search for sudden wealth. Often they died there of hunger and exposure, or came back haggard and frostbitten, to prepare for the next expedition. I am not sure that finding gold was their main purpose: really they were just chasing a dream, and caught up in the process of searching. In effect they well deserved their name: they were possessed men.

Now and then one of them would make a strike and come back to town with small bags of gold dust. Then he would go on a fantastic spree, an absurd exuberant Russian alcoholic binge which was known as *chertogon* (literally "devil-chasing"). A really good *chertogon* would shake a town to its foundations. As though driven by some biological urge for self-destruction, these men would squander their sudden wealth in the most preposterous orgy of suicidal drunkenness and hell-raising until they were either put in jail (and robbed there), or died of sheer alcohol poisoning (and then robbed). And even if they survived, they were doomed: the next time they went into the taiga, they would be closely followed by other "possessed," and murdered by them as soon as they reached their secret taiga Eldorados. Murder and gold have always lived side by side in Siberia, as anywhere else, for that matter.

Only once, as a very small child, did I catch a glimpse of a *chertogon*, but the picture has stayed in my mind ever since. Some ten hired *drozhkis* went past our house in Irkutsk at a moderate speed. The first one contained a wooden gold-washing trough, the next a pickaxe, the third a pair of taiga boots, the fourth a taiga fur hat, and so on. The last one was occupied by the lucky Croesus himself, drunk as a lord. His red flowing beard was thick with vomit, and he held a *chetvert*, or a gallon vodka bottle in his hand. He was roaring something incomprehensible at the top of his voice. Around his *drozhki* several breathless accordion players were running at full speed trying to play something, but producing only some ear-splitting cacophony. What impressed me was that the adults around me were watching this ugly scene with deep admiration, and when the mad cavalcade disappeared from sight, our bow-legged Buryat policeman shook his head and said, "The dirty dog sure knows how to spend his money beautifully, ulcers to his mother's soul."

I was surprised to hear that this sort of thing still survived in Siberia, after fifty years of socialism. I knew that private gold prospecting had been declared illegal many years ago.

"But aren't they afraid of being arrested—burning campfires like that?" I asked.

"Why?" The stewardess was obviously bewildered by my question.

It took me several minutes to understand that the term "possessed" had another meaning now, even though it described the same disease. Now it was applied to young geologists who wandered all over the Siberian wilderness looking for gold, diamonds, oil, coal, iron, copper, tungsten, or any other useful natural deposit. Discovery would make their names famous overnight. They were graduates of universities and came from comfortable homes, but these young men and women volunteered for this lonely and dangerous life.

"The possessed." Geologists on their way into the tundra.

Later I met some of them, husky, tough-looking boys and girls with university badges pinned to their rough taiga clothes, intent, taciturn, dedicated young people—the new "possessed." Siberia owes much to them. It is through their labor that every known natural element has been found in the country within the last fifteen years. Many of them have perished in the wilderness, but new waves of volunteers take their place and continue this unending search.

The Soviet press, often in ridiculously rhapsodic terms, forever speaks of the "mass heroism" of Soviet youth, and attributes this to the new socialist education. Undoubtedly this is partly true. New Soviet generations are constantly indoctrinated with the spirit of sacrificial devotion to the new society, but it must be said here that this heroic, even suicidal, streak has been a part of the Russian national character for many centuries, making the Russians extremely resilient in the face of hardships and suffering. Their entire history proves this: no other nation has been subjected to such a series of national disasters. Yet they have survived them all, and today have worked their way to the forefront of the modern age.

So the Soviet youth of today are in many ways following in their fathers' and forefathers' footsteps. The undeniable fact is that the development of Siberia is primarily the work of young volunteers. They often perform prodigious tasks under most extreme hardships which no ordinary hired worker would tolerate for a single day.

It has been cynically suggested that this enthusiastic response of the Soviet youth to "the call of the motherland and the party" is based on their desire to escape the boredom and regimentation of socialist society, and this may be partly true. Youth, any youth, is always in emotional rebellion against any routine, any rigidity, against everything in fact that might be imposed on it by older generations; this is a universal, organic process. This is a matter of biology, I believe, more than of sociology or of any politics. The young all over the world want to do their own living, their own thinking, to make their own mistakes; they are impatient to take over from the older generations, to sweep them aside. The population explosion on one hand, and increasing longevity on the other, sharpen this conflict and fill the young with a sense of biological frustration: they have an enormous amount of excess energy and no way of expending it, with the older people clogging all the avenues of life.

In this, I believe, the Soviet state is more fortunate than any other society. It has Siberia—an entire new world to be built, which can absorb millions of young enthusiasts, giving them a matchless opportunity to participate in life, an exciting creative life of accomplishment calling for near-heroic effort, which feeds their romanticism, and uses their physical and emotional energies.

In some special cases, army conscripts are mustered out sooner than their two-year service term if they volunteer for the "shock construction projects" in Siberia. Young soldiers take advantage of this opportunity by whole squads and companies, and provide the Siberian projects with disciplined, closely-knit groups of workers. Most of these demobilized soldiers never return home. They stay in Siberia, marry there, and become honored "veterans" of this new frontier. It is, I think, a wise use of young manpower, which is so often wasted in preparation for destruction instead of construction; and as one Siberian engineer pointed out to me, it teaches future soldiers, should they ever be called back, the value of the things they might be called on to defend. A soldier must have a perfect service record in order to be allowed to serve part of his army term in Siberia, so that the country is supplied with potentially the best future citizens.

When the history of new Siberia is wrtten, many names will be in it: planners, builders, but mostly, geologists. They are the "advance scouts." Often dropped by parachute, hundreds of miles from the nearest settlement, they work their way step by step through treacherous wilderness. Assaulted by cold, wild animals, and clouds of murderous *g'nuss* in summer, fighting off fits of the "taiga madness" (a peculiar disease akin to "desert madness"), many of them perish, but there are always new volunteers to take their places.

There are many names, unknown to the outside world, that have already become a part of the new Siberian lore. The Siberian writer, N. Meisak, tells us about one of them:

... Trains speed along the Southern Siberian Railway only recently cut through the trackless taiga. Approaching the station of Koshurni-kovo, each train lets out a long blast of its whistle, to salute the memory of the man who first went through this taiga surveying the route for the new railway. Sudden savage frosts caught the party in the middle of nowhere, and all the men in it, except one, died trying to ford a dangerous stream. Alexander Koshurnikov, the only survivor knew he was doomed. His wet clothes froze to his body, and he lost his supplies, his radio, and his matches in the icy river. But to the last moment, he continued his work: when they found him, frozen to death, he still had the pencil in his hand.

And this is another example:

Young professor, Kyra Sobolevskaya, had crossed and criss-crossed the Altai and Sayan ranges in quest of medicinal herbs. She walked, rode horseback, sailed on rafts. Her tent was often snowed under during sudden storms. At one point she had to negotiate a 9,000-foot high mountain pass. The local guide refused to lead her, and so she went alone, leading the pack mule that carried her priceless herb collection. The path was so narrow that the pack on one side was scraping the mountain while another end was actually hanging over the precipice. By a miracle she survived, and now all Siberian libraries have the copies of the capital work by Professor Sobolevskaya entitled *The Flora of the Tuva*. Many of the herbs found by her are now widely used by Siberian physicians.

Yes, many of "the possessed" are women; the story of modern Siberia is largely the story of women. In the lean post-war years when young men were scarce, women often led geological parties, and even today there are as many female explorers as there are men.

What makes these young men and women abandon their often comfortable homes, their friends and families, and strike into the unknown?

I spoke to one of these "possessed" in the dining room of the Yakutsk Lena hotel. He was a huge blond youth with a handsome weather-beaten face, and his name was Fedor. It was six o'clock in the morning, and Fedor and I were the only people in the dining room of the hotel. Both of us were fighting Siberian hangovers, I with coffee and Fedor with glasses of soured milk, called *keffir*, which is the usual Siberian breakfast.

Fedor was born in Leningrad and was graduated from a geological institute there. He planned to marry a fellow student and settle down in Leningrad, but somehow it did not work out, the girl changed her mind, and so Fedor volunteered to go to Siberia. This was his third year in the Indigirka River basin, one of the most desolate corners of northern Yakutia. He and his party had not made any startling discoveries—just "exposed" some alluvial gold areas, strictly pedestrian stuff.

He was in Yakutsk buying supplies for his party: three men and three girls who were waiting for him near Chokurdakh, a tiny Yakut settlement some 500 miles above the Arctic Circle. The four-month-long polar night was just ending there, and they would have six months of practically uninterrupted sunlight now—the time of year in which they did most of their work. During the long "night" they had been caught in polar blizzards that continued for seven weeks; they had eaten up all their supplies, their reindeer, and even their dogs. They were saved by a supply helicopter when they were starving.

During this period they came across the frozen body of a lonely Yakut trapper who was himself trapped by a huge block of sliding ice which had crushed his leg. They found a passport on him, and among other things, Fedor had to visit his relatives in Yakutsk and break the tragic news to them.

"It was awful," he said. "After I saw his mother last night I got dead drunk. What else could I do? And now I must sober up, or the pilot won't take me back."

Siberian aviation wages a relentless war against alcohol. Often pilots must take blood tests before flights, and no passenger who is drunk is taken aboard.

"What's your hurry?" I asked. "You can stay a day or two in Yakutsk, see some new films, find a pretty girl, maybe."

"No, I hate this place. I want to go back."

"Why?"

For a moment he seemed to be lost for an answer.

"I don't know. I suppose there is something about the tundra that gets you. At first you feel stunned, terrified. It's so evil, so empty, so dead. But then you get used to silence, to emptiness, and then it becomes a part of you, ulcers to its soul. And it's better than the taiga."

"Why?" I asked again.

"The taiga is like a prison. You're surrounded by trees and you can't see beyond them. And what would you see if you could? More trees. Billions of them, for hundreds of miles in every direction. The endlessness of it gets you, your nerves become as tight as guitar strings. Some people break. They just get up and go. And then the taiga begins to whirl them around."

"Whirl them around?"

"That's what the taiga people call it. A man starts walking. He walks and walks, and he always comes back to the same place. So he gets terrified, and starts running, and still he comes back to the same place, over and over again. Until he drops dead, or steps into a marsh hole and drowns. The holes are covered with moss, and you can't see them. I had four months of that, when I first came here. Never again."

Fedor was describing the "taiga madness." I have heard about it since childhood. Even experienced taiga hands have been known to succumb to it.

"And the tundra?"

"It's different. It's open. You can see the horizon, and maybe a mountain in the distance, and you know where you are and where you are going. It doesn't drive you mad. It doesn't kill you."

"It killed that trapper."

"He was a fool. You never go anywhere alone in the tundra. He must have been after sables, out of season—his greed must have killed him."

He went back to the counter to get another glass of *keffir*. By this time two or three other men were in the room. People rise early in Siberia, and the "buffet" opened at five-thirty. In Moscow they do not open until eight.

"Are you ever going back to Leningrad?" I asked when Fedor came back.

"I don't know. Maybe. But I don't think I could live there now. . . . My mother's calling me back, she has three daughters, but I'm the only son, but no . . . I don't like Leningrad."

"It's the most beautiful city in Europe," I said.

"Maybe. . . . But I don't think I can live in any big place now. Mother says I can get a job there. . . . And become an ink soul? No."

The "ink soul" is the Siberian way of describing a bureaucrat.

"No," he repeated firmly. "I'll never go back until we find a gold deposit of All-Union significance." He smiled, and sang in a low voice a verse from a song popular among the Siberian geologists: "We shall discover a deposit of All-Union significance ... we will become laureates and will earn money by shovelfuls ..."

The geologists who make important geological discoveries receive generous cash bonuses and often special awards which make them "laureates," which is a special Soviet title of distinction. Were financial benefits the main attraction of this work, I asked Fedor.

"No," he said. "It's important, of course, but it isn't all. It's finding gold that's important—it's like nothing else in the world. It makes you tremble, even cry. Last spring we thought we found a large deposit.... We didn't sleep for three days and nights digging and taking samples, and we weren't even tired —we could have gone on for a week. But it wasn't anything important—just a good gold 'sign.' We've made a pact, the six of us, not to go back to 'the big land' until we make a really important strike."

The term 'the big land' was used by the Soviet guerrillas operating behind the German lines to describe unoccupied Russia, and now the Siberian geologists have adapted it as well, even though their "land" is infinitely bigger than their former homes.

"And then—if you make the strike?" I asked.

"Then I suppose we'll stay there to develop it."

Clearly I was dealing with one of "the possessed."

"But isn't it depressing to live for months in the dark?" I asked.

"Well, it isn't really dark. Maybe for two weeks. Then the sun comes to the horizon, even if it does not rise. Then there are the Northern Lights, they are beautiful, and because it's rarely cloudy, we get starlight and it makes the snow glow. You get used to it. If we don't find anything this summer, we'll go to the Chukchi—there's plenty of gold there. When the north gets into your blood—it stays there."

At this point Fedor suggested a small glass of cognac. For some reason the Siberians do not consider drinking cognc early in the morning as anything unusual. I declined, but he got 200 grams for himself: liquor is sold by weight throughout the Soviet Union.

Obviously he had decided to take my advice and stay in

Yakutsk for another day. There was another plane leaving the next morning, he said.

The very sight of the cognac made Fedor talkative. Talking to strangers is a favorite indoor sport of the Siberians. The very fact that they will never see the person again plays a part in this—it becomes a form of confession, and they speak about things which they would never discuss with a friend.

Fedor spoke about gold—this was his specialty. He was absolutely sure that he and his friends would one day stumble upon their Eldorado. (There is a gold mining town in Siberia actually called "Eldorado.") They even had a name for it already, "Electra." Why "Electra?" It was a combination of their first names: Elena, Evgenyi, Constantine, Theodor, Raissa, and Anna, with Elena supplying the first two letters for the future town. Elena was Theodor's wife. Yes, he was married; all three boys in the party were married, and their wives were with them. All three girls were graduate geologists, and one even "a candidate of geological sciences." Fedor and Elena had a baby daughter Vila—the name composed of the initials of Vladimir Ilyich Lenin, but they called her Vera. She had stayed during the winter in a nursery in a town called Batagai, but they were taking her into the tundra for the summer. All three boys met the girls in Siberia; they were assigned to the same party, and the pairing off came naturally. "It was too cold to sleep alone," according to Fedor. The other two couples had no children, but Fedor suspected that one of the girls, Anna, was pregnant.

Someone has said that the Russians are unconscious of racial differences. In Siberia at least, they seem to be unconscious of sex difference as well: men and women are often placed together in conditions of physical intimacy which would be considered embarrassing anywhere else. A girl, coming to work on a building project, might find herself sleeping in the men's barrack for a night or two, before she gets a room in a women's dormitory, and this does not seem to surprise anyone. And of course, men and women work side by side in all jobs, sometimes in desolate camps, miles away from civilization. Does it lead to sexual laxity? I asked Fedor, though the subject is considered to be extremely delicate in Russia.

"Well," Fedor said, "people are people of course—they are not made of wood. Some men pester girls. Some girls even like it. But the collective usually watches those things. If a man is accused by the girls of 'hooliganism,' he gets a warning first, then a strict warning, and then he is expelled, or even sent for trial. I heard of a case in a mining camp—a boy got drunk and took a girl by force in the forest. Had she reported him, he would have gotten ten years maybe. He was frightened, he was kissing her boots. Finally they signed up and they gave them a room, but she left him—she wouldn't live with such a dungheap."

Marriage is referred to as "signing up" in common Soviet parlance: it is a simple procedure of registering the union at a special office. However, since divorces have been made difficult, especially if there are children involved, "signing up" is no longer as lightly considered as it was once.

Then there are periodic public meetings held in all enterprises, during which anyone may be "candled" like an egg, so to speak, for anything wrong in his professional or private life. This public denunciation, if substantiated, may lead to drastic consequences for the culprit, especially if he is a Communist or a Komsomol member.

"That doesn't mean that people don't make love," Fedor continued. "They do, but a man must be careful. Even kissing a girl against her will may bring real trouble. . . . So it's not worth it. It's best to sign up and settle down. And when you get two salaries together, you can afford things which a single man can't afford. And there's a special tax on bachelors as well. All in all, it's best to find a good girl and sign up."

Fedor and his friends were earning good money, even though, he insisted, "the long ruble" was not the reason they chose this work. What did they do with their money in the tundra? They were saving it. Their ambition was to buy "collectively" a snow truck, known as *vezdekhod*, literally "go anywhere." With that marvelous machine they could cover ground faster in search of their golden dream. They were all members of the Komsomol, the Young Communist League, when they came to Siberia, but none of them was a party member. Why? First of all, it was not easy to join the party while traveling in the tundra: each candidate had to have two sponsors, members of the party, who had known him intimately for at least two years previously. And then, Fedor said, membership wasn't so important in their work. It was different for those who worked in the cities. If and when they made their strike, they might apply for party membership, and then they would easily be accepted, but now it was not important. They were conscientious Soviet citizens, and that was the most important thing of all.

No, none of them had any plans to go back to European Russia, even though none of them was Siberian by birth.

"It's like this: if one doesn't go back during the first two years, he's stuck. It's funny: you can tell almost exactly how long anyone has been here. If he says, 'this damned Siberia'— that's the first year. And if he says just 'Siberia,' he's been here more than a year. It takes a year to swallow Siberia, to accept it."

"And after that?"

Fedor grinned. "After that a man begins to brag about Siberia —'with us in Siberia it's this, and with us in Siberia, it's that.' Then he's stuck. Even if he did go back to the big land, he'd come back. He would brag so much about Siberia that people would chase him away. It's like smallpox: once you get it, you're marked. Hell, going back to Russia after Siberia is like eating borsht after you've had ice cream. Incidentally, I'm getting some ice cream for myself. Shall I bring some to you?"

I declined, and Fedor went back to the counter, and I noticed that he got a glass of cognac. Ice cream is immensely popular all over Siberia; people eat it at any time of day or night, in summer and winter alike.

By the time Fedor was through with his second cognac he became sentimental. Fedor talked of his love for humanity, and because I was an American, he wanted me to know how much he loved and admired America.

"If only the Americans would get together with us. There's enough of everything here for everybody . . . Look at Japan. Their country is ten times smaller than Yakutia alone, they have no natural resources—no gold, no diamonds, no coal, no oil, nothing, and eighty percent of their land is mountains, and still eighty million people live there! So what are we all fighting about? Every time I come here and read the newspapers, I get sick, and I want to go back to the tundra and stay there. . . . It's big and it's clean—hell, it's wonderful. . . ."

Suddenly and without any transition, Fedor was overcome by acute homesickness. "I'm a criminal," he said, "sitting and drinking here when I have Elena and Vila waiting for me . . . This place here is a madhouse, damned madhouse, with all those people rushing around, all this noise and the gasoline smell. . . ."

"We must build a new world. Decent. Clean. You should see some of the mining towns up north. They say the cold there kills microbes, that people don't get sick there in winter. Well, I'll tell you something else—it kills a lot of things. Egotism. Greed. Envy. When it gets to sixty or seventy below, you must trust people, trust life. You must stick together. They say they're building Communism here. Utter rot. It's *we* who are building it—not these ink souls sitting in offices and sleeping with their secretaries. I'm choking here. I'm going back this morning, and nothing will stop me. Do you understand—nothing."

But Fedor didn't go home that day. Our conversation was interrupted by the appearance of a squat young Yakut, wearing a leather jacket and fur boots, his fur hat with flaps hanging down framing his round Mongol face. He stood in the doorway scanning the room.

Instantly Fedor pushed his empty cognac glass over to me. "That's Andrei, my pilot. Don't tell him I've been drinking."

Now Andrei saw Fedor and walked over to us. He and Fedor embraced and kissed.

"I have all my gear in the lobby, Andrusha!" Fedor said energetically. "It won't take a minute."

"No hurry," Andrei said guiltily. "I'm not flying today. That doctor, ulcers to her soul, grounded me for twenty-four hours. And I ate two raw onions last night to kill the alcohol in the blood . . ."

For a moment Fedor appeared stunned, but then he embraced his friend.

"To hell with it!" he declared. "Elena, ulcers to her soul, can survive one day without me! Let me get you two hundred grams, Andrusha—they have some four-star Armenian stuff here. Melts in your mouth."

He and Andrei went to the counter. Would they leave the next morning, I wondered?

Was Fedor typical of the thousands of "the possessed" discovering Siberia? Probably. He was certainly "captured by Siberia," as they call them there, committed to it for life. Like so many other young men and women who came here looking for a temporary romantic adventure, he had found his destiny here instead.

I left before Fedor and Andrei were back at the table with their grams.

According to the best available figures, only about twenty-five percent of Siberian territory has been fully prospected for geological resources. Many large deposits of various ores, coal, etc., even though found, are still classed as only "exposed" but not "surveyed." The search goes on relentlessly. Several thousand geological teams are in the Siberian wilderness at any given moment. What has been found so far has vastly exceeded the most

Geologists surveying.

optimistic expectations. According to experts, there now exists in Siberia a geological base for the creation of the greatest industrial empire on earth.

Despite the feverish building going on in Siberia, the job of turning the country into a vast industrial region will take many years. The difficulties are enormous—the climate, the terrain, lack of communication, lack of labor and of capital. Still, what is being accomplished is the greatest job of industrial development ever attempted by man on this planet, and the Siberian geologists have been largely responsible for it.

What has been found in Siberia so far? The answer, in short, is *everything*. Now Siberia exports over fifty raw material items, as well as a whole line of manufactured goods.

Today, on the basis of surveyed and evaluated geological findings, Siberia has the greatest reserves of any country of the following items: coal, iron ore, manganese, natural gas, lead, nickel, cobalt, tungsten, molybdenum, bauxite, antimony, diamonds, sulphur, apatite, asbestos. Even though no exact figures are known, it is believed that with the recent gold strikes in the Magadan and Chukchi regions of Siberia and the Muruntau gold deposit in Uzbekistan (discovered less than five years ago), the gold reserves of the Soviet state will far surpass those of South Africa, at present the largest gold producer in the world. And some of the gold-bearing regions of Siberia still lie largely unexplored.

The work being performed by "the possessed" is really enormous.

And still the search is going on.

Just to get an idea of the titanic work done by the Siberian geologists, in 1967 alone they had drilled through 9,800 miles of rock—a distance which is over 2,000 miles longer than the earth's diameter. In 1968 this figure was exceeded, but no exact figures have been published. Some of the finds have been truly remarkable.

"The possessed" are continuing to blaze trails into the very heart of Siberia, into regions that were absolutely unexplored. In Transbaikalia, for instance, some 500 miles from the railway, a fabulous copper deposit has been discovered among the impassable marshes. To explore it, the first geological party had to be parachuted there. The Udokan copper, millions and millions of tons of it, is still untouched. One cannot exploit mining deposits by parachute drops. Udokan, along with hundreds of such rich potential regions, must await the completion of the new Trans-Siberian Railway.

Not all of the geologists are prowling the taiga and tundra. There is scientific work being done in the regional Geological Centers of Siberia, which plan and direct this assault on nature. Such centers are located at Omsk, Novosibirsk, Krasnoyarsk, Irkutsk, Tyumen, Chita, Ulan-Ude, and Yakutsk. They employ thousands of scientists who study the geological structures of Siberia and map the areas of exploration, often pinpointing the exact spots where important discoveries are to be made. Both Siberian diamonds and Siberian oil have been found on the basis of the painstaking theoretical calculations of the scientists working in their offices.

It is thought that Siberia will become the richest country in the world, and in time, a highly industrialized area fully capable of supporting a population of 250 million people or more.

This is the dream of "the possessed" who dedicate their young lives to blasting the way into the future. The old Vladmirsky Road running out of Moscow to Siberia and across it was known as "the chain highway" for two centuries: countless thousands of chained prisoners walked its endless miles, many of them dying on the way. It was closely connected with the darkest pages of Russian history. There was a day, for instance, when the mad Tsar Paul, dissatisfied with the parade performance of one of his crack guards regiments, dismissed it with a short command: "About face! Forward march—to Siberia!" Only his assassination a few months later interrupted this dreary march along the Vladimirsky chain highway, when the soldiers were nearing the Urals.

After the revolution the Vladmirsky Road in Moscow was renamed, along with many other streets of the capital. Its new name is symbolic. It is now called "The Road of the Enthusiasts," and it was a prophetic bit of inspiration on the part of some unknown city planner, for it still leads to Siberia.

13.

The Snow Queen and Her Frozen Realm

AS I looked through the plane window, a golden glare suddenly appeared in the black void.

"Yakutsk . . ." Liudmilla, our stewardess, said breathlessly.

The shimmering vision was nearer, and now I could distinguish the straight lines of electric lights crisscrossing in orderly rows. The city looked huge from the air—much larger than I had expected it to be. Even though Yakutsk is the capital of the largest autonomous republic in the Soviet Union, it is a small town by new Siberian standards. Its official population estimate as of January 1, 1968, was 98,000, and its growth has been modest.

Yakutsk is not a new town; in fact it is one of the oldest in Siberia. It was founded in 1632 by a band of Russian adventurers who reached it by way of the Upper Lena and the Vitim Rivers, and built an *ostrog* here. One wooden tower of the fort is still standing, although the rest burned down some 200 years ago.

For 300 years, Yakutsk slumbered in complete neglect, a God-forsaken Siberian town, and a dreaded name among the prisoners and exiles who were sent there. And suddenly this orderly electric checkerboard! I certainly did not expect it.

The plane made a wide lazy loop coming in for the landing.

"Comrade passengers. . . . Fasten your seatbelts. . . ."

Nobody bothered, and the stewardess did not insist. The passengers were collecting their bundles from the baggage racks. My two companions, Lev Nosov and Stanslav Ilyin, and I were the only "foreigners" on the plane. The rest were Yakuts, and they, like Liudmilla, were coming home.

"What sort of town is it?" I asked, still looking out of the window.

"The best," Liudmilla said. "I went to Moscow last year, and it's nothing in comparison. People have good hearts here.... I wouldn't live anywhere else for all the money in the world."

The winter noon at Yakutsk. The city has about four hours of sunlight in January; up to nineteen in July and August.

"Were you born here?"

"Oh, yes. My father and my mother, too, and their parents. I'm a real Yakutka!"

"But you're a Russian."

"So what? There are many Russians here, but they are Yakuts as well. There are Russian villages down the river where they speak Yakut. I can speak it too."

"Have you ever seen your Snow Queen?" I asked.

"Who?"

"Ovchinnikova."

"Oh," Liudmilla said. "Alexandra Yakovlevna? Of course I've

seen her. Many times. Only we call her the President. We're a republic, you know."

Technically, Liudmilla was right. Alexandra Yakovlevna Ovchinnikova is the chairman of the presidium of the Supreme Soviet of the Yakut Autonomous Soviet Socialist Republic. She is the highest executive of this huge land, but she has been affectionately known as the Snow Queen in Siberia for years.

Street scene at Verkhoyansk, where temperatures of −90.4°F have been recorded.

Yakutia is an enormous land, indeed. It covers 1,198,216 square miles. It is one-third as large as the United States, but its population as of January 1, 1967 stood at 646,000, and might be just reaching 700,000 at this writing, or roughly the population of New Orleans or Pittsburgh.

The explanation lies in the country's remoteness, and in its climate. Yakutia is the coldest place in Asia. Two Yakutian towns, Verkhoyansk and Oimyakon, claim to be the "poles of cold" of the northern hemisphere. Both have registered an official temperature reading of —90.4°F.

(This is not the lowest temperature recorded on earth. That honor is claimed by the Soviet weather station Vostok in Antarctica where on August 24, 1960, the thermometer plunged to an unbelievable —126.9°F, but then Vostok is located at an elevation of over 11,000 feet while Verkhoyansk and Oimyakon have a mean elevation of about 350 feet above sea level. Then, of course, Antarctica is not populated, but both Yakutian towns have about 3,500 people who live there permanently and raise silver fox on huge state farms.)

Can man live under such extreme conditions? The answer is yes, but not comfortably. True, the temperatures quoted were meteorological freaks, but in January and February temperature readings of —70°F are not uncommon throughout Yakutia, causing human breath to freeze instantly with a crackling noise which is locally known as "the whispering of the stars"—a poetic name, but a highly uncomfortable phenomenon. In fact, on frosty days all Yakutian towns are enveloped in man-made fog caused by the exhalations of men and animals, a weird phenomenon not found anywhere else.

The winter is long all over Yakutia, lasting for at least seven months, and the summers are short, but, paradoxically, extremely hot. The summer temperature can even rise over 100°F which, coupled with almost perpetual sunshine then, gives Yakutia a growing season for hardy crops such at oats, rye, and northern wheat, as well as vegetables. But still Yakutia cannot produce enough food for its small population, and much has to be imported. The area will never be developed as an agricultural land, but it has other resources to fall back upon, and they are unique.

First of all, 42 percent of the land area is covered by forests—412,000,000 acres of them representing a lumber reserve of some 10,000,000 cubic yards, 85 percent of which is composed of the highly regarded Dauria larch. Because of difficult transportation, lumbering is not yet a highly developed industry. A more important item is furs: squirrel, polar fox, and hare. Silver fox, ermine, and kolinsky are abundant, and silver fox is also produced on huge government animal farms. Sable, once almost exterminated, has been reintroduced and is fast multiplying,

Map of Yakutia.

and so is muskrat. There are huge herds of reindeer, both do-
mesticated and wild. Reindeer herding was the traditional occupation of the rural population, and still is.* But this is all secondary compared to the geological resources discovered in Yakutia.
Diamonds and gold make it "the valuta factory" of the Soviet
Union, and there are also immense deposits of coal, iron, tin,
copper, mica, and natural gas. Mining and, later, metallurgy
will be Yakutia's future in the economic life of Siberia. It is a
fabulously rich land, and great areas are still not even surveyed.

During the Tsar's time, Yakutia was the most backward part
of Siberia which, in turn, was the most undeveloped part of the

* Over 85 percent of the Arctic reindeer population of the world is in Siberia;
75 percent in Yakutia.

empire. It was a totally forgotten land. The native Yakuts, and several northern tribes who called themselves Yakuts since they were unconscious of their real national identity, were slowly dying out from sheer neglect. Whole taiga communities were wiped out by tuberculosis, smallpox, spotted typhus, scurvy, and periodic famines. The local Russian settlers fared hardly better, except for those who lived in Yakutsk itself which was a small garrison-*cum*-prison town. The mortality among taiga-born children was astronomical; less than one child in five lived to be an adult. The illiteracy was appalling: only seven men in a thousand could read and write—in Russian, of course, since the Yakut language had no writing. At the time of the revolution there were only two Yakut women known to be literate.

The purely Russian names of the Yakuts usually surprise foreign visitors. The Yakuts were Christianized shortly after the arrival of the Russians, i.e., almost 300 years ago, and were arbitrarily given traditional Russian names. The names clung, even though the great masses of people reverted to their primitive shamanism almost immediately. The peaceful coexistence of the Yakuts and the Russian settlers was not based on any attempts of the Tsarist administration to promote it, but on the fact that the local Russian settlers lived with their Yakut neighbors in perfect harmony and common misery, so much so that many of them adopted the Yakut customs and even the language. In the whole history of the Russian penetration into Yakutia there is but a single episode of conflict. According to old Yakut legends, a powerful Yakut chieftain by the name of Tygyn was disturbed by the fact that the Russians were building an *ostrog* on the land which he considered to be his, and he tried to rouse his tribesmen against the newcomers. But since the Russians were armed with rifles while his men had only bows and arrows, he thought better of it, and decided to make a deal. He asked how much land the Russians wanted. The Russians said that a space covered by one ox hide would be sufficient. Tygyn thought that the request was extremely reasonable and gladly granted it. But when he returned in the morning he saw that the Russians had meanwhile cut the ox hide into thin strips and encircled a rather large plot of land with it. But the deal had been made, and Tygyn, who apparently possessed the keen sense of humor characteristic of the Yakuts, accepted this with good grace. This was the only account of any friction. Yakuts and Russians have found their coexistence mutually profitable. While the Russians taught the Yakuts how to till the soil and use firearms for hunting, the Yakuts helped their new neighbors to cope with the climate, which was too severe even for the hardy Russians.

A mail-call in the Yakutia tundra.

Who are the Yakuts? In the absence of any written history, the Yakut folk legends are the only source of information about them. According to these legends, a rich and powerful man called Omogoy once came down the Lena River in a raft, and settled on the site of the present city of Yakutsk. Omogoy had several beautiful daughters but no sons. A year or so later, a very handsome young man called Ellai also came from the south, and became Omogoy's son-in-law, apparently on a bigamous basis. So Ellai and Omogoy's daughters were the ancestors of the present-day Yakuts.

This legend, apocryphal as it may be, gives a clue to the obvious ethnic dualism of the Yakuts. They are Mongol in appearance, but they speak a language of Turki origin, and a remarkably rich and well-developed language it is. It included words that described articles and animals that never existed in Yakutia, such as "camel," "lion," "tiger," as well as words for various agricultural implements never used by the Yakuts until the arrival of the Russians. Philologists and ethnologists are still struggling with the problem, and the precise answer may never be found.

Much of what I have learned about Yakutia and the Yakuts came from Nikolai Mikhailovich Sibiriakov, the secretary of the Yakutsk Union of Journalists who was our host in Yakutsk.

He met us at the airport and took us into the town. The weather was surprisingly mild, and Sibiriakov was distressed by the fact that we were going to see his beloved Yakutsk during an unseasonal thaw which was turning many of the city streets into quagmires. This, he told us, was untypical, since usually in April the ground was still hard-frozen. We asked him not to worry—we knew that Yakutia was no French Riviera.

Strangely, this remark seemed to upset him. "No one should feel sorry for us," he declared. "I'm a Yakut and I know that I'm speaking for all Yakuts when I say that we are proud of our country and would never trade it for any tropical paradise. There is not a single Yakut who has ever emigrated anywhere, though many have had the opportunity, and now this opportunity is open to all. This is our motherland and the word 'mother' has a special meaning for us Yakuts—and always has had."

This patriotism, I was to discover, is strong in Yakutia, and it includes both the native Yakuts and the Russians living there.

We came to the Hotel Lena, a venerable old Siberian establishment with the double entrance that is usual here. Between the two doors is a sort of chamber which prepares one in winter for the sharp change in temperature encountered coming in from bitter sub-zero cold to the heat of the lobby. The Siberians overheat their houses in winter to a remarkable degree. Apparently they believe in storing up heat before braving the winter weather.

I was assigned a large suite in the hotel. The place was hot, and the first thing I did was to turn off the heat, much to the amazement of the matronly "floor hostess." They are a customary feature of all Soviet hotels. Twenty-four hours a day, one of these ladies sits at a desk facing the stairway or elevator on every floor. They take an almost maternal interest in the welfare of their charges.

Despite some maladjustments in the plumbing, I found the Lena home-like and charming. What surprised me were beds in the halls on every floor. These, I was told, were for the convenience of the drivers of the supply truck convoys. They arrive in Yakutsk almost daily in winter, then have to spend a night there. There was no charge for these beds. It was a courtesy extended by the city of Yakutsk to the men servicing the winter lifeline from the south. In summer most of the supplies are delivered by boats along the Lena River, one of the great Siberian waterways.

There was also a contractual arrangement between Yakutsk and Tashkent in Uzbekistan for the daily delivery of fresh fruit and vegetables by air. Such arrangements exist between all far north cities and their southern counterparts, with the result that the far north is well supplied with fresh fruit in winter, even when it is in short supply in Moscow.

Before the revolution ninety-five percent of all the Yakuts were nomads, following their reindeer and horses all over the taiga and tundra. Now almost seventy percent of the population are settled in urban communities, and all children attend school.

It was eleven o'clock, and we were hungry—we had had our last meal in Mirny, more than nine hours before. We went downstairs to the hotel restaurant, and here Sibiriakov had to leave us—his wife and his children were waiting for him at home. But he did not leave before securing a table for us, no mean feat in any Soviet restaurant, and this one was crammed with diners even at this late hour. The place was jumping. The three-piece orchestra was playing with such vigor that conversation was difficult, and the young people were twisting. Here one could see an illustration of complete racial equality: young

Yakut girls in miniskirts were dancing with Russian students and young officers, and I spotted Liudmilla, our stewardess, dancing with a tall bespectacled Yakut youth. There was a hum of voices, a clatter of dishes, and the popping of champagne corks; it was hard to believe that all this revelry was taking place not far from the Arctic Circle.

The atmosphere was most informal and uninhibited; it was really all one party. Table-hopping was going on all over the place, perfect strangers were toasting each other, kissing and hugging—all men of course, for women preserved a certain decorum. Anyone could dance with anyone he wanted to, but each man had to ask the permission of the woman's escort before inviting her.

As we ordered the meal—which included boiled deer and horse meat, and some local fish called *chir*, a kind of river perch —the orchestra discontinued its efforts and the couples scattered to their tables.

Almost instantly singing started in different corners of the room—another Siberian custom and the repertoire was typical —the "Holy Sea, Sacred Baikal" gave way to a nostalgic Ukrainian song, "Winds are blowing, tempestuous winds," and then a blonde woman sang in Yakut a monotonous and strangely haunting tune with the same words repeated over and over again. The effect was magnetic. Yakut is a harsh sounding language when spoken, but something happens to it when it is sung; it becomes beautiful and melodious. The same thing, I have noticed, happens with modern Greek.

The accordion player suddenly broke into the wild Lesghinka, the dance of the Caucasian mountaineers, which requires near-acrobatic dexterity. It is often mistakenly called Kazatsky in the United States, where it was often performed in quasi-Russian night clubs by whirling "Cossacks" with daggers in their mouths, but the genuine Lesghinka is quite different; it is probably the most exuberant and wild folk dance in the world, definitely not for amateurs. It is native to the tribes of the high Caucasian ranges. They were Moslem warriors who resisted the Russian advance into their mountains for over seventy years of bloody warfare. However, they eventually became the loyal mounted warriors of the Tsars.

This was not music of Yakutia but apparently it had been requested. A young man in a wrinkled brown suit suddenly leaped to the center of the room and became a whirling dervish. Every joint seemed to move separately and violently, and yet it was a disciplined performance of rare grace. There is no more exciting dance to watch than a well-performed Lesghinka, and the entire room became silent watching the man, who paid no attention whatever to his audience. The tempo became faster and faster; sweat ran down the accordionist's face because of the volcanic heat in the room, but the dancer appeared to be undisturbed by it. Men and women clapped rhythmically and chanted *"tash—tash—tash!"* This word, from some obscure mountain tongue, is supposed to be chanted during a Lesghinka performance, which was always popular in Russia, and apparently still is.

Presently the lone dancer was joined by a very tall young man and a very tall young girl, both of them at least six feet and both Russians. Their performance, too, displayed both exquisite exuberance and rare control of every violent move. This was easily the best-performed Lezghinka I have ever seen, and to see it in Yakutsk, of all places, was to understand the true meaning of the amalgamating spirit of Russia, which draws together people of various races, colors, and creeds, and transforms them into a multiracial, multilingual unity.

Nikolai M. Sibiriakov called for us the next morning and took us for a walk around Yakutsk. The weather was still balmy, and the streets very muddy, but the sights were remarkable. Most of the city is still composed of old wooden houses leaning in different directions at crazy angles, and the same phenomenon affects wooden fences and gates: it looks as though the town had just suffered a violent earthquake. However, as Sibiriakov explained, this is caused by the permafrost. In the torrid heat of the summer the soil partially thaws, causing all structures to tilt and sag, and until recently there was no way of correcting this. It was considered a normal thing and people had learned to live with it. But not any longer. New concrete buildings all over town stand straight. This had not always been so: the first large buildings constructed in Yakutsk split like over-ripe watermelons in summer, and had to be demolished. Another building technique was tried: constructing on iron pylons sunk deep into the permafrost, but this was a fiasco, too. These reinforced buildings did not split open, but they cracked just the same, because the heat from the buildings traveled down the pylons and thawed out the permafrost around them. The problem was finally solved by building on pylons but raising the buildings some six feet above the ground so that the pylons had air circulating freely around them and cooling the iron. Now all the buildings in Yakutsk are constructed this way. The pylons are usually sunk into the frozen ground in winter when they are instantly gripped by the ice: in order to do this, the pylons are first heated, then sunk. The buildings are finished in summer, even though some construction goes on twelve months of each year. In winter, the cement and mortar must be warmed before they can be used.

It was a sunny day and it was Sunday. Streets were crowded with strollers, both Yakuts and non-Yakuts. Young mothers were pushing baby carriages, and the Yakut children, like all Oriental children, look like dolls. They seem to be bursting with health, their round cheeks apple-red, and their black eyes sparkling. It was hard for me to realize that half a century ago, most of them would have been dead before they reached the age of one. If modern medicine needs publicity, here it was—a perfect example of what it can do.

No wonder that the people of Yakutia swear by the Soviet system. If one studies the work done here by the Tsarist administration during the 250 years of their rule, it is understandable why the average Yakut has no nostalgic memories about the "good old times."

I remembered the letter that the Yakut editor, A. A. Semenov, wrote to Maxim Gorki in 1921, asking the famous Russian writer to help some of his countrymen:

On both sides of the Verkhoyansk mountain range (in the coldest spot in the world), there lives the Lamukhin tribe of the Lamuts comprising 350 souls.... A terrible disaster befell the tribe.... Out of 3,278 deer which they had, 1,543 died, and now wolves are decimating the rest of the herd.... During the tribe council held on January 27, the Lamuts asked me to appeal to the government for the grant of 2,000 deer, the only thing which could save the tribe from certain

She might be the future president of the Yakut Republic. Women are traditionally greatly respected by the Yakuts.

extinction. . . . If the tribe dies out, it would be impossible to revive life here again—there is no tillable soil, no meadows, and not even water in winter because the local streams are frozen solid here, but for the Lamuts this is their motherland. . . . I know that you cannot refuse help to these primitive people who have preserved through centuries their child-like decency and honesty. . . .

The tribe was saved, but how many of such tribes had perished in the frozen wilderness in the "good old times" when there was no one to appeal to?

The reindeer roundup. More than eighty percent of all the reindeer in the world are found in Siberia.

We were passing a magnificent building; the Geological Department of the Yakut Academy of Science. It was one of the handsomest buildings I had seen in Siberia, and we stopped to admire it.

"In ten years the whole of Yakutsk will be like this," Sibiriakov said. "Now that we have learned to build on the frozen ground, there won't be any stopping us. We'll have a beautiful capital for our beautiful republic."

This was a large order, I thought. Yakutsk was extremely interesting, even exciting, but it was not handsome. The ab-

sence of any foliage was one reason. The city was built on earth
so rich in salts that it killed all plants unless they were planted
in specially prepared beds of imported soil. Some of the largest
deposits of high-grade rock salt in the world have been found
in Yakutia, but that only pleases geologists and economists, not
city planners.

We walked along the banks of the Lena River. It was still
covered by ice. Handsome white steamers were securely imprisoned in their berths. Yakutsk, like all Siberian cities, is
basically a river town, and the Lena was its sole connecting link
with the outside world before the advent of air travel.

The Lena (*Elueneh* in Yakut) is one of the world's great
rivers. The Lena begins some 3,000 feet above sea level, only
five miles from Lake Baikal. It works its way north through
mountains and taiga for 2,680 miles until it reaches the Arctic
Laptev Sea. It drains part of Irkutsk Province and then Yakutia.
With its large tributaries, the Vitim, Olekma, Vilyui, and Aldan,
as well as hundreds of smaller streams, it forms the central
water axis of Yakutia. Flowing in a deep channel cut in the
permafrost, it is navigable for some 2,000 miles for 170 days
annually in the higher reaches, and 120 days near its enormous
delta. Supplies for Yakutia arrive by way of the Arctic sea
route, and a good portion of the exports—furs, tin, lumber—
go out the same way. The Arctic port of Tiksi serves as the
outlet for this trade. In summer, ocean-going cargo ships dock
there. In winter the river serves as a frozen highway for truck
convoys from the south. In effect, the Lena is Yakutia's main
lifeline, and it is one of the most picturesque rivers of Siberia,
especially in its mountainous higher reaches where the scenery
is often stunning in its savage beauty. The "Lena Pillars," where
sheer cliffs drop straight into the river in the form of enormous
columns of granite, are considered one of the foremost beauty
spots of Siberia.

Three other important rivers of Yakutia are the Indigirka,
the Yana, and the Kolyma. They all flow north into the Arctic
Ocean like all large Siberian rivers, except only the Amur, which
flows into the Pacific.

Yakutsk, the largest town on the Lena, is the home port of

a large river fleet of modern steamers that connect the capital with the outlying regions of the republic.

We visited the local museum, a collection of articles and relics pertaining to the history of Yakutia—ancient costumes, utensils, weapons, a mammoth skeleton, and the mummified body of a Yakut woman wearing ceremonial clothes. There is art work by early Yokutian artisans: the most striking are the articles carved of mammoth bone, which are incredibly delicate. Bone carving is the national art of the country, and the craft is still practiced even though mammoth bone is now scarce. Endless tons of it have been unearthed, mostly from the banks of local rivers. Much of it has been sold abroad. But mammoth skeletons are still found now and then during excavations. Once these huge beasts were as numerous here as polar squirrels are now.

My meeting with Madam President, Alexandra Ya. Ovchinnikova, was arranged for the next morning, and I tried to find out more about her. No records of any kind were kept in Yakutia when she was born, probably just a few years before the revolution, which would make her near 60. Her father was a tundra cattle-breeder, and both he and his wife were pure Yakuts, belonging to the original Saha tribe of the country. There were sixteen daughters in the family, and two sons; I could not find out how many of the children survived, but little Alexandra went to school—the first Ovchinnikova girl to do so. Upon completion of her studies she went to the Road-Building Institute and was graduated as a road builder. Subsequently for seventeen years she worked at building roads all over Yakutia. She was also active in politics. When the first President of the Supreme Soviet of Yakutia (also a woman) resigned, she was elected to this post. For over twelve years now she has served in this capacity with distinction. Much that has been done in Yakutia is due to her determination and energy.

She received us the next morning in her large modern office in the new government building. She was dressed in a very well-cut suit, with her jet-black hair combed straight back and her handsome Mongol face smooth and unwrinkled. Alexandra Yakovlevna (as she should be properly called in accordance with polite Russian usage) looked surprisingly youthful, and had a delightful smile. She spoke precise classical Russian, rarely heard nowadays.

When I told her how much impressed I was to learn that the president of Yakutia was a woman, she laughed:

"What is so unusual about that? The president of Tuva is also a woman, and so are the presidents of some national districts in the Caucasus."

"If more women were in responsible positions in politics, this might be a safer world to live in," I said.

Alexandra Yakovlevna did not protest. She just laughed. "You're just a feminist," she said. "But it is really fantastic what has happened to Yakut women in just a few years—you should go to the tundra and see."

I said I would, one day.

"Come back in summer," she urged me. "This is a very beautiful country—our mountains are just as majestic as those of Switzerland, and the Lena River is something to see—it's like no other river in the world. In fact Yakutia is a jewel, both in summer and in winter, but not in the spring—this mud can drive one insane. But some day we'll find a way of defeating this enemy."

Indeed Yakutia has defeated many enemies during the last fifty years. Mrs. President overwhelmed me with figures. Once the most ignorant people in Siberia, the Yakuts are not only 100 percent literate today, but there are 50,000 of them with university degrees, fully one-half women. More than 50 percent of the members of city and regional Soviets are women as well, and Yakutia is represented in the Supreme Soviet in Moscow by two women. Ignorance has been defeated. There are 1,500 schools with 200,000 students. In 1917 there were 13 doctors in the whole of Yakutia. Today there are 1,500; and 293 hospitals in addition to 517 maternity clinics. Trachoma and tuberculosis, two scourges of prerevolutionary Yakutia have been completely eliminated. "We are terribly rich," Ovchinnikova said, "but our greatest wealth is people. Gold, diamonds, coal, timber are nothing compared to this wealth. Come in ten years and you'll be dazzled—absolutely dazzled."

I said I'd try.

Meeting the Snow Queen of Siberia was a remarkable experience which I am not likely ever to forget. Instead of the fifteen minutes which she had told me she could give me, we spoke for an hour and a half. I can't remember having been more charmed during my travels throughout the world.

The Permafrost Institute at Yakutsk.

We next visited the Permafrost Institute. What actually is permafrost? It is an enormous cushion of hard, frozen earth lying between the warmth of the sun and the molten core of the earth, and here in Yakutia there is not a square yard that does not rest upon it. Some incredible wealth is locked in it, as well as whole zoological eras—mammoths are found in it, and some prehistoric microbiological forms. It is a gigantic form of cold storage, and holds a wealth of information about the past.

How deep is the permafrost in Yakutia? We were bombarded with figures. In some spots in northern Yakutia it goes down 1,300 meters (about 4,265 feet). In the basin of the Vilyui river it varies in depth from 1,640 to 1,968 feet, and in the Yakutsk region from 570 to 1,300 feet.

This was inconsistent with the figures I knew. Just before coming here, I had looked them up in the Guinness Book of Records, and it stated that the deepest permafrost on earth was discovered in July, 1963, at Winter Harbor in the Northwest Territories in Canada, and it went down 1,620 feet. When I mentioned this to Katanosov, my informant at the institute, he became very upset.

"It's not true. How many tests did they run in northern Canada? We take hundreds every year, and our figures are accurate. They are always trying to talk us down abroad, but this time they have gone too far. We should know best—fully 43 percent of the entire territory of the Soviet Union rests on permafrost, and here in Yakutia we have the best and the oldest permafrost in the world. Please write to them and ask them to correct their figures."

I promised him to do so (and I subsequently did).

I asked him how the soil could stay frozen at such depths. What about the thermal influence of the earth's core?

Katanosov explained that here in Yakutia underground salt water acted as insulation. He disagreed with the theory that northern Siberia had once been tropical, until some long-ago geological catastrophe overwhelmed it and almost instantly froze all life in it. He claimed that the mammoths who once lived here were of a polar variety and had disappeared gradually, hunted down by prehistoric man, and starved out by lack of fodder.

But what about the mammoths who were found here intact, frozen in the ice? Some had undigested food in their stomachs.

Katanosov agreed that there had been finds like that, but not many—just two, and both animals had broken legs. Apparently they had fallen through thin ice and were frozen. The important fact they helped prove was that the Yakutian permafrost is at least 30 million years old.

He took us into the underground tunnels dug in the permafrost under the institute. The huge underground chambers had no supporting shorings of any kind. The earth was as hard as rock, and there was no danger of caveins. The air was musty and frosty. Permafrost has a constant temperature of just about four degrees below freezing; in winter it is in fact the warmest place in Yakutia, as well as the most dependable cold storage in summer. Each home in Yakutia has such a storage area dug under it. Yakutia is a poor territory for refrigerator salesmen.

Permafrost has other uses. Pipelines for natural gas can be just drilled into it, and the gas sent through without pipes. Eventually, underground roads and even electrified railroads can be built in it—just as soon as the problem of proper ventilation can be solved, so that the permafrost is prevented from thawing.

The Permafrost Institute is working on a wide variety of technical problems connected with mining, building, and construction materials used here. Oil-well drilling, for instance, presents a problem because the oil becomes thick and viscous going up through thousands of feet of the permafrost; the pipes have to be electrically heated. One practically inexhaustible source of heat here is the thermal water under the permafrost. It could

The natives of the Siberian far north—especially the men—are natty dressers as well as functional ones. The "Kukhlianka," a deerskin overcoat with a hood (left) is very much "in." The design is traditional, and it successfully resists the bitterest cold.

be brought up and used to heat Yakutia. One large city in Siberia, Petropavlovsk-Kamchatsky, already is being heated completely in this way, and the technique may change living conditions in Yakutia drastically. Yakutia also needs a huge amount of electric power, which is now supplied by small and uneconomical thermal-electric stations that burn brown coal, which lies practically on ground's surface. The power now available is insufficient. If and when the Lower Lena hydroelectric project is constructed, it will solve all Yakutia's electric power problems.

14.

"The Golden Bottom"

THIS is an exact translation of the Russian expression *zolotoye dno,* used to describe something particularly rich, either a locality or even something intangible such as some sphere of knowledge, etc. It can be idiomatically translated as "inexhaustibly rich."

The Russians have applied this term to Siberia for many years, long before the Russian revolution. Besides furs, "the soft gold" of the early Tsarist economy, "hard" gold has been found in Siberia since the middle of the seventeenth century, shortly after the Russian conquest of the country.

The first indications of the existence of silver and gold deposits in Siberia were obtained in 1677 from the native tribesmen of Transbaikalia by the warden of the Nerchinsk prison. In 1704, the first silver and gold smelting plant was put into operation there, using convict labor. Its productivity proved to be low, and in 1734 it was shut down as uneconomical.

But by that time many other promising locations had been found, and the government permitted private mining. In the Altai region considerable deposits of silver and lead ores were discovered, which yielded better showings of gold than the Transbaikalian operations. However, gold remained a secondary consideration, while silver and lead were smelted.

The first pure gold deposit was found in the Urals in 1745 by a peasant, E. Markov. This was the famous Berezovski vein, which is being worked up to this day. The first gold mine was put into operation there in 1747.

During the next fifty years quite a few gold-bearing areas were found along many Siberian streams. But the first really important strikes occurred in Transbaikalia where a deposit of loose gold running for 14 versts (versta = 3,500 feet) along the Kara River was discovered in 1838. In 1850, another deposit was found, 17 versts long. Other large strikes were made in Transbaikalia in 1854 and 1863. The "gold rush" to Siberia was on.

Other discoveries were made along the southern rim of Siberia, from Transbaikalia almost to the Urals. Many mines that began operations during that period are still producing gold today.

The discovery of the famous Lena gold deposits in Irkutsk province in the middle of the nineteenth century marked the beginning of the "big time" of Siberian gold. Foreign capital was invested; a number of gold-mining companies were formed; and soon gold became the number-one industry of the country. Siberia became "the golden bottom."

How much gold was mined in Siberia up to the revolution? There are no accurate figures, but Russia was classed as an important gold producer, and it is estimated that in some years as much as 200 to 250 tons were produced. The Tsarist government had an important gold reserve in 1914 when Russia entered World War I. Much of it was transferred abroad during the war to pay for war supplies, and when the Soviet government came into power in 1918 it found itself gold-poor—and with practically all the gold-producing regions of the Urals and Siberia in the hands of the white armies and foreign interventionists.

The civil war which raged until 1922 in Siberia left the country in shambles. The Soviet government was faced with the gigantic task of the reconstruction of all of Russia and found itself in desperate economic straits. Russian industry could not be rebuilt and revived without large purchases aboard, and the young Soviet state had no credit standing at all. In fact, it found itself a victim of well-planned international economic squeeze. Few countries would deal with it, and those who did required payment in gold, often in advance.

Reconstruction of the Siberian gold-mining industry, as well as prospecting for new sources of gold, became a life or death necessity. Thousands of geologists and experienced prospectors were sent into the battle.

Their achievements during the last forty years are truly remarkable. Not only were the old gold works rebuilt, modernized, and enlarged, but large new gold fields were discovered that drastically changed the economic standing of the Soviet Union.

The discovery of the fabulously rich Aldan gold belt in 1923 by the geologist V. P. Bertin, and of the so-called "golden Kolyma" in 1930 by Y. A. Bilibin, made Soviet Russia potentially the greatest gold producer in the world.

But bringing gold out of the desolate frozen tundra, with Arctic storms raging for months and months on end, was a formidable task. The exact spots had to be found and surveyed. Then heavy machinery had to be brought in. This battle goes on to the present day, but the new fields are so rich that any capital and labor investments are insignificant compared with the results.

Even the terrible world war of 1941–1945 did not interrupt this work. Women replaced men in prospecting, in geological groups, in mines, and in smelting plants. By the end of the war the gold production of Siberia was paying for the reconstruction of Russia, which had been left in ruins after the German invasion. While Siberian troops took a conspicuous part in every great battle of the war, from Moscow to Berlin, it was Siberian geologists and gold miners who provided the gold to pay the bill. Now they are supporting the industrialization of their own country. Siberia is proving to be a true "golden bottom," both figuratively and literally.

It is generally believed today that the government gold reserve of the Soviet state closely rivals that of the United States, and is growing at a prodigious rate as the Siberian gold-mining industry develops. New large strikes are periodically reported. Within the last ten years no fewer than fifty gold-bearing areas have been located in the Kamchatka peninsula alone.

This preoccupation with gold seems strange to many foreign observers. "What does Russia need all that gold for and what is she doing with it?" is a question often asked.

What indeed? Surely gold as such plays little practical part in a socialist economy. It is a remarkable metal, of course. It is beautiful, non-corrosive, and also the most malleable, or ductile, of all metals. One ounce of gold can be drawn in the form of a continuous wire thread to a length of 43 miles, and a cubic inch can be beaten into a sheet to cover 1,400 square feet. But, more important, it has been accepted as a symbol of wealth ever since it was first discovered, and has taken a peculiar hold on human emotions. Even today in Siberia, when local enthusiasts rave about the Yakut diamonds, about the "oceans" of Siberian oil, of "mountains" of iron ore, the mention of the "golden Kolyma" evokes the greatest emotional response of all. The Kolyma has become a symbol of the new Siberian age, its power, wealth, and future. For the Kolyma gold basin, just being put into operation and not yet completely surveyed, is the true "golden bottom," topping by its potential all the other gold workings and resources of Siberia put together.

With the Soviet Union conducting practically all its foreign trade on a reciprocal or long-credit basis during the last few years, this incessant accumulation of gold seems to be rather strange, if not actually senseless. I asked an intelligent Soviet friend in Moscow about this. He said:

"We *must* be rich; it's more important for us than for a capitalist state. Once you're rich, and people know it, you needn't touch your wealth. It's only the poor that must have money. The rich can live on their reputations. We don't forget the time when we were poor, and had to pay with gold or blood for every needle and every nail we bought abroad—that is, if anyone would sell them to us. Well, we never want this to happen again. Today any foreign firm will make long-term credit deals with us; they know we have our own Fort Knox and perhaps even better stocked than yours. This is why we need gold."

Gold is a rare metal. Yet is it more widespread than any other; it is found virtually everywhere. A ton of any ore on earth contains about 0.005 gram of gold; sea water contains gold; plants and animals, and even human bodies do, too. It is finding gold in commercial quantities which is difficult. Unlike other elements, gold does not tend to blend with other metals, and this is why it often forms concentrations—nuggets. But finding nuggets does not necessarily prove the commercial potential of any given locality. A year or so ago, a virtual treasure-trove of nuggets was found in a small taiga river in Amur Province. There were 112 nuggets, the largest of which weighed over 15 pounds. But the Gari River was not found to be a commercial mining possibility. As a rule, the alluvial or "sand" gold is lightly regarded by serious gold prospectors. The rock or "lode" gold permits a truly economical exploitation, and the Kolyma basin is particularly rich in this kind of gold.

Fully seventy percent of all gold mined in the Soviet Union is still taken from alluvial deposits, since mining it is infinitely easier than extracting gold from rock. But only veins of rock gold justify the use of heavy industrial machinery. Nuggets, for instance, are spectacular, but one cannot build a gold-mining industry on them. In fact, all the nuggets found in the Soviet Union are preserved in a special "nugget fund" for scientific purposes, and never melted down into bullion, and today Russia possesses some of the largest nuggets in existence, among them the "Large Triangle" weighing over 75 pounds. This is not the largest nugget ever found—Halterman's Nugget, found in Australia over 100 years ago, weighed over 200 pounds, but that unfortunately was almost immediately melted down.

But scientific gold prospectors do not search for nuggets, or even rich alluvial deposits, but for the natural rock deposits which justify intensive industrial mining.

There are nineteen large gold-mining regions of "All-Union significance" known to exist in Siberia today, all working full blast, but it is the Kolyma that is the real star.

The Kolyma region was claimed for the Tsars as early as 1643 by a small band of Russian *zemleprokhodtzi* (literally "land-farers") led by a man called Michail Stadukhin. How these early adventurers could cover thousands of miles without proper transport or equipment is a mystery, but cover them they did, overrunning the whole of Siberia in a remarkably short span. Stadukhin and his men, for instance, came to the mouth of the Kolmya by way of the Arctic Ocean—an extremely precarious trip even for modern ice-breaking craft now. They sailed up the Kolyma River and found no people, but abundant sable and blue Arctic fox. This was at a time when furs represented a third of the Tsar's treasury's income. Stadukhin built three small *ostrogs*, or log-forts, naming them Verkhne-, Sredne-, and Nizhne-

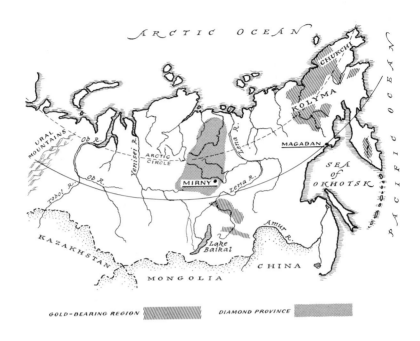

GOLD-BEARING REGION [hatched]   DIAMOND PROVINCE [shaded]

Kolymsk, or Upper, Middle, and Lower Kolymsk. The forts soon developed into fur-trading posts and an orgy of wild-life extermination began. Nomadic Yakuts killed countless thousands of the fur-bearing animals and traded the skins for salt, powder, and, unfortunately, alcohol. Soon most of the animals were killed off, and by the 1670s the whole region was dying economically.

It would probably have returned to its original desert conditions had someone in St. Petersburg not developed the bright idea of turning the three God-forsaken settlements into penal colonies for the particularly dangerous criminals condemned to exile to "the most remote places, unsuitable for habitation," to quote the official criminal code of the era. Thus started a new page in Kolyma history which was to last for over 200 years, during which the region gradually became the most dreaded name in all the Russias.

Indeed there was very little to recommend it besides the profitably short life expectancy of the convicts sent there. The huge region of over 500,000 square miles was one frozen desert in the winter which lasted for nine months of the year, and a *g'nuss* —infested marshland in summer; the very uncomfortable home of a few hundred nomadic deer-herding Yakuts, some Russian prisoners, and their guards, who usually were assigned as a punishment for some breach of discipline. No one suspected, of course, that this land could be one huge treasure-trove. In 1892, a lonely explorer, I. D. Chersky (the man whose name is given to the Chersky Mountain Range), found large open deposits of coal here, but the idea of mining it in this wilderness seemed ridiculous. Who needed coal, or anything else for that matter, in the Kolyma? The most valuable commodities there were onions and garlic as a cure for the scurvy which decimated the ranks of both prisoners and guards each winter.

The present story of the Kolyma began in 1908—and it is connected with the name of one man, Yuri Yanovich Rosenfeld, the Estonian-born employee of a rich Siberian merchant, Shustov. Shustov, an enterprising merchant, knew that the Kolyma prison camps were supplied only once a year by way of a tremendously difficult overland route from Yakutsk. This cost the government a good deal of money. He also knew that at the height of the scurvy season there a single clove of fresh garlic could be exchanged for a sable skin, and so he conceived the idea of finding an overland route to Kolyma from the fishing village of Ola on the Sea of Okhotsk, then the regional center of the whole huge territory. Should such a route be found, Shustov could get a government concession to supply the Kolyma prison camps, and carry on some profitable trade on the side.

This was worth a gamble, and Shustov sent Rosenfeld to Ola to scout the possibilities. What he did not know was that in Rosenfeld he was dealing with a potential "possessed."

Rosenfeld, who must have been a man of iron constitution and will, spent several years crossing and crisscrossing the tundra, sometimes with a guide, though often alone, sometimes on horseback though often on foot. He followed the tundra streams. Originally eager to go to Siberia because he had a dream of gold, Rosenfeld now looked for that instead of searching for an overland route to the Kolyma. Though he was not a trained geologist, he was impressed by geological formations along the riverbanks that showed massive veins of quartz, laced with pyrites and ochre. He abandoned the idea of returning to Shustov.

But since he had no equipment and no knowledge of prospecting, in the spring of 1914, he returned to Ola and formed a partnership with three local "possessed," Kanov, Geifullin, and a man known as Boriska, for "Boris." Supplied with primitive equipment and modest provisions they went into the tundra.

They reached the headwaters of the Booyunda, a large tributary of the Kolyma. From there they decided to continue in a makeshift raft. So Boriska was left there in charge of the horses, while Rosenfeld, Geifullin, and Kanov sailed down to the Kolyma and then to the mouth of the Djegian where Rosenfeld saw some especially spectacular quartz veins. Since the three men did not have any heavy equipment they could not get to the veins, but instead took sand samples all around the place which showed mere "signs" of gold, i.e., microscopic particles of no commercial value.

Meanwhile Boriska also took some tests on the Booyunda and also found some gold "signs." So when Rosenfeld and his companions returned, he declared that he had decided to stay here over the winter and do more prospecting. Kanov stayed with him while Rosenfeld and Geifullin went to the village of Yamsk, near Ola, to get some better equipment.

In Yamsk they learned that World War I had broken out and that Russia was in it. Both Kanov and Boriska were subject to military service. Boriska refused to go. But Kanov and Geifullin went back to Yamsk, and eventually into the army.

Working on his own, Boriska reached the mouth of a small nameless brook, and there he made his strike. (This place is now known as "Boriska's Springs.") No one bothered Boriska here for a long time. Then, in late autumn of 1916, three Yakuts came across Boriska's frozen body near the brook, and on him, a few small bags of gold dust. No one knows how he died. There was food in the hut, and the presence of gold dust on his body made murder for robbery improbable. The three Yakuts buried Boriska and then reported their find to the authorities, at the same time surrendering the gold dust.

Rosenfeld, after losing his three partners, decided to go it alone. He went back to look for his fabulous quartz veins, which he called "Gorelovsky." They are called that to this day. But he got sick, and lost all his precious equipment in the tundra. He was not able to reach his "find."

But like a true "possessed" he did not give up. He decided to go back to Shustov and try to interest him in the large-scale gold-mining potential of the Kolyma. But when he got back to Vladivostok, he learned that the once-wealthy Shustov had gone bankrupt.

Rosenfeld now went to Petrograd (the erstwhile St. Petersburg, and now Leningrad) with an idea of interesting the Tsar's government in the Kolyma project and made endless rounds of various government departments. Finally, in January 1917, he succeeded in talking the Ministry of Transport into financing an expedition, not as a gold-prospecting venture, but as an overland route survey—Shustov's original scheme.

This time it was the revolution that disrupted all these plans. Rosenfeld returned to Vladivostock just as Siberia became an arena of foreign intervention and fell under the rule of the counterrevolutionary white government.

But even that did not stop Rosenfeld. He composed a lengthy "Report about the gold-mining potential of the Okhotsk-Kolyma region," and submitted it to a consortium of Vladivostok merchants. Once again, he described his Gorelovsky veins with their "mighty, lightning-like, zig-zag formations" and expressed his willingness to lead an expedition to them. He expressed his absolute conviction that the Kolyma was the most promising gold-bearing region of Siberia.

However the local capitalists could not be induced to invest in a venture located in a region which they suspected would soon come under Communist control. Their fears proved to be correct. The white armies of Admiral Kolchak were defeated, and his government collapsed.

Vladivostok was still occupied by Japanese troops, and a nominal Far Eastern Republic was set up, a frankly interim regime since the Soviets did not want to come into open conflict with any foreign country. The indefatigable Rosenfeld now resubmitted his report to the new temporary authorities. They showed interest, but just about then, the Japanese troops began to leave Vladivostok. Before the Soviet troops entered Vladivostok, Rosenfeld went abroad.

For two years he tried to interest foreign capitalists in securing a concession from the Soviet government but his Kolyma claims sounded too extravagant to interest serious foreign investors.

So Rosenfeld finally gave up. He returned to Siberia and took a job as a government tungsten prospector in the Transbaikalia.

Meanwhile the news of the luckless Boriska's gold strike had slowly spread among the Siberian "possessed" by mysterious ways known only to them, and scores of them had gone there to dig. Most of them were completely unsuccessful, but there were a few lucky ones. Some gold dust was brought into Ola and went to the Chinese and Japanese ships that stopped there, all, of course, on the black market.

This finally attracted the attention of the Soviet government. The young Soviet state was in acute need of foreign exchange. It could secure no credits and had to pay with gold for anything purchased abroad. So the government gave the highest priority to the development of new gold-bearing regions, and a special agency, called the Soyuz-Zoloto, was organized to handle this operation.

The Soyuz-Zoloto made no attempt to stop private prospecting in Siberia as long as the gold was delivered to the government at a fixed price. But the Kolyma "possessed" continued to sell their dust abroad at a much higher price.

Meanwhile Rosenfeld's report to the temporary Far Eastern government was sent to Moscow with all the rest of the bureaucratic files, and was gathering dust there. Then a young Leningrad geologist, Bilibin, read it. Bilibin had been studying the geological formation of the Siberian northeast and noticed that the general geological structure of the region was similar to that of many known gold-bearing areas. To him Rosenfeld's report made sense, and he recognized in it more than the raving of a greedy adventurer.

Bilibin talked his superiors into financing an expedition to the Kolyma basin to study its potential. On June 12, 1929, the small group, led by Bilibin, sailed from Vladivostok for Ola.

The arrival of the expedition in Ola was met with open animosity. The local prospectors immediately suspected that their "free life" was coming to an end, and Bilibin and his men were almost lynched at the diggings, but finally he convinced some prospectors working there that he was merely doing a geological survey, and for a little while the two groups coexisted in harmony.

In the middle of September a representative of the Soyuz-Zoloto arrived, with a large group of workers, and posted a notice that the entire Bezimiannyi region was now a government preserve and that all the gold found there was to be turned in at a fixed price of 1.50 rubles per gram.

There was a near riot until the prospectors recognized the inevitable, and submitted. They realized that their free gold route to Ola had been cut off and they had no choice. So a government-controlled gold work camp was set up here—the first of such camps in the Kolyma.

Bilibin realized that the Soyuz-Zoloto representative had no knowledge of geology and was a poor administrator. He was also convinced that the Bezimiannyi region, the current scene of diggings, was not a particularly promising place.

He had noticed a bare mountain near a river called Bas-Ugunya. He sent an aide to prospect there.

The aide and a companion moved slowly up the stream taking samples and reached a small nameless tributary of the Utinnaya and pitched their tent there. The sand showed two grams of pure gold. Translated to cubic yards this meant 200 grams for each, an absolutely incredible figure. Another test, and another, and still another, and each showed the same fantastic result.

Then they found nuggets: in an hour they filled a cigarette box with them.

At this point the aide's assistant said:

"Listen. This happens once in a hundred lifetimes. . . . This is a mad fortune. . . . Let's keep quiet about it, resign, and then come back here on our own . . ."

Since private prospecting was still legal, there was nothing actually criminal about this suggestion. But the aide Rokovsky, was a very dedicated young Communist. He said:

"Look here, Petya. Let's say you haven't said anything and I haven't heard it. Understand?"

With this he turned his back to his friend. This was the classic moment in gold-prospecting partnerships which usually ends in murder, but Rokovsky's companion was no murderer. According to Rokovsky, he became ashamed of his momentary weakness.

The friends worked for a few more days scouting the region, and came across a quartz lode running for three miles in an unbroken line, and with breaks, for almost ten miles. They took samples of it, but they had no rock-crushing equipment, and could not determine the gold content.

Bilibin took nuggets and samples to Moscow, and the quartz samples showed such high gold content that Bilibin was afraid to report it in full, and simply cut it in half. Even then the figures were phenomenal: this lode alone, properly worked, should bring in 400 percent more than the entire current gold production of the Soviet Union.

The inefficient Soyuz-Zoloto was dissolved and the whole project was transferred to a new organization called the Dalstroy which operated under the Committee of Labor and Defense—a paramilitary organization. The Dalstroy was given almost unlimited funds for necessary technical development, and the use of convict labor from the so-called "corrective labor camps."

The Dalstroy acted swiftly and drastically. The entire region was cordoned off and all private prospecting was declared illegal. The "possessed" were swiftly driven off, and the history of the present "golden Kolyma" began.

A sweeping new survey of the whole region was initiated, with hundreds of geological teams thrown into it. Nothing was overlooked. And this is how Rosenfeld, the man with good intuition and bad luck, once again entered the story.

The Dalstroy operation was a part of the prison camp empire initiated under Stalin. Today's Siberians do not like to remember that, but unfortunately it is a part of recent Siberian history and it can't be erased by not mentioning it.

Stalin's "corrective labor camps" have been discussed and written about all over the world, but no accurate figures have ever been made known. Some exaggerated claims put the prison population of Siberia under Stalin and Beria as high as 10 million, but that is undoubtedly a wild figure. Siberia just could not possibly support and maintain such masses of prisoners. But in itself the existence of such "corrective camps" is a black page in recent

Soviet history. The practice was cruel, and as all such practices are, wasteful and uneconomical. The productivity of all forced labor is extremely low.

Originally, "corrective labor" was supposed to be the way to reeducate the country's "antisocial elements," i.e., all those who failed to accept a socialist way of life and who actively resisted it. But there were terrible abuses; the poor wretches were subjected to all sorts of hardship and privation, and many died not so much from intentional maltreatment as from the lack of proper housing, proper clothing, and proper food in the severe climate. How many of them died and are buried in the Siberian permafrost will never be known, but the figure might be shocking. And as they perished, new victims had to be found to take their places since the prison administration was interested in just one thing, the fulfillment of various "plans" and "norms." To fulfill them it needed laborers. It was a vicious circle: the demand was begetting the supply. Soviet courts throughout the country were meting out sentences at forced labor reputedly just to fill prison trains leaving for Siberia.

Fortunately, this is a thing of the past. All such corrective camps were closed after Stalin's death, with the inmates either allowed to go home or induced to remain on the spot as free employees with all the benefits and privileges of workers working in the far north, i.e., high pay and early, pensioned retirement. I have been told, but could not verify it, that many people chose to stay in Siberia. It is reasonable: many of the former prisoners were strong-willed non-conformists and they might well choose to stay where bureaucratic supervision was not nearly as strict as in the large European Soviet cities.

But Dalstroy, despite all efforts, was not producing enough gold to satisfy demands, and nothing could be overlooked to improve the production figures, nothing at all. And that is how Rosenberg's report came to light.

His report, written more than thirteen years before, impressed the Dalstroy people. Who was this Rosenfeld, and where was he? A country-wide search flushed him out, still in his obscure job as a tungsten surveyor in the Transbaikalia.

Rosenfeld was immediately ordered to report to the Kolyma and lead a geological expedition.

So in the summer of 1934 he arrived in the Kolyma again. All the necessary transport, supplies, and equipment were now available. Rosenfeld suddenly became a key man, and his dream was about to be turned into reality, even though at no profit to himself.

But his bad luck continued to dog him. Despite an extensive search, no sign of his Gorelovsky veins could be found. The expedition found some very indifferent quartz formations, that showed no gold, and nothing even remotely resembling the formation described by Rosenfeld in his report was found.

Rosenfeld was flabbergasted. Had nature itself turned against him? In truth, everyone familiar with the Kolyma region knows that all riverbanks are subject to almost yearly landslides caused by the intense freezing in the winter, when wedges of ice form in the crevices and pry off masses of earth and rock. Land contours are often changed beyond recognition. But the Dalstroy administration did not know this, and took a dim view of his failure. He was accused of intentionally misleading the authorities in order to preserve his "find" for himself.

And so poor Rosenfeld was given five years of "corrective labor education" in the Kolyma, and had to spend them swinging a pickaxe along with all other prisoners.

At the termination of his sentence, he chose to remain as a free government surveyor. He was now an old and broken man. However, fate was not through with him. It prepared a tragic end for the lonely "possessed" who by sheer intuition had pointed out to his country an area of enormous wealth.

One cold morning he did not report for work, and he was missing for a few days. Then his naked frozen body was found under a wooden bridge on the local creek. His skull was crushed. Apparently he had been murdered for the clothes he wore, not an unusual occurrence in this region which was teeming with runaway camp convicts.

Some thirty-five years have passed since then. Today the Kolyma is still a grim place, but no longer the wilderness which Rosenfeld knew.

It is still a lightly populated province, but no longer completely isolated from the rest of the world. Snow-truck convoys reach all settlements and the air is alive with planes and helicopters bringing supplies to geological parties. Many of these geologists are women. As everywhere in Siberia, the presence of women tempers the brutalizing effect of a hard climate and loneliness.

The modern city of Magadan has been built beside the little log-hut village of Ola which once served as a base for the early "possessed." It is the industrial and supply hub of the entire region, the "open door" to the Kolyma, and now has 90,000 people.

A main street in Magadan. This city did not exist thirty years ago.

Magadan is built on the shore of the Nagayevo Bay, the best deep-water harbor of the Okhotsk seaboard. During the summer season hundreds of ships dock here with food, supplies, and equipment for the entire Kolyma region. Most of it is shipped by truck convoys into the Kolyma basin. The Magadan truck park is the largest in northeastern Siberia, and has thousands of machines, extensive machine shops, and repair facilities. There are also shipyards and ship repair docks here, and marine engine factories, and a whole complex of industrial plants to serve not only Magadan Province, but Kamchatka and the Kurile Islands as well.

Magadan's airport is one of the busiest in northern Siberia. Flights arrive daily from Khabarovsk, Irkutsk, Vladivostok, and Sakhalin, and it is also a center of polar aviation.

Magadan, though rather monotonous in appearance, is a modern city of well-built stone and cement buildings. The scarcity of electric power is its greatest handicap for further industrial development. There are no hydroelectric projects anywhere in the region and electricity is produced by comparatively small stations, but the Lankovsky brown coal deposits located near Magadan are being developed, and they will substantially relieve the present power bottleneck of the region.

The entire province, with the exception of a narrow seaside strip along the Sea of Okhotsk, is located in the deep permafrost zone, with all the difficulties that this represents. Not only does this make agriculture extremely difficult, but it increases the cost of all industrial and residential construction enormously. At present this is more than covered by the gold production of the region, but development of other industries is hampered. For the foreseeable future, Magadan province is destined to remain "the gold factory" of Siberia rather than an all-around industrial region. Tungsten mining is the only other industry that has good prospects for development. There are fur farms for silver and blue fox, mink, and squirrels. Fish wastes and small noncommercial fish are fed to the animals, and they seem to flourish on this diet. There is commercial fishing, but the rich fishing banks are further east, along the Kurile and Kamchatka shores.

The predominance of married couples with children at mining camps gives the Siberian "gold rush" a vastly different aspect from Sutter Creek and the Klondike. And often women run these settlements, and run them very well indeed.

The present gold production figures of the region have not been published, but an educated guess puts them close to 1,000 tons per year, and rising.

It is interesting to note that many hidden hoards of gold and

The Golden Kolyma: a dredge at work for gold.

jewelry have been literally unearthed in Siberia during the present construction boom. During the revolution, many wealthy families in Siberia buried their valuables when they fled the advancing Red armies. Probably they hoped to come back for them later on. Many of these hidden treasures are found during demolition and excavation operations and, of course, are taken over by the state. However, in accordance with Soviet law, the finders are entitled to 25 percent of the value of each find, so treasure-hunting can be a profitable business.

The Kolyma "golden bottom," rich as it is, may be eclipsed

even before the region has reached its full production capacity. A recent rich strike has been reported, not in the Far North, but in the burning sands of Uzbekistan, which lies south of Siberia proper.

News about this new Eldorado is still fragmentary. For many years archeologists have been aware of prehistoric excavations in the Kuzylkum desert, a region which has never, in recorded history, been known to produce gold. These ancient diggings remained a complete mystery until late autumn of 1967. Then a Soviet geological team, prospecting for oil, came upon what may be the greatest concentration of gold anywhere on earth. What is more, these deposits were found so close to the surface that they can be worked by the most economical method of open pit mining, making this, in effect, the "cheapest" gold in the Soviet Union.

The place is called Muruntau, and it is doubtful if many geographers have ever heard of it. But if the initial claims are found to be correct, it is bound to become a household word in a few years. While the survey is still going on, a brand-new city is being built in the trackless desert. The Soviet designers plan to make it the most beautiful modern city ever built. It will house 50,000 technicians, miners, and their families, and will be called Zaravshan.

The full story of the Muruntau strike is not yet complete. It may well astound the world.

15.

The Land of the White Bear

THE northern seaboard of Siberia is its longest and most desolate frontier, and its most important one, because of the practically limitless natural resources locked in the frozen soil all along the Arctic Ocean.

One day railroads will be built there, probably on steel pylons sunk into the permafrost, and weather-controlled, enclosed towns will dot the tundra. One of the North Siberian cities, Salekhard, the capital of the Yamal-Nenets National District and the sea gateway to the Ob-Irtysh River basin, is already connected with the rest of Russia by a railroad which loops its way over the northern edge of the Ural mountain chain. But Salekhard, despite its location, has a milder climate than the rest of the Siberian Arctic seaboard. It benefits from the warmer Atlantic currents. But other North Siberian cities must depend on the so-called Great Arctic sea route, their lifeline and the most vital connecting link with the outside world now.

The Arctic sea route originates in Murmansk and ends at the small port of Provedenniya on the southern tip of the Chukchi peninsula, just sixty miles from Alaska's St. Lawrence Island. The route has some 7,000 miles of the roughest possible sailing, along the frozen edge of the world.

Murmansk, the northernmost port of Russia, is, by a quirk of geography, the only open sea port of the entire Soviet Union which remains ice-free throughout the year. Murmansk, with its satellite towns of Polarny, Soveromorsk, and Kola, can be

The great Arctic Sea Route: Siberia's northern lifeline.

justly called the gateway to northern Siberia, and it has become
so closely connected with Siberian destinies as to become virtually
a part of Siberia—if not geographically, then certainly economically.

The history of Murmansk is closely connected with the two
great wars which Russia has had to fight within the last fifty
years, and because it is so vital for the development of today's
Siberia it should be briefly mentioned in the context of this book.

Murmansk, once a tiny fishing village, became enormously
important to Russia during World War I when both the Baltic
and the Black Seas were blockaded by the enemy. The only
supply routes open to the country were distant Vladivostok
which was not an ice-free port in winter, and the then one-
track Trans-Siberian Railway. Obviously that was insufficient,
and another route had to be found. It was then that somebody

Sailing over Siberia's frozen "top" is a hazardous enterprise, even in summer. How did early Siberian discoverers negotiate these waters in their flimsy craft? The question still baffles historians and today's Siberian polar seafarers.

remembered that there was a spot in northern Russia which was free of ice for twelve months of each year.

Accordingly in 1915 the Russians started building a railway from Petrograd to Murmansk, then called Romanovsk-on-Murman. This almost brought Sweden into the war, because the Swedish government suspected that instead of just developing a small obscure fishing village into a new port, the Russians were planning to occupy northern Norway and seize the Norwegian port of Narvik. This did not happen. The railway was completed in two years, and Murmansk became a brand-new Russian supply port. However, before it could be used effectively, the Russian revolution took the country out of the war. For a while Murmansk was all but forgotten.

Then, in World War II, its importance was again fully appreciated. The "Murmansk ship convoys" became almost the sole means by which supplies were delivered to Russia. The convoy

routes became the favorite hunting grounds of German sub-
marines, which took a tremendous toll of shipping and lives.

I had once visited Murmansk in the winter of 1917, a few
months before the Russian revolution. My father was involved
in the building of the strategic railway line to the town. I
vividly remember the dismal little settlement of log huts and
houses with gas lamps glowing in the Arctic night. The entire
population of the town, as I remember it, was about 2,000 people,
mostly Chinese construction workers who were brought in from
Manchuria. Some 200,000 coolies were brought in to do the work,
but most of them deserted the section gangs, and scattered all
over Russia. Only a few of them returned to their homes. Some
of them stayed permanently in Russia. Many had died on the job.
Eventually the railroad was finished by crews of mostly German
and Austrian prisoners-of-war who were paid full wages for
their work.

Today Murmansk is a modern city of 300,000 people and a
great northern port. Cargo ships, many of them of foreign reg-
istry, assemble here every spring to sail the Arctic sea route to
various ports of northern Siberia—Salekhard, Dudinka, Igarka,
Khatanga, Tiksi. The navigation season lasts for some 100 to 110
days, and during these days the Arctic sea route is a busy sea
lane with hundreds of ships carrying supplies to Siberia, and
bringing back lumber, furs, zinc, and copper.

This is a difficult and dangerous route. Storms and drifting ice
menace the ship convoys even in July and August. Ice-breakers
lead these convoys. There is a whole fleet of them, the most
famous of which is the atom-powered giant, *Lenin*, the pride
of the Soviet Arctic fleet.

Arctic sea traffic is directed from a central station at Dickson
Island on the Taimyr Peninsula. Meteorological information is
supplied to Dickson by a number of all-year-round weather
stations located all over the long Siberian seaboard, as well as
weather planes that patrol the area. The convoys are warned of
sudden storms and general weather conditions.

Now the northern seaboard of Siberia is closed to foreign
tourists, and for information about life and work there we must
go to Soviet sources.

There are women steamboat captains in Siberia, as well as

The Arctic Sea Route is constantly patrolled by the planes of the Ice and Weather Service.

women pilots flying polar aircraft. The presence of women in the crew of any Soviet ship is taken for granted. The old superstition held on sailing ships, about women aboard bringing bad luck is not accepted in Siberia, and particularly not in the far north, where the only danger women seem to represent is to young bachelors.

A correspondent for the Workers' Press Agency in Warsaw describes a trip on the *Lenin:*

All around us lies the Arctic Ocean, which is always full of unexpected surprises. The ice movement on the sea lanes is constantly reported by hydro-meteorological stations and weather planes. But the situation may be changed almost instantly by the greatest ice-breaker of them all, the wind. It can shatter the largest ice fields and sweep them into the sectors that had been reported free of ice only a few hours before. This happened to us. We expected to meet our first ice near the Kara Strait leading into Siberia, but we met it much earlier.

Suddenly there was a sharp temperature drop. Out of the fog caused by this drop, ice fields appeared. The *Lenin* plowed through them without any visible effort. Only the slight vibration and the snapping sound of breaking ice reminded us that we were moving through the

Arctic Ocean. This sound accompanied us to the end of our trip. I have made a tape recording of it. The sound is not particularly pleasant, but soon one becomes unconscious of it.

The speed of our ship decreased insignificantly—from 18 to 17 knots, even though the ice was many inches thick. Later when it became several feet thick, we were moving at 10 to 12 knots.

Gradually the fog lifted and the sun rose over the sparkling field of ice. On one side we could see the distant contours of the Novaya Zemlya, but everyone rushed to the opposite side, bringing their cameras. An enormous white polar bear stood there motionlessly watching our ship without any sign of alarm.

Not long ago, these animals were very numerous here. The Norwegian explorer, Kore Rodal, wrote in his book about a hunter he had met in Greenland who had shot 700 polar bears. But according to zoologists, the number of bears on the sea lanes has decreased 90 percent during the last 30 to 40 years.

In the Soviet Arctic Ocean, bears are protected by the law. One can kill a white bear only in self-defense or facing hunger. A polar bear is a virtual storehouse of meat, and its fat contains anti-scurvy vitamins. The average weight of a grown polar bear is about 1,500 pounds.

It is estimated that the entire bear population of the Arctic now is 5,000 to 8,000 animals. On Wrangel Island there are about 200 known bear lairs. Our bear was migrating north to escape the summer "heat." Polar bears are known to swim for hundreds of miles, and our friend was much more at home in the water than on the ice.

Some people from Dickson Island told me a story of a movie cameraman. He carried his rifle unloaded because he did not believe in polar bears. One day, returning from a picture-taking expedition, he suddenly heard some puffing behind him. He turned around and saw a polar bear standing erect a few feet away. He threw his camera at the beast who grabbed it and held it against its chest. Then the cameraman hit the bear on the head with the rifle butt whereupon the animal dropped the camera and ran away. The cameraman shot a few memorable feet of film, but afterwards suffered from nervous shock. . . .

While in Siberia I heard many stories of young men and women volunteering to work in the far north, and according to these stories, many of them reenlisted after the completion of their contracts. They live and work hundreds and even thousands of miles from the nearest large town, in complete darkness for many months every year and amid almost constant savage storms. Why?

A white bear cub on the Chukchi Peninsula.

It may be the strange quality of human relationships in Siberia. The severe climate—and the climate of Siberia, even its southernmost parts, is very cruel—makes people cling to each other, and they form relationships that endure for a lifetime. It is a warm, friendly place on the human level, just as it is bitter and unfriendly outside.

This is why many people go back. Once a person becomes "captured by Siberia," as they call it there, one becomes committed to it. Apparently there are greater values in life than sunshine and gentle breezes, and then, of course, Russia is a cold country in winter as well—even though not as cold as Siberia.

My whole life I have been fascinated by geography, and the Siberian North particularly intrigued me. But traveling there in my time was all but impossible. It is easier now with airstrips built in practically every far north community, but not for foreigners—since it is still a closed area for international travel: no facilities for tourists.

Two places especially fascinated me—the promontory of Chelyuskin, the northernmost point on the Siberian continent, and the town of Uelen, located at the extreme east of the Chukchi peninsula, facing Alaska across the Bering Strait. This is the easternmost town on earth—each day begins there: when it is midnight of Monday in Uelen, it is midnight of Sunday in Wales in Alaska, only fifty miles away. The very name, Uelen, intrigued me—it sounded so peculiarly un-Russian, and very romantic, for some reason. However, in all my travels I have never met anyone who has been there—even though Soviet polar aviation connects it now with Yakutsk and other large Siberian towns.

There are three versions about the origin of this name. The captain of the first schooner which dropped anchor here had a wife who was called Elena. While in port she moved ashore to be further away from the boisterous crew. The husband, quite naturally, preferred the marriage bed to his drafty and lonely cabin. So when someone asked "Where's the skipper?," the usual answer was *"U Eleny,"* "at Elena's" in Russian. The second version is more plausible. The world *uelen* means "black rock" in the Chukchi language. And there are dark, snowless hills to the west of the settlement. Some believe that the name is based on the English word "whale." There are thousands of whales around Uelen.

The town is located on a strip of snow-covered land jutting out into the sea—two seas, in fact, the Chukchi Sea to the north and the Bering Sea to the south. So Uelen divides two oceans— the Arctic and the Pacific.

16.

The Polar Baghdad Revisited

IN the beginning of the sixteenth century, all over Europe, especially in commercial circles, a new and strange name was mentioned more and more often. The name was Mangazeya.

None of the European merchants had ever visited it, but many had grown rich trading with it. Hundreds of thousands of sable, ermine, silver and blue fox skins and countless tons of precious mammoth and walrus bone flowed each year into Europe from Mangazeya, a fabulous polar city built in the wilderness of northern Siberia. It was a few miles above the Arctic Circle, in the middle of nowhere on the tundra river Taz. Founded by the *pomori*, the Russian vikings of the Arctic Ocean, it had become, in a few years, probably one of the richest trading towns on earth. Not only the products of the Arctic shores, fur and bone, but also precious cargoes of silk, porcelain, and rare fabrics came to Mangazeya from Central Asia and China, were shipped up the mighty Yenisei river, and from there to Europe. Mangazeya was a virtual Baghdad of Siberia, a city-state, all but independent of the Russian Empire in its wealth and utter isolation.

The history is interesting. The *pomori* (the word means "sea people" in old Russian) originally came to the shores of the White Sea from Novgorod late in the fourteenth century. They fished and hunted, following the pods of seals through the White Sea into the Arctic Ocean. Over a period of years they learned to build a special kind of seaworthy craft suitable for sailing through floating ice, yet light enough to be dragged across land. They sailed this craft all along the Siberian Arctic seaboard, "towards the sun," "following the spring," and there are indications that they had even reached Alaska before Siberia was officially "conquered." Many of them perished, but others came back loaded with precious skins.

Once they had sailed down the Ob Bay and then into the Taz River inlet they came upon a beautiful spot, surrounded by dense forest. It was well protected from storms. Game and fish were plentiful, and they could rest here and repair their boats, or spend a winter there when caught by an early freeze. But best of all, the place was teeming with fur-bearing animals and the local nomad tribesmen had no idea of the true worth of the skins—for a fistful of salt one could get a dozen choice pelts. So more and more *pomori* came, and some of them eventually settled. They called the place Mangazeya, a corruption of the name of the local tribe, Malganzei.

The fame of the place finally spread to Russia, and in 1601, the Tsar Boris Godunov ordered a Russian *ostrog* (fortress) built there, and appointed a *voyevoda* (governor) to administer it. Within a few years it became the richest international trade center of northern Siberia.

Today, Mangazeya cannot be found on any map. It was as utterly destroyed as Troy or Carthage, by direct order of the first Russian Tsar of the Romanov dynasty, Michail, who in 1619 forbade the *pomori*—the only people who knew how to reach Mangazeya—to sail their northern routes. The Tsar's order decreed that all who disobeyed were to be "put to the hardest possible death, and all their homes and families destroyed branch and root." Navigation markings were torn up. Surveillance posts were set up along the Arctic shores to intercept and kill all who broke the terrible order.

What was the reason for this destruction? There were two reasons. The first was an international one. The reputation of Mangazeya, the only northern outlet of the mysterious Siberia of that time, was beginning to attract the attention of European rulers, primarily those of England, Poland, and Sweden. The Tsar feared, and not without reason, that Mangazeya might be seized by one of the powerful European trading nations against whom the weak Russian state could not offer defense. This would mean the end of the Russian dream of conquering Siberia. The second reason was an internal one. The *voyevodas* of Tobolsk and Tyumen, and the Ural merchants, had demanded the destruction of Mangazeya. It was siphoning off the fur trade of Siberia. Mangazeya had to die if they were to prosper, and to the Tsar they were more important than Mangazeya, over which he could exercise no control and whose trade bypassed Moscow and reached directly into Europe. And the volume of this trade had been growing spectacularly from year to year.

ROUTES...
FROM ARCHANGEL TO MANGAZEYA
FROM MANGAZEYA TO DICKSON I.

The secret route to Mangazeya.

Every summer (Mangazeya could be reached only in June, July, and August) hundreds of the *pomori* ships, built especially for this trade, lined the river in front of the city, and the spacious *gostinnyi dvor*, the commercial exchange, operated on a round-the-clock basis buzzing like a beehive. Big commercial deals were celebrated at fabulous feasts that lasted for days, and featured the best European wines and local delicacies like sturgeon, caviar, mushrooms, berries, and venison and other game.

The life span of Mangazeya was short, but fabulous. A few descriptions of the town survive, and paint it as the "golden Mangazeya," a city of spacious homes and incredible riches. Throughout each winter huge piles of sable and ermine skins, and other furs, as well as loads of mammoth and walrus bone, would accumulate in its enormous warehouses, from Siberia tribesmen who would travel hundreds, even thousands of miles, to bring furs to Mangazeya. There they would trade them for salt, weapons, household utensils, and, of course, alcohol. All the accumulated merchandise would be sold during each short summer and shipped out.

And so Mangazeya lived and grew richer from year to year in its splendid frozen isolation. It was estimated that by 1615 its trade volume had surpassed the entire foreign trade volume of Russia, and not a kopeck of it was reaching the Tsar's treasury.

The meteoric rise of Mangazeya would not have been possible without a special combination of historical factors. Russia was going through the "time of confusion" after the death of Tsar Ivan the Terrible. His heir, a weakling son by the name of Feodor, died, whereupon Feodor's brother-in-law, Boris Godunov, usurped the throne from the lawful heir, Dimitri, the youngest son of Ivan, whom he ordered put to death in the town of Uglich. In due time, a young lay monk by the name of Gregori Otrepiev declared himself "the miraculously saved" Dimitri, and challenged Godunov. Godunov died, and the false Dimitri, helped by the Polish army, captured Moscow, killed Godunov's son, and proclaimed himself the Tsar. Almost immediately he was overthrown, murdered, and his body loaded into a cannon and shot in the direction of Poland. That proved to be a mistake, because another pretender appeared and declared himself the "miraculously saved" Tsar Dimitri. Russia was thrown into utter confusion with two Tsars' courts actually functioning at the same time. The powerful Boyards were changing their allegiance from day to day. Finally, in 1613, the Council of the Moscow Boyards finally elected 17-year-old Michail Romanov the new Tsar, and his dynasty was destined to rule Russia for the next 304 years.

It took five years for Tsar Michail to consolidate his rule. Then he turned his attention to Mangazeya, this fabulously rich oddity, which had sprung up in the Siberian North. True, Mangazeya was ruled by a local *voyevoda* nominally representing Moscow, but Moscow could not exercise any control over him, and the Tsar feared, again not without reason, that this governor might be seduced into breaking away from the Russians. In 1619 he dealt the city its death blow by cutting its lifeline through the Arctic Ocean.

The plan worked. Mangazeya began to die. Though the Ural merchants attempted to sail down the Ob River toward it, they did not have the skill of the *pomori*. Their ship convoys were often smashed by savage storms in the treacherous Ob inlet, which stretches for some 400 miles into the heart of Western Siberia. The operation began to be unprofitable. The new Mangazeya *voyevoda* moved his residence to Turukhansk on the Yenisei, the rich merchant families left the city, and by 1678, under mysterious circumstances, the city was turned into charred ruins. For a while it was known among the local Nentsi tribesmen as Tagarevyhard, or "destroyed town," and then even that name became forgotten. The very site of Mangazeya was swallowed up by the tundra.

It was not until the summer of 1967 that it was rediscovered. A Soviet writer, Michail Skorokhodov, and a retired polar hunter and navigator, Dimitri Butorin, decided to retrace the route of the ancient *pomori* from the White Sea to the Ob and Taz inlets, and find the site of the lost town. All that they had to guide them were old maps drawn by the *pomori*, and the vague and inaccurate descriptions of their travels which had survived in the museums.

It would be a fascinating and difficult adventure. They decided to construct a *karbas*, a sail and oar craft like those used by the *pomori*, which could pass where even a modern ice-breaker would be stopped, and they would follow the summer thaw as the *pomori* had done. Every spring the southern winds drive the ice away from the shore, and a channel about twenty feet wide is opened along the shore. Only a small craft can navigate it. In the course of their journey, the *pomori* had to drag their boats across two peninsulas jutting out into the Arctic Ocean, one called the Kanin and the other the Yamal, since sailing around them was impossible. Two men could not hope to drag any craft across dry land unless it was quite light in weight.

The modern explorers had several advantages over the original *pomori*. First of all, they had an auxiliary gasoline motor. Then too, their route was no longer deserted; there were many Arctic villages and weather stations where they could stop and rest, and summon help if necessary. And since the region is now well covered by Soviet polar aviation, they could be flown home upon the completion of their trip instead of spending the Arctic winter in Siberia.

Their boat had classical *pomori* dimensions, 20 feet long and 7 feet wide at the widest point. They christened it the *Schelya*, and they had a skiff called the *Schelianochka*, or "little *Schelya*." They had a good supply of fuel, but not food. With two rifles and fishing gear they knew that they would never go hungry. They fitted the boat with red sails—a customary color for the Arctic—and all other necessary gear. They did not have to take fresh water because they were "to follow the spring," and the thawing ice would supply them with water. This is how Butorin, the veteran of the polar regions, described it:

Nowhere in the world is spring as beautiful as in the Arctic. We will be following the breaking ice, and our spring will last not two-three days, but weeks. Scoop up some water from a thawing ice floe—it's like nectar. The young of the migrating birds all drink it—it has some magic to it. Look at that goose—it gambols in the air, sweeps up and swoops down like an eagle—and this, after thousand of miles of migratory flight.... Or at the White Sea seals ... they had followed the thawing ice with their young, to drink the ice water ... for millions of years.

The Arctic spring is sudden, and so dramatic. Overnight the warm southern winds melt the snow, and within two or three days the earth bursts into blossom, with myriads and myriads of bright flowers suddenly in bloom. The combination of warm air, moist soil, and long Arctic summer days produce this fantastic display. But one must be careful, since a sudden freeze can trap one and one's boat. However, Butorin had spent most of his life in polar regions, and knew them intimately.

The Arctic spring—the beginning of the uninterrupted "day" which can last for weeks—is often swift, dramatic, and beautiful. Flowers bloom amid ice slabs, icebergs melt into fantastic shapes, and animals gambol in cold sunlight.

They started in May, 1967, from Archangel and headed north. Because of the Gulf Stream influence, spring in the far north starts in the Berents Sea, and if one follows the breaking ice along the shore, spring lasts for weeks. This was the secret of the old *pomori:* they followed the *pripai,* the shore ice, which disappears first in the Arctic.

The adventurers followed the spring. Since they had no radio with them, they were cut off from civilization for weeks.

They dragged the boat across the Kanin Peninsula and passed through the treacherous Yugorski Shar channel. Early in July they reached the enormous Yamal Peninsula. Here they had to drag their boat again. This "dragging" did not involve carrying the boat across the 100-mile width of the Yamal's land. The *pomori* had traveled up the Mutnaya River to the three lakes in the center of the peninsula (one of which had the local name of Lutzi-Khomo-To which means in translation "a place where Russians died"), and from these lakes there was a small river that flowed into the Ob Bay on the other side of the peninsula. This route had not been used for over 300 years.

By now it was hot—the thermometer would rise to +90°F at noon—and as they went up the Mutnaya, they discovered that the water was low. In many places they had to unload their boat and then drag it across stretches of the sandy riverbed. By this time the news of their adventure had reached the press and most of the Soviet Union knew about their trip.

Butorin and Skorokhodov planned to cross the peninsula in five to seven days. However, two weeks passed without any news from them. They were considered lost. An official search began.

Actually, they had discovered that the river which was supposed to lead from the central lake into the Ob Bay had practically dried up, too, and they had to drag the boat foot by foot. Their fuel was exhausted. But food was plentiful, since Arctic regions are the home of enormous swarms of aquatic birds in summer; wild ducks, geese, and swans. And the rivers, wherever there was any water, were thick with fish.

Finally they were spotted by a helicopter flyer as they were nearing the Ob Bay. Another helicopter landed and made contact with them.

They crossed the Ob Bay and entered the Taz inlet and then the Taz River. According to old records, Mangazeya once stood nearby. . . . Here, at the Manashevsky promontory the *pomori* ships were supposed to have loaded and unloaded. Skorokhodov noted in his diary: "It is here that Mangazeya once stood. . . . A beautiful place . . . the western part of the town was located along a little brook called the Mangazeyka. . . . The clearing is surrounded by birch, larch, and cedar trees, and covered with bushes of ripe red currants. For several hours we walked through the grass, which was almost as high as we were, trying to find some sign of the former town, inhaling the aroma of flowers and the vanished centuries . . ."

For a while it seemed that the search would be fruitless . . . But then they found an old iron object—a weight for scales. . . . So this was the right place!

That evening Butorin and Skorokhodov and a group of journalists who had joined them sat around roaring campfires, cooking fish soup, the celebrated Siberian *Ukha,* and singing. Early the next morning Butorin went to the river to swim and soon returned. He was very excited. He had found an old Orthodox baptismal cross, a copper arrowhead, and two rusty nails.

The group found various other objects, all concentrated along the river shore. There were rings, baptismal crosses, earrings, arrowheads, and a great many small things which could not be properly identified. There was a silver coin with St. George on one side and unreadable Slavic lettering on the other. By evening a pile of "treasures" had been unearthed, among them twenty-six Russian and foreign coins, some of them bearing the dates and names of ancient Russian feudal princes. Mangazeya was finally rediscovered, after over 300 years of oblivion.

17.

The Brotherly People in the Sunny Land

CROSSING Lake Baikal, or traveling around its southern rim by the scenic Transbaikal Railway, one enters the last part of traditional Siberia, which is called Transbaikalia. Beyond it lies the area of Siberia called the Far East.

Transbaikalia is the old Prison Land. It was the only part of the former Russian Empire where an attempt was made to develop a productive prison colony. Some 250 years ago the first silver mines were set up there, as well as gold diggings, which were run by the Prison Authority. But neither was very profitable, or efficiently run: the huge cost of maintaining the prison establishment, the flagrant corruption, and the low productivity of forced labor, combined to make the project a loss.

Under the Tsarist administration it was known as Chita Cossack Region, and was a part of the huge Irkutsk Government General. It was a frontier region, with Mongolia on the south and Manchuria on the east. Both these were under Chinese domination then. For defense the Transbaikalian Cossack Troop, made up of Russian settlers was organized. Most of them were former soldiers who were given land, and freed from all taxes, in exchange for service as a part of the Tsar's military establishment. They supplied three mounted and one infantry regiment for the regular army, and in the event of war or national emergency they were the first to be called up. So Transbaikalia was basically Cossack, rather than peasant country. It was prosperous, by the standards of that time.

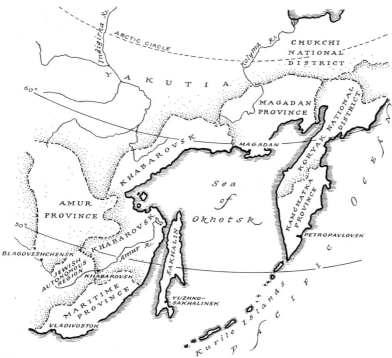

This map shows the six Siberian provinces that together are known as the Far East: Amur, Khabarovsk, Maritime, Sakhalin, Magadan, and Kamchatka. The Chukchi National District is part of Magadan Province, and the Koryak National District a part of Kamchatka. The Kurile Islands are part of Sakhalin Province, and the Jewish Autonomous region part of Khabarovsk Province.

It was also the home of the largest national minority of Siberia, the Buryats.

The Buryats are often inaccurately called Mongols. They are Mongolian in appearance, their language is close to that of the Mongols, they have been Buddhist-Shamanists for centuries, but they are a distinct ethnic unit. The Buryat nation was formed around the tenth century of some tribes that had migrated from Mongolia, and integrated with the native tribes who had lived around Lake Baikal since prehistoric times. In the merging process, the Buryat nation absorbed some Evenk and Even tribes of Tungus-Manchu origin. In the thirteenth century, the armies of Ghengis Khan occupied Transbaikalia and held it for almost three centuries. When the Mongols were finally driven out by the Russians in the early seventeenth century, the Buryats joined with the Russians to fight against the Mongols. According to Russian history and tradition, the Buryats joined the Russian state voluntarily, and have remained loyal to it ever since. On July 3, 1959, the 300-year anniversary of this event was celebrated.

After the Russian revolution, Buryatia was proclaimed an Autonomous Republic within the Russian Federation, and its present borders were defined, though even today the Buryats comprise only about 20 percent of the republic's population. The Siberian provincial town of Verkhneudinsk was designated as the capital of the new state, and renamed Ulan-Ude.

But since the Buryat population spread into all the territories around Lake Baikal, two additional Buryat National Districts were set up: one, the Aga National District in Chita Province, another the Ust-Orda District in Irkutsk Province. Both these districts, unlike the republic itself, have a large and predominantly rural Buryat population.

The Buryats, originally cattle-raising nomads, were known to the early Russian people as the *Bratski narod*, or "brotherly people" because of their friendship and kindness to the newcomers in their territory. They are still known as "the brotherly people" to old Siberians who hold them in particular affection. Unlike other ethnic minorities of Siberia, the Buryat women often married the early Russian settlers. There were many interracial marriages and liaisons which produced a distinct East Siberian anthropological type, Russians with a marked mixture of Buryat blood. Many Transbaikalian Cossacks were practically indistinguishable from the Buryats, except that the Cossacks spoke Russian and were Orthodox Christians (no Cossack was permitted to profess any other faith). These East Siberian types were known as the *bratskovatye* in Siberia, or "brotherly-like" people, and this appellation was used solely to describe their facial type.

However, even though the Buryats had been generous in sharing their womenfolk with the Russians, few Buryat men ever married Russian women (there were very few of them available in any event), and therefore they preserved their ethnic purity.

Despite the most cordial relations between the Buryats and the Russians, the Buryats were completely neglected by the Tsarist administration which made no effort to educate them or to integrate them into the economic life of the country. The best that could be said about the Tsar's administration is that the Buryats were left in peace. They raised their reindeer herds and lived according to their ancient tribal traditions, marked by the feudal rule of tribal chieftains and by shamanism. Nowhere in Siberia did the shamans have greater power or influence than among the Buryats.

Though generally respected and liked, the Buryats were considered to be hopelessly primitive and ignorant to the point that there were no attempts even to convert them to Christianity, the usual Tsarist gambit in all newly acquired territories.

As with many national minorities of Siberia, the advent of the Soviets was an unmitigated blessing to the Buryats. The revolution not only gave them a national identity, but also gave them practically unlimited educational opportunities. The Buryats proved to be such talented and avid students that they amazed the Russian educators who came to work among them. Buryat writing was developed, and the Buryats were the first of all the small minorities of Siberia to eliminate illiteracy completely. By 1935, the Buryats were proclaimed to be 100 percent literate.

What is more, their country proved to be not only scenic, but extraordinarily rich in natural resources of all kinds. Today the Buryat Autonomous Region may well be considered one of the most successful economic units not only of Siberia, but of the Russian Federation as a whole.

The country lies around the eastern and southern shores of Lake Baikal, and then stretches westward along the Mongolian frontier to a point where it borders the Tuva Autonomous Republic. Its territory occupies 135,540 square miles, and its population is estimated to be slightly over 800,000 (789,000 as of January 1, 1968). The population includes Russians, who predominate (about 75 percent), Buryats (about 20 percent), and other smaller national groups, including a few nomadic Evenks, some Mongols, and some completely Russified Chinese. The Russian language is taught in all schools, along with the Buryat, and all Buryats are bilingual.

About 45 percent of the population lives in urban centers, primarily in Ulan-Ude, which today is a thriving industrial city and railway center of 232,000 people. It had less than 20,000 population in 1923 when the republic was formed. It has the largest locomotive and rolling stock manufacturing and repair works in Siberia, and one of the largest groups of meat-processing plants—it has been called the Chicago of Western Siberia. Other industries are the natural leather-tanning and shoe industries, and a whole complex of consumer-goods factories.

Not only is Ulan-Ude an important point on the Trans-Siberian truck line to the Far East, but a branch railroad leads from there to Ulan Bator, the capital of the Mongol Republic, and from there on to Peking. So Ulan-Ude is an important gateway of trade with China which, despite political differences, is still quite important.

Buryatia is a modern state, and one of the most advanced by Siberian standards.

Despite the fact that Buryatia is predominantly a mountainous country, agriculture is well developed. There are 40 large agricultural *sovkhozes* (state farms) and 81 *kolkhozes,* or collective farms. No individual peasant holdings remain. Animal husbandry is predominant. There are large herds of horses and, in the north, reindeer herds. Both horses and reindeer are used for food by the Buryats, along with cattle, pigs, sheep, and goats.

Some two million acres are under cultivation. Wheat, rye, and oats are the main crops. Some sugar beets are grown as well as corn, buckwheat, and also berries. Truck gardening is important. All in all, Buryatia produces enough food for internal consumption, a happy situation for any Siberian region, and this production can be considerably extended if necessary.

The natural mineral resources of the country are very large. Gold is found in many places, particularly along the Barguzin River. There are large deposits of molybdenum, tungsten, coal, asbestos, and graphite. Practically inexhaustible supplies of bauxite have been found, which are all-important for the aluminum industry now being developed in Siberia. The mineral resources of the country, particularly in its southwestern regions, are only partially surveyed, however.

Lumbering is an important and fast growing industry. Forests cover four-fifths of the land, and some contain very high-grade cedar and Daurian larch groves.

Since the republic borders sixty percent of the Baikal shore, the fishing industry is well developed. There are several large rivers in Buryatia (the largest one of them, the Selenga, flows into Lake Baikal), and all of them are rich in fishing grounds. The Selenga is also navigable for its entire length in Buryatia, about 300 miles, but it freezes in the beginning of November and remains frozen until the end of April or even the beginning of May. Altogether there are over 9,000 rivers and streams in Buryatia.

Buryatia has a great volume and variety of fur-bearing animals: sable, squirrel, kolinsky, polar hare, wolverine, and bear populations are large, particularly in mountainous regions, as well as of mountain deer and goat, moose, boar, and others. The very best sable in Siberia is found in the Barguzin River Preserve —it is rigidly protected by law, and hunting is forbidden. The sable are captured alive and shipped to regions in Siberia where they were once numerous, to build up the sable population. In the plains of Buryatia there are foxes, wolves, ermine, polecats, deer, and rabbits. The muskrat has been introduced, and its population is growing rapidly. There is a profusion of game birds such as geese, duck, partridge, and wild turkey. Over forty varieties of food fish are found in lakes, rivers, and streams, in addition to the varieties in Lake Baikal.

Buryatia, along with the southern part of Eastern Siberia, has a typical continental climate with a wide range of temperatures. The mean temperature for January is —3° to —5°F, the mean temperature of July is +55 to 60°F. The seasonal temperatures vary widely: near Lake Baikal they are moderated by this tremendous body of water. The high mountain reaches and the mountainous southwestern "horn" of the republic are marked by short cool summers and long, severe winters. In the town of Örlik in the Sayan Mountains there are only 35 to 38 frostless

The Siberians call furs—one of the foremost export items of the country—soft gold. Here a shipment of mink and blue fox has just arrived at the state fur center in the Altai region.

days a year. However, there is hardly any population here; only about 30,000 people live in the entire southwestern third of Buryatia.

In the agricultural regions the growing season lasts for 150 to 160 days per year, sufficient for most crops, especially as it is accompanied by almost uninterrupted sunshine. Buryatia, along with neighboring Chita Province, is the sunniest place in Siberia, and one of the sunniest in the entire Soviet Union.

The city of Ulan-Ude is hub of Buryatia's population concentration. It is located at the confluence of the Selenga and Uda rivers 55 miles east of Lake Baikal, and was founded in 1666 by the first Russian settlers, and called Udinsky Ostrog, later renamed Verkhneudinsk. At the end of the eighteenth century it became a trade center of western Transbaikalia. Since 1768 large yearly fairs have been held here with furs and gold traded by merchants from all over Siberia. However, until the time when the Trans-Siberian Railway reached it in 1903, the town's growth was very slow: the census of 1897 listed its population as 8,000. The railway brought new life to the town. By 1923 its population stood at 20,000. From then on, and particularly after it became the capital of Buryatia, Ulan-Ude's growth has greatly accelerated; its population is expected to reach 300,000 by 1970.

Today Ulan-Ude is considered to be one of the most picturesque cities of Eastern Siberia. While the old part of the town, located along the Uda River, retained its early Siberian character, the new city was built on a high plateau over the Selenga with rows of fine administration buildings and blocks of new apartment houses from two to four stories high. The streets are laid out along the terraces facing the two rivers, with the mountain ranges of the Ulan-Burgas and Tsagan-Daban serving as a backdrop. Dense pine forests surround it. The streetcar network connects all parts of the town and two bridges have been built across the two rivers which form the natural city limits.

Ulan-Ude is justly famous for its nearby scenery, and particularly the wildly picturesque valley of the Berezovka River. Here, amid pine forests, are the country hourses, or *dachas*, of well-to-do Ulan-Udenians, as well as rest homes and large berry farms. Soviet law allows ownership of such *dachas* by private individuals, and the people of Ulan-Ude, which is a prosperous industrial center, take wide advantage of this privilege.

There are no other large cities in Buryatia. The next town of historical importance, Kyakhta, is located in the extreme south of the republic, on the very border of the Mongolian Republic. It was founded in 1728, some 180 miles south of Ulan-Ude. Until the beginning of the twentieth century it was an important center of international trade between Siberia and China. But with the construction of the Trans-Siberian Railway its importance decreased because Chinese tea, the town's main commodity, was delivered by the railway through Manchuria. The railway from Ulan-Ude to Ulan Bator and Peking has also by-passed Kyakhta by some fifteen miles, and the present population of this old Siberian town is estimated to be only 10,000.

The largest town, next to Ulan-Ude, is Gusinoye Ozero, located in the mining region near the famous lake of the same name. Prior to the revolution it was the center of Buddhism in Buryatia, with the biggest temple, or *datsan*, located there. The town's population is 15,000. Buryatia has over 300 registered mineral springs. Some of them have been found to possess important curative properties. Only a few are now exploited. Generally the waters belong to six categories: (1) thermal waters with azote and methane gas contents; (2) carbon-acid thermal waters; (3) carbon-acid cold waters; (4) radioactive cold waters; (5) cold waters with iron contents; and (6) hydrogen-sulphate cold waters. The curative properties of these springs have not yet been completely studied, but some of the spas are already famous all over Siberia, and have been for centuries. The shamans used the waters of various mineral springs to treat their patients and perform "miraculous" cures.

However, the main wave of large-scale industrialization has barely reached the Baikal and Transbaikalian regions.

Buryat ethnologists and sociologists are worried about the rapid process of absorption of the Buryats into the Russian mainstream. They fear that they may lose their national identity and language. This danger is real. Young Buryat boys and girls, who go into school and learn the Russian language, soon become largely Russified, and the very fact of the historical affinity between the Buryats and Russians, and the easy way in which they mix and intermarry, may in time lead, if not to complete Russification of Buryatia, then to the creation of a Slav-Mongol mixture, primarily based on Russian culture. Like the Russians, and unlike other national minorities of Siberia, the Buryats seem traditionally international in their attitudes, and the elimination of Buddhism and shamanism has severed their historical connection with their past, slight as it was in the first place.

Further east lies Chita Province. It has been emasculated both economically and geographically by separation from Buryatia, and is now a small province by Siberian standards, and still largely untouched by the modern age. But it is a country of old traditions, and many of these traditions are organically connected with the old prison system of Siberia.

Its territory now is 131,700 square miles, slightly smaller than that of Montana, and its population stood at 1,092,000 in 1959, during the last census, and it may be around 1,200,000 now. The region's growth has been comparatively slow.

Chita is primarily a mining province. Silver, gold, and iron ore have been mined here for over two centuries, and the work was always primarily done by convict labor. Recently a whole list of nonferrous deposits has been found. But much of the region, and particularly its northern areas, are not even surveyed. The remoteness of the province from the industrial centers of Western and Central Siberia and the Pacific seaboard has made it a forgotten land in Siberian planning.

The climate is another drawback. Although Chita is located in southern Siberia, with its southernmost regions lying on the same parallel as Vancouver in Canada, Nuremberg in Germany, or Paris in France, the climate is typically continental—short hot summers with the thermometer rising to +95°F or even higher, and extremely cold winters, even colder than the Arctic Ocean islands, with temperatures of —40° to —50°F lasting for weeks. But the Transbaikalian winter is an unusual winter. Though cold, it is dry and sunny. The air transparency plays tricks, even on the coldest days. In the areas under the direct rays of the sun, the snow may melt or evaporate, and because there is generally very little snow in winter, the Transbaikalian plains present an unusual sight. I remember how, before World War I, crossing Transbaikalia by train, we would watch the landscape out of the car window, and it would present almost an African appearance. The snowless plain would stretch to the horizon, covered with yellow grass as though burned by the sun, the sky would be brilliantly blue, and on the horizon as often as not one could see a camel caravan. And the temperature outside would be —40°F or even lower! Camels from Mongolia and the Gobi Desert were a familiar sight. There was a special breed of long-haired dromedaries which were used to the climate, and frozen grass was their favorite food in winter. Now, only a few of them are raised or used.

Thus the climate, though severe, is by no means savage. But it is not conducive to large-scale agriculture even though the soil is, in most places, extremely fertile. Rye, oats, potatoes, and even some wheat are grown, but the lack of rain and early and sudden cold snaps, which can ruin crops, hinder agriculture. The autumn is short but delightful—sunny, warm, and dry—but it does not last long, and the farmers must harvest their crops very quickly, often working around the clock to beat the winter which may set in overnight without any warning.

Chita province lies along the watershed between the Lena and Amur Rivers, and among other rivers are the Vitim, Olekma, Shilka, Argun, Khilok, and Chikoi. In the southern regions, however, there is only one large river, the Onon. There are several hundred lakes, none of them large. Most of them freeze to the bottom in winter and almost dry up in summer, and many are salty. So water is a problem.

About one-half of the territory is covered by forests, primarily larch (84 percent). The animal population is large. Particularly in the remote northern regions, many lakes are favorite nesting grounds of migrating birds—ducks, geese, swans, and cranes. There is an abundance of berries and mushrooms, and fishing is generally good in rivers and lakes.

Before the arrival of the Russians, the nomadic Buryat and Daur tribes followed their flocks of sheep and herds of horses and camels over the southern steppes of the region. Even today, sheep-herding offers the best opportunity in animal husbandry; because of the almost total absence of snow cover, it is often possible to graze flocks throughout the year. Sheep-herding represents over one-half of the income of the collective and state farms, and the Transbaikalian breed of sheep has been considerably improved of late. It is estimated that the present sheep population of the province is over 5,000,000 head, i.e., over 50 percent of all the sheep in Western Siberia.

The province produces enough food for local consumption, and exports wool to other parts of Siberia.

The capital city is Chita, located in a beautiful scenic valley of the Ingoda River with the high Stanovoi mountain range in the background. It is not a new town. It was founded in 1653 by Russian settlers attracted by stories of rich silver mines. Starting in 1700, mining for silver, lead, and then gold was the main occupation of the population, until the area was taken over by the Prison Administration. Several smelting plants were built, including one at Nerchinsk which was the first silver and lead smelting plant in Russia. It is also here that the first tin in Russia was found and smelted. There was a great deal of private prospecting done primarily by escaped convicts. Transbaikalia was the dreaded place of forced convict labor. Old Siberian songs are full of references to it. A whole set of prisons was built around Nerchinsk. This forced labor mining was wasteful and primitive, and only the richest deposits were worked.

By the beginning of the twentieth century this activity was almost all discontinued: in 1904 the last smelting plant was closed. But private gold prospecting continued until the revolution, and probably goes on even now. Transbaikalia is rich in gold which can be found along almost every taiga stream, but professional exploitation is hindered by the lack of transportation and communication in the northern regions, which are the richest in mineral resources.

Chita remained an absolutely unimportant small town, the capital of the Transbaikalian Cossack Region, until 1903 when the Trans-Siberian Railway arrived. On the eve of the revolution, it had a population of 52,800 and was, by Siberian standards, an important city.

Today Chita's population is estimated at 208,000 and it is a center of local mining and agriculture. Several other fair-sized towns have sprung up in Transbaikalia in recent years: Petrovsk-Zabaikalski—35,000; Balei—30,000; Khilok—20,000; Magocha—17,500; Sharlovaya Gora—15,000; etc. The old towns, however, remain unimportant and small: Nerchinsk, once the capital of a virtual prison empire, has perhaps 15,000 people now, as has another historical town, Sretensk.

It is believed that the mountainous regions of the province, particularly in the north, possess tremendous mineral deposits. A fabulous deposit of high-grade copper ore has been found at Udokan, in the extreme north of the province, but a complete lack of roads or even trails makes exploitation impossible. It is being held in reserve. When the proposed North Trans-Siberian Railway reaches northern Transbaikalia, which at present remains a virtual terra incognita, the area is expected to blossom

into a large industrial "complex" along with southern Yakutia
on which it borders. But this is still Siberia's "tomorrow" and
will not become "today" for some years, or even decades, to come.

Transbaikalia is one of the most scenic and beautiful regions
of Siberia. Several high mountain ranges cross it and the scenery
rivals that of the Rockies, but the region is remote and inaccessible. It was not for nothing that in Tsarist times run away convicts were never hunted. Finding and recapturing them was
practically impossible. Some of them made important gold strikes,
and founded prominent Transbaikalian families, making no
secret of their history as *varnaks,* or escaped convicts. If anything, this was considered to be a status symbol. It was an un-
written law that any man not recaptured within three years
from the date of escape could not be rearrested. Some of the
successful ones entertained their former prison wardens in their
fine homes in Chita.

In fact, here old Siberia still lives, though it has all but disappeared elsewhere. This is still a part of the Siberia unspoiled by
modernization, and it is of interest to students of early Siberian
lore. Some ancient prison songs are still sung here and the peculiar
early Siberian idiom in speech is still used.

Despite the blood curdling stories of the prison past of Transbaikalia, relationships between the prisoners and the administration were governed by a set of local traditions peculiar to the
region. The lot of convicts was undeniably hard, but as a rule
no undue cruelty was practiced. The majority of prison administrators were decent people—as often as not sent here as a
form of disciplinary exile, usually for misbehavior like unpaid
card debts, small-time misappropriation of funds, or amorous
misadventures which had provoked the ire of their superiors.
Guard duty was done by soldiers, most of them peasant conscripts, who had also erred while in service. So in a way of speaking, they were all in the same boat with the prisoners.

Shortly after the revolution, early in 1918, my family became
closely acquainted with the family of one Colonel S., a former
chief warden of the dreaded Kazakovskaya Prison which was a
part of the Nerchinsk Prison District, the toughest in Transbaikalia. The good Colonel, now out of a job, was living in Chita
with his wife and two pretty teenage daughters who had been

born and raised in the prison. They spoke about it with deep nostalgia.

"The convicts, as a rule, are good and kind," Mrs. S. assured us. "We got mostly murderers in Kazakovskaya. . . . They would take care of our baby daughters like real nursemaids. And honest. All servants at our house were convicts, and I never locked or hid anything. That would be an insult to them, and never, not once, was anything stolen."

"This is true," the Colonel supported her. "There was a certain code of behavior, a *katorga* code of morals to which the prisoners adhered." (The word *katorga,* of Greek origin, was used to describe forced labor prisons in prerevolutionary Russia.) "Of course there were bad ones among them, some real troublemakers, but their fellow prisoners kept them in check—especially the old-timers. Every time we took a work party out we asked them whether they would give us their '*katorga* word of honor' not to try to escape. They would confer among themselves and either give us this word or not—as the case might be. But whenever the word was given it was never violated. Murderers were especially dependable—they commanded the respect of their fellow prisoners, and would kill anyone going back on a given word. So when we received such a word, which was not always the case, we called off all guards and left them to work on their own."

Mrs. S. said, "Here in Chita I'm afraid to go into the streets after dark. And back at Kazakovskaya I never even had a key for our front door . . ."

After the revolution, the prisons were closed and the prisoners set free. Actually, this amnesty was supposed to cover only political prisoners, but in fact all the soldier guards simply removed their uniforms and left, and so did the inmates. So Colonel S. and his family came to live in Chita. They had no home there, and stayed at a hotel. All their belongings were kept in the hotel storeroom.

One night this storeroom was broken into and all its contents stolen. Colonel S. went to the office of the local militia, and discovered that the Commissar in charge was one of his former prisoners. The Commissar was indignant when he learned about the theft.

Within a week, every article had been returned. The Colonel also received a short scribbled note through the mail:

Your Excellency! Please forgive this error. We did not know the stuff was yours. Please give our regards to Her Excellency and the young ladies, your daughters.

Respectfully,

Pavel Kozel

Pavel Kozel, Colonel S. told us, was a man sent to Siberia for murdering a family of six during a robbery in Tula province in Russia. The robbery netted him two rubles. This was old Siberia, and Pavel Kozel is a true name. I can use it because he was killed a month later fighting against the counterrevolutionary troops, when they invaded Transbaikalia from Manchuria.

18.

The Strongest Weaker Sex

WOMEN in Siberia do every kind of work: laying brick, plastering, mending roads, running bulldozers and cranes, digging ditches, cutting wood. They are teachers and doctors, and engineers and geologists. By law and by custom, men and women are equal. Some 51 percent of all jobs in Siberia are filled by women.

Historically, the role of women in Russia has been unique from earliest times. Among the Slavic tribes which eventually united to create the huge Russian nation, women were never in the degrading position of being considered a sexual commodity, as was the case in many primitive societies. They were needed and respected workers. The reason for this was economic, as well as geographical. The question of survival in an agricultural society—and the Slavs had been agricultural since the dawn of time—in a severe climate with a short growing season, made all able-bodied people important. Climate played an important part as well: among the most northern tribes of aboriginal Siberians, matriarchy was once the rule. The very survival of tribes and families depended on the ability of women to manage during long and bitter winters. For seven or eight months of every year, home was the only place where a man could survive, and home was run by the woman.

In early Russia a wife was not a sex symbol, but an economic necessity. A hard-working wife was infinitely more valuable than a pretty one; in fact, a woman's beauty was often a detriment to her chances on the matrimonial market—it made prospective husbands suspicious that she might prove to be frivolous, and therefore a poor working helpmate. Strong legs were more important than shapely ones, and a strong back more sought after than a pretty face.

This attitude helped to produce a breed of hardy, independent women. In Russia, husbands were known to maltreat their wives, especially when drunk, but that was not sanctioned by custom, and as often as not such family quarrels were two-way affairs— the woman gave as much as she took, and often more.

In Siberia, of course, the role of the woman was an especially peculiar one. Under Tsarist administration the country had been developed primarily as a penal colony, and the women sent to early Siberia from Russia were of a special kind. Fully 80 percent of them were exiled for the murder of husbands or lovers, according to prerevolution statistics. Murder in Tsarist Russia was not a capital offense. Murderers were sent to Siberia for forced labor, and then for forced residence there, usually for life. In the case of women, the law was lax. Unlike men, they were not imprisoned in prerevolutionary Siberia, or expected to do forced labor. They were just expected to relieve the chronic woman shortage among the male prisoners. In fact many murderesses, after getting rid of abusive and bothersome husbands (usually by poisoning them), found their "happiness" in Siberia with good men of their choice.

Anton Chekhov wrote about prison conditions in 1890 on Siberia's "Devil's Island" of the era, Sakhalin. He described the system as follows:

There is no forced labor for women on the island. True, women sometimes wash floors in offices, work in vegetable gardens or sew bags, but any regular forced work does not exist for them, and probably never will. The prison has surrendered their women to the colony. When they send them here, no one thinks of punishing or reforming them, but merely of their ability to bear children and to help men maintain the households. All such women are distributed among the settlers as "domestic workers," but this is merely a legal euphemism— such a woman is not a servant, but first and foremost the mistress of the household, a common-law wife, and this is done with the full knowledge and blessing of the prison administration: all such unions are officially registered as "joint households" or "free families." One can say that all women arriving here, with the exception of those who come here voluntarily with their convict husbands, become common-law wives of the settlers. This is a firm rule. They told me that when one woman, upon coming here, declared that she wanted to work, in accordance with her sentence, everyone was astounded . . .

Obviously, women who came to Siberia in the early days of its development were not the kind who could be mistreated with impunity, and men knew this only too well.

Traditionally, Siberian women have always been strong, willful, and independent. This was not only true of the penal colonies, but also of the immigrants and free settlers. Only strong women would go there in the first place, and only the toughest of them would stay; others would persuade their husbands to return to Russia. And because there was a chronic shortage of women in the early days of Siberia, women could write their own ticket, so to speak.

Chekhov describes this in his *Sakhalin Diaries:*

When a party of convict women arrives at Alexandrovsk, the administrative center of the island, they are ceremoniously conducted to the local prison. Bent under the weight of their miserable belongings, they trudge slowly along the road, listless and still nursing the after-effects of seasickness, and whole crowds of men, women and children follow them the way they would follow wandering performers at country fairs. It reminds one of the herring run on the Aniva when whales, seals and dolphins follow the schools of fish hoping to feast on the fat egg-filled herring. . . . The men have simple and honest thoughts: they need women for their households. The women want to see whether there are any relatives or friends among the new arrivals from home. The clerks and prison guards are after girls. This usually happens towards the evening, and the women are locked up for the night. Meanwhile, all over the town there are discussions about the blessings of family life, about the impossibility of maintaining a household without a woman, etc., etc. The next day, while the steamer is still in port, the women are assigned to various districts. This is done by the Alexandrovsk administration, and therefore their district gets the cream of the crop, as regards both the quantity and quality. The neighboring Tymovsky district gets second choice, while the southernmost, the Korsakovsky, which was the best district, gets the discards—the oldest ones and those who "have not won masculine attention."

This is done with utter disregard for the economic needs of the colony, and therefore women are distributed extremely unevenly—in districts which are economically least promising there are more women than in those which could be successfully developed for agriculture. In the poorest Alexandrovsky district there are 69 women to every 100 men, in the more attractive Tymovsky, there are 47, and in the best, Korsakovsky, only 36.

Then Chekhov describes the confrontation at the prison in Korsakovsky, the district least favored in this distribution of women:

Here again the women are locked up in special barracks while the administration decides who among the settlers deserves to get a woman, good workers and men of stable character getting preference. Then those lucky prospects are notified that on such-and-such day and on such-and-such hour they are to come to Korsakovsky for their women. All along the road leading from Naibachi one can see these men, known here as "bridegrooms," walking towards the prison. They indeed look like grooms—one is wearing a flowing red shirt, another some unusual planter's hat, and still another a pair of shiny boots acquired under some mysterious circumstances. When they arrive at Korsakovsky, they are admitted into the barracks and are left there with the women. During the first quarter-hour everyone feels timid and ill at ease; men walk about looking at the women who are sitting on their cots with their eyes cast down. Each man is making his choice—without any frivolity, "with humanity," as they call it, paying no attention to age, lack of beauty, of miserable prison appearance, but trying to guess what sort of helpmate this or that woman would make. Once some young or aged woman attracts him, he sits beside her and starts a heart-to-heart conversation with her. She asks him whether he owns a samovar, and whether his house has a wooden or thatched roof? He answers that he indeed owns a good samovar, that he has a horse and a calf, and that his house has a wooden roof. Only after this thorough property status examination does she ask the final question:
"And you wouldn't mistreat me?"
The deal is made. The woman gets assigned to the man as a "joint householder" and they depart together, the happy groom usually hiring a horse cart, often spending his last money for it. Upon coming to her new home, the woman first of all sets the samovar going, and the neighbors, watching the rising smoke, comment with obvious envy that so-and-so finally got a woman for himself . . .

From that point on the woman became the queen of her new shabby realm, and her "husband" lived in dread of losing her. Even though assigned to him, she could abandon him and become assigned to another man, and that would be an unmitigated disaster for the poor wretch. However, according to Chekhov, these strangely-arranged unions were often successful, oddly enough. Some women claimed that, for the first time in their lives, they were genuinely happy. "Thank God, I am living with a good man, and he treats me well."

This was eighty years ago, and in a penal colony. But things were not much different elsewhere, among the free immigrants and settlers in Siberia. Woman had always been queen in Siberia. True these queens had to work like horses, but there was no question of their being dominated or ill-treated by their menfolk. If anything, it was the other way around.

In the fifty years before the revolution, a considerable middle class had developed in Russia, in addition to the aristocracy and the intelligentsia. For them the position of women was different: women were mostly indolent, helpless, and supported by their husbands or fathers. The revolution eliminated these classes, or drove them out of the country. Russia was left with working women and peasants, poverty-stricken and tough. The new Soviet state, which had proclaimed the complete equality of women, opened all educational and employment opportunities to them.

The Russian revolution took place in 1917 after years of a bloody and frustrating war, which had killed millions of men. Then the new Soviet state had to fight a civil war and armed foreign intervention. This decimated the male population, and caused a complete collapse of the economy. This, in turn, led to a catastrophic famine that took millions of victims. In order to rebuild the economy and turn the Soviet Union into an industrial country, every pair of hands had to be employed. They were mainly women's hands. Later, the forced collectivization of agriculture was tantamount to another civil war, with almost the entire class of well-to-do peasants dispossessed and killed or deported. Then followed a whole series of the so-called Stalinist repressions which claimed countless victims. Then came World

War II when 20 million people died in the Soviet Union between 1941 and 1945, most of them men, and most of them young.

This unparallelled series of national disasters was borne primarily by women, who had to replace men in all spheres of life. The survival of the country undoubtedly should be credited to the resilience and endurance of the Soviet women.

The end of World War II left the Soviet Union with 25 million more women than men. So, obviously, women had to continue to take on men's work in all spheres of life to rebuild the country. But that was not all. To avert a demographic catastrophe, women not only had to rebuild the country, but to repopulate it as well.

The magnitude of this demographic disaster has never been fully appreciated or understood by the outside world. Again it was the women who had to bear the brunt of coping with it.

How was this achieved? It is a fascinating, unique story. Shocking perhaps, and yet the method adopted was the only practical one to save the nation. Women who had not found husbands, because of the lack of available young men, were encouraged to bear children. Socialist planning came into play. In July of 1944, when the war was drawing to a close, a law was passed which in effect made all children born out of wedlock the wards of the state. The fathers were expressly relieved of responsibility for their support. The men were no longer required to pay the money that divorced men, for instance, had to pay to their wives for the support of their children.

This law (which is still in existence) served its purpose: millions of young unmarried women had children. They produced the new generation that is now taking over the task of the development of the country, including, of course, Siberia. How many such babies were born? No exact figure is available since the label of illegitimacy is not used, nor permitted to mar the children's lives. But the number of unmarried mothers claiming state support is known. In 1945 there were 280,000 of such single mothers. By 1950, this number grew to over 1,600,000 and by 1957 to over 3,000,000. From then on the number decreased and has been decreasing ever since. The new generation has almost reached parity between the sexes, and there is great pressure at present from sociologists, demographers, and jurists for the abolition of this emergency law which, according to them, no longer serves any purpose except to protect male sex predators.

It should be remembered that the number of single mothers receiving state support by no means indicates the accurate number of such children. Many women gave birth to more than one child, and many did not apply to the state for help, preferring to support their children on their own.

One thing that the Russian revolution achieved was to free woman from economic dependency on men. Now economic

Women engineers working on the construction of the Bratsk Dam on the Angara River.

matters rarely if ever play an important part in the relationship between the sexes. It is often said that Soviet women work along with their men not so much because of a desire to do so, but because of economic necessity—a man rarely earns enough to support his wife and raise a family. Though it is true that Soviet salaries and wages are low by Western standards, in a majority of cases women work because they prefer to, especially a woman who has a profession. A Soviet divorce petition might state that a husband insisted on a wife not working. This is a serious accusation. First of all such an existence places her in an awkward social position; she has no social status and cannot claim many benefits to which a working woman is entitled. Being just her husband's wife is not considered socially admirable, and of course, it does not give a woman the security in old age which a full pension would give her. The latter consideration is very important—retiring on pension is an undeniable blessing for the older generation in the Soviet state, and a large part of the population today lives on pensions. In effect, an average Soviet worker earns two salaries; the one he uses while he works, and the other he receives at his retirement, when he is pensioned off for life.

This is especially important in Siberia where on many projects each work year is computed as 18 months toward the retirement total of 25 working years for men and 20 for women. This serves as an added incentive for bringing volunteers to work in this uncomfortable climate, often under extremely primitive and difficult conditions. Many women prefer hard work computed at the additional retirement age rate in order to retire earlier, and to build up their future pension which is computed on the basis of salary earned during the work years. If a salesgirl, for instance, earns a salary of 80 to 100 rubles a month, someone operating a crane or laying brick can earn twice as much or more, and therefore a respectively higher pension on retirement.

Hundreds of thousands of young men and women come to Siberia every year. Often they are placed in situations of constant intimate contact. How does all this affect their sex life?

This is a hard question to answer. No sex statistics are published in Siberia, and the question is rarely discussed. Early mar-

A shipwright at the Tyumen shipyards who is studying at night to become an engineer.

riages are a rule, and the sex disproportions among the younger generations have almost been eliminated. (There are still close to 19 million more women than men in the Soviet Union, but almost all of them belong to older groups.) While in the whole of the Soviet Union there are 87 marriages every year for every 10,000 of the population (exactly the same percentage as in the United States) in certain parts of Siberia, this figure is considerably higher—in Kamchatka, for instance, it reaches 130.

Basically, economic considerations play almost no part in the matrimonial choice. Few men and few women can be considered good matrimonial catches, and in a vast majority of cases women continue to work after marrying. So love plays an important part in marriage here—the mutual sex attraction uncolored by economic considerations and also friendship, a sense of free camaraderie which is a striking facet of relationships between young people in Siberia.

Outwardly, any public manifestation of sexual activity, like kissing or petting for instance, is not tolerated. A petting couple in a public park would be arrested and charged with "hooliganism." In this respect, Soviet society is rigidly puritanical, though this does not mean that the activity does not take place in private. It does, of course: single girls do not become mothers by holding hands with men, which is the extent of tolerated public display between the sexes.

Sex is not a subject for public discussion in Siberia, but it's there, and it is important. Loneliness and isolated places and a sense of high adventure only sharpen these normal human reactions and urges.

It is my impression that sex relations between young people in modern Siberia are easy and devoid of any morbidity, are not based on economics and, what is more important, are free of fear of consequences. Pregnancy almost always leads to marriage; the concept of female virginity at marriage is practically nonexistent, is considered utterly degrading, and justly so; and if a girl happens to change her mind, abortions are legal and easily arranged under proper medical conditions. And if a girl decides to have a child and become a single mother there is no stigma attached to this, and she receives the full benefits which any married woman would receive—up to 112 days off at full

pay for confinement and postnatal recovery, with no medical
bills of any kind to pay.

Any mother, either married or not, can avail herself of a
whole network of nurseries operating in all factories and enterprises. The children are cared for by professional nurses while
their mothers work. The cost is nominal. Here again being a
working woman becomes an advantage—non-working mothers
are charged a substantially higher price for this service—if they
can get room in a nursery for their children. Since they are not
working, they are presumed to be able to care for their children
themselves.

Divorces, once very easy, then very difficult to get, were
made less difficult in 1965. But they are still difficult especially
if there are children to be considered. First of all, the procedure
entails expense. It is the duty of the divorce courts to try to
discourage applicants. A certain waiting period is required.
Then, if a man or a woman is a member of the party, or of the
Komsomol, he or she might be under pressure from his or her
comrades to reconsider and stay married—sexual laxity is a
serious sin on the Communist list. If children are involved, divorce is a costly arrangement for the fathers: support payments
are automatically deducted from their pay, and the payments
continue regardless of the former wife's financial status until
the child is 18. The rate is standard—25 percent of the man's
salary for one child, 33 percent for two, and 50 percent for
three. If there are more than three children, divorce is virtually
prohibitive.

This had led to bitter complaints from estranged husbands
who consider it utterly unfair that while they are being made to
pay, the unmarried Casanovas go scot-free if they sire a child.
True, all bachelors pay a nominal tax for the privilege of staying single, but this tax is in no way sufficient to repay the government for the care of fatherless children.

Undoubtedly there is some justice in all these complaints. But
Soviet laws are quite inflexible.

However, as we have seen, these strict laws do not seem to
discourage marriage. Why? The answer lies in the fact that
married couples get housing and employment privileges. Also
unmarried sex is rather difficult because of limited housing and

other circumstances. Any single woman, for instance (and any single man, for that matter), who entertains visitors of the opposite sex at home (usually a room) might lose her precious housing if the neighbors complain of his or her behavior. The majority of young unmarried workers are lodged in dormitories, where such activities are almost impossible. Then, such sex is not considered admirable if there is any promiscuity about it.

A young woman employee at a chemical plant in Krasnoyarsk.

Commercial prostitution is practically nonexistent in Siberia. Not so much because of strict morals as of the practical difficulties. First of all, a professional prostitute would find it impossible to secure any housing since all housing is state-controlled. Then, even if she could contrive to rent a private room somewhere, her income status would be questioned. All unearned incomes (i.e., not derived from work) are illegal. And finally, even if she could somehow legitimize her status (by getting, for instance, some part-time work), there is simply no class of males who could afford expensive commercial sex. Prostitution would not be financially worth-while.

If marital obligations do not deter people from marrying, do the strict divorce laws discourage divorces?

Yes, but only to a certain degree. In the early years of Soviet power, when divorces were very easy to obtain, over fifty percent of all marriages ended in divorce. If one takes the average statistical figures for the last ten years for the entire Soviet Union, one discovers that there has been 1 divorce for every 5 or 6 marriages. (In Siberia, however, this figure is substantially lower because of the flurry of early marriages among the young people there; it is estimated that in 1968 this divorce ratio was 1 to 10.) How does this compare with other countries? This is a lower percentage than the United States (1 divorce to 4 marriages), but higher than many European countries. In France, for instance, there is just 1 divorce to every 11 marriages, and in England 1 to 11 or 12.

Alcohol is probably the major destroyer of marriage, perhaps even more so in Siberia than in Russia. Roughness and bad manners of the husband come next. This is a peculiar postrevolution phenomenon. While women, always better mannered than men, have acquired some social graces along with education, men somehow have resisted this patina of culture. Swearing and abusive language and rough "peasant" manners are common among men despite their new education. In the early revolutionary years great stress had been put on the "correct class background," and everyone tried to speak and act like a country lout. Unfortunately, it has become a style, and while women have freed themselves from this affectation, many men have not. One has only to remember the manner of Nikita Khrushchev, a brilliant man, to understand this phenomenon.

This, combined with alcohol, may lead to excesses, and the modern Siberian woman, completely independent economically, will simply not tolerate such behavior from her husband.

Both men and women often cite the loss of affection for the spouse as a reason for wanting a divorce. This reflects the Russian belief that marital cohabitation without love is purposeless and even degrading in the socialist society. Neither husband nor wife is presumed to have any conjugal rights and such rights cannot be enforced by law. It is held as an unalienable right of a woman to refuse access to her body to any man, including her husband. Loveless marriages are not considered worth preserving.

Refusal to produce children is a serious complaint, but it is hard to understand how birth control can be practiced since contraceptives, even though not illegal, are rarely available. No Soviet factory produces them, and few are imported or sold. It is in this sphere that shamans and folk medicine practitioners were often consulted in the past, and might occasionally be consulted even now.

Homosexuality as such is not generally recognized, tolerated, or seriously discussed. It is considered a peculiar Oriental perversion, once practiced in the Caucasus and the Moslem regions of the country. It is a theme of many jokes and off-color stories in Siberia, but I have never heard it discussed as a serious medical problem.

Generally, despite the declared absolute equality of sexes by law, women get a better deal in Soviet courts and legislation, on a purely biological basis. Because she has the all-important function of bearing children, she is given certain allowances which men cannot claim. No one seems to contest this.

So much for sex in Siberia. Despite the lack of outward display of it, it is certainly a very important part of life here as anywhere else. What does *not* exist is commercial pandering to it, or stimulation of it by artificial means. There are no "sexy" posters, ads, or magazine or book covers. Pornography in any form is a serious crime and is prosecuted implacably.

It is dangerous to generalize, but it seems to me that sex relationships among young Siberians are generally wholesome, and I believe the credit for this goes to the women.

And they certainly know how to deal with any man who becomes bothersome. If they are the weaker sex in Siberia, they are certainly the strongest weaker sex that can be found anywhere. Their physical stamina and moral courage are almost unbelievable, and men well know it. Women are universally admired and respected in Siberia. On March 8, the official Woman's Day of the Soviet Union, it is difficult to find an altogether sober man anywhere between the Urals and the Pacific Ocean.

19.

The River of Discontent

EACH part of Siberia has a river backbone: one great waterway along which the original Russian penetration was made. All such rivers, the Ob, the Irtysh, the Yenisei, the Angara, and the Lena had served as high roads for the advancing Russians. After the collapse of the original Mongolian khanate, no one opposed them. The Russians spread out along the riverbanks. A country larger than the United States was conquered within a few short years by a handful of armed adventurers.

But another great river, the Amur, had a different story and it took the Russians 200 years to move along it to the sea, and to cross over it at the most important point.

It did not take the Russians long to discover that their new Siberian empire had no practical sea outlet. All Siberian rivers flow north and empty into the Arctic Ocean. The stretch of the eastern seashore, on the Sea of Okhotsk, north of the island of Sakhalin and in Kamchatka, which they secured in the seventeenth century, was ice-bound for most of the year, and was extremely difficult to reach from the interior. There were no navigable rivers that could serve as highways to it. In effect, the Russians were bottled up in their new domain.

In the original grand sweep across Siberia, the Russians discovered that there was one great river, that could serve as an outlet to the Pacific Ocean. It was navigable along its entire length and somewhere it did flow into the Sea of Okhotsk, and therefore into the Pacific. That was the Amur.

How did the river get its name? There is still disagreement

among historians on this point. Since the Chinese were the first
to discover it it would have been logical to borrow their name
for it, the Hailungtsiang ("the River of the Black Dragon") or,
if this proved too difficult for the illiterate Russian Cossacks,
the Hai-Heh ("the Black River") which was its alternate Chinese
name. But no. Even in the very earliest Russian reports it is
referred to as "Amur" (pronounced "Amoor").

Some historians believe that this is a corruption of the word
Mamu, the name the river was given by the aboriginal tribes
living along its lower flow. Others believe that the Mongol name
for it, Khara-Muren (Black River), was used by the Russians
as the basis for the river's name. Still others believe that it has
come from a contraction of two ancient Tungus words *za-mur*,
both meaning "river." Whatever it is, it is known today as the
Amur on most maps of the world.

The Amur is a great and lovely river. It ranks eighth among
the great rivers of the world by its length (if one includes the
Shilka in this computation), and tenth as to its drainage basin,

The Amur River beach at Khabarovsk.

with only three rivers in Siberia surpassing it in this respect—the Ob, the Yenisei, and the Lena. The Amur proper is formed by the confluence of the Shilka and the Argun Rivers in Chita Province, near the village of Pokrovka. From there, for some 850 miles, it forms the border between Siberia and Chinese Manchuria. Near the town of Khabarovsk, however, it swings sharply north and goes some 500 miles further, before it empties into the Sea of Okhotsk, near the northern end of Sakhalin island. Here, in the Tatar Strait, between the mainland and Sakhalin, it is hard-ice-bound for about five months each year, and therefore it is hardly an ice-free outlet.

But near Khabarovsk, another river, the Ussuri, flows into the Amur from the south. Between the Ussuri and the Sea of Japan lies a wide, long stretch of land dominated by the Sikhote-Alin mountain range. The Ussuri rises near a fine natural harbor.

The Amur and particularly the maritime stretch south of it, and east of the Ussuri, could be developed for agriculture to feed the chronically hungry Russian fur-collecting posts along the Lena, the Sea of Okhotsk shores, and in Kamchatka. It is this stretch of land with a comparatively mild climate, and the fine harbor, which attracted the Russians from the earliest years of Siberia's discovery.

Without this outlet to the sea the whole Russian enterprise in Siberia resembled, to use an old Far Eastern simile, "a turtle in a clay jar."

The earliest Russian forays into Amur territory were made by two Russian empire-building freebooters. Poyarkov from Yakutsk, and Khabarov from Irkutsk. What they saw impressed them enormously: a deep, wide river teeming with fish (the Amur has the greatest variety of food fish found in any Siberian river—99 species) flowing through beautiful and fertile lands; the woods alive with fur-bearing and food animals, including the matchless Siberian tiger; game, including clouds of pheasants; and best of all, good weather for farming. There were practically no people, apart from some nomadic tribes. Even though the Amur was claimed by the Manchu empire, the entire length of the river had not a single Manchu or Chinese settlement or farm. One of the richest plums in Asia lay there and could be had for the taking.

So, in the spring of 1650, Khabarov, with some free Cossacks and some government troops, swept all the way along the Amur to the present site of Khabarovsk, which was named after him. He claimed the vast territory for the Tsar without firing a shot. This was a conquest of incalculable value for Siberia. For the first time, there was Siberian land lush in summer, with a sufficiently long growing season to afford wide-scale agriculture. Better still, the Amur promised an eventual outlet into the big sea, the Pacific. It is true that Khabarov had no idea where the Amur eventually flowed into it, but it flowed east and *not* north like all the other Siberian rivers. Here was a chance for the turtle to get out of the jar.

So Khabarov built a Russian *ostrog* at Albazin on the Amur. But the Manchus, who by then had succeeded in imposing their dynasty upon China, intervened. Manchu troops sent from the south attacked Khabarov and were defeated in a pitched battle. During the next 15 years, Albazin was attacked and besieged again and again, burned down and rebuilt by the Russians. The Manchus, unsuccessful in battle, now brought pressure on the Russian government in Moscow, supported by the *voyevoda* and the merchants of Irkutsk who, by this time, had developed an overland trade route with China across Mongolia, and were intensely interested in protecting their trade.

Generally the Moscow government, still desperately weak after the "time of confusion," was unhappy about the actions of the Siberian adventurers. It placed almost no value on the territories won by them. And Moscow wanted no trouble with China. The overland route seemed to be the best, if not the only way of supplying Siberia, and the military power of China was then vastly overestimated in Moscow. So in 1667, an embassy delegation of Russian functionaries was sent to Peking with instructions to settle the Amur controversy peacefully. If necessary, it was to give up the entire territory. The Manchu emperor, Kwang Hsi, put up an impressive show in Peking for the Russians, including a dress parade of some 20,000 Chinese soldiers. The Russians were impressed. A treaty was arranged, after years of negotiations, which confirmed China's claim to the entire Amur basin, in exchange for trade privileges.

The Russian garrison of Albazin was left to the mercy of the Manchu armies and, after a long siege, the Cossacks there surrendered and were taken to Peking as prisoners. The Amur outlet was lost to Siberia.

There followed a great deal of diplomatic activity as well as sporadic military action on a very minor scale. Finally in 1689, there was a new treaty concluded at Nerchinsk which, though confirming some of the Chinese claims, left large tracts of territory unclaimed by either side.

After this, the Russians started to explore the possibility of opening a trade sea route via the Arctic Sea. Vitus Bering, a Dane in the Russian service, sailed through the present Bering Strait and confirmed the fact that Siberia was not connected with Alaska, as previously was believed. This was in 1725, and explorations continued until the 1740s, until the fact of the existence of a theoretical sea route over the top of Siberia and into the Pacific was well confirmed. But it was also learned that the route was impossible to use because of the climatic conditions— it was ice-bound practically the entire year.

And all this while the Amur outlet remained deserted—no Chinese or Manchu settlers colonized it, and China did not make the slightest attempt to use it.

It was not until the first half of the nineteenth century that the Amur again attracted the attention of the now St. Petersburg government. Russia, after defeating Napoleon in 1812 and after marching into Paris two years later, became a recognized world power with imperial ambitions. At the same time, a series of tragic events for China proved that country's extreme vulnerability. In 1839, the English started the Opium War with China, occupied Canton, and defeated the once-mighty Celestial Empire with surprising ease. The Treaty of Nanking in August of 1842 opened China to British trade. This, in turn, led to the Taiping Rebellion, the bloodiest civil war in history, which claimed an estimated 40 million lives and devastated the entire center of China and almost toppled the Manchu dynasty. The British, led by "Chinese" Gordon, came to the help of the Manchus, and the rebellion was finally suppressed in 1864. This established the major role that Great Britain was to play in Asia.

The Russians, still smarting from their defeat in the Crimean War by the coalition of Turkey, England, France, and Sicily in 1853–1856, now considered "perfidious Albion" as their deadliest potential enemy. The British penetration into China gave rise to suspicions in St. Petersburg that Siberia was in danger of British annexation. (It is true that in 1854 the British and the French attempted to land in Kamchatka and were beaten off. This was only a small-scale demonstration in support of the Crimean campaign, but logically the foray could be repeated, and be supported by an overland attack from Manchuria and Mongolia.)

Since the Chinese still had not made the slightest attempt to colonize the Amur River basin or the land stretching south of it, the Russians decided to act. By this time the territory had been thoroughly surveyed by Nevelskoy, acting for Count Muraviev, the Governor-General of Eastern Siberia, and this survey had proved the absence of any Chinese settlements there. In 1858, the Nerchinsk Treaty was abrogated, and Muraviev, acting with extreme boldness, simply occupied the northern bank of the Amur all the way to the sea. He founded the town of Nikolayevsk-on-Amur near the river's mouth. The following diplomatic activity confirmed the Russian claims to the left bank of the Amur, and by the treaty of Tientsin of 1859, all the territory lying between the Amur, the Ussuri, and the Pacific was declared to be a condominium between the two states. But this was just the territory which Russia needed—affording them an outlet to the sea, and so Muraviev boldly moved south and founded Vladivostok, giving it its "imperialistic" name. (Vladivostok translates into Russian as "rule over the East.") And here occured, according to historical legend, the strangest "conquest."

When he sent the map of the new Chinese-Siberian border to Peking, Muraviev simply tinted this region—the present Maritime province east of the Ussuri, and the part of the Khabarovsk province south of the Amur—in the same color as Siberia. The Chinese government verified it without question. Whereupon Muraviev moved a permanent Russian garrison to Vladivostok.

Before the Chinese could check on their geography, streams of Russian settlers were sent into this southernmost part of Siberia. They were mostly immigrants from the Ukraine who were considered to be the most talented farmers in Russia. They were given Cossack "status"—that is, that of armed peasants organized on a paramilitary basis. Thus two new Cossack troops were added to the troops already in Siberia—the Amur and the Ussuri

Cossacks. There is no record that China ever protested about the encroachment. There were reasons for this. She bitterly resented gun-boat penetrations of the Western powers into her central provinces, and she considered Russia, which was violently anti-British, her best potential ally. The tea trade with Russia was becoming the main source of her foreign income, and after all, the territories over which Russia was spreading had never been a part of traditional China. They were distant and valueless colonies. It was a small price to pay for keeping Russia away from the camp of the "white devils" which were cutting China to pieces.

In 1867, Russia sold Alaska to the United States, and concentrated on developing her Siberian holdings, and primarily the newly acquired territories, as a bulwark against the spread of British and French power in China. Immigration to the territories was encouraged. Vladivostok was developed into a fortress and the Russian garrison there was reinforced. But still the Siberian Far East remained the "Godforsaken frontier," and an assignment there was considered tantamount to exile. The early settlers there were exploited by the local administrators; they, in turn, exploited the local tribesmen.

Early Russian settlers in the Far East, especially in the Vladivostok region, had become known in Siberia by the strange name of the Lantsepoops. The origin of this meaningless word is interesting. According to a popular story, a French warship was slated to pay a courtesy call at Vladivostok. The local commandant decided to "show the flag" to impress the visitors. However, his garrison at Vladivostok composed of perhaps 500 soldiers, was in completely unpresentable shape. Their uniforms were shabby, half of the men did not even possess boots, having traded them for vodka, and all the men wore long, untidy beards and looked like savages. So about 100 of them were chosen, ordered to cut their hair and wash, and then they were dressed in whatever clothing could be found by stripping the other men. They were drilled to act as guard of honor to the visiting Frenchmen. The rest were ordered to disappear and not to show themselves to the foreigners.

The French ship duly arrived, and the French officers went ashore. They were met by the Commandant and his officers, some of whom could speak French. The guard of honor pre-

sented arms, and all went well until one of the Frenchmen
noticed some bearded savages hiding in the bushes. They were,
of course, the half-naked soldiers who could not overcome their
curiosity.

"Who are those?" one of the Frenchmen asked.

The Commandant had to think fast. "Oh," he said, "those
are the local tribesmen ... native ... completely savage and
hardly human."

The Frenchman brought out his notebook. "What are they
called?"

"Oh ..." the Commandant mumbled, "they are called—er—
the Lantsepoops."

"Les ... Lantsepoups ..." the Frenchman nodded, putting this
down into his book.

So, presumably, somewhere in the archives of the French Navy
there is some short mention of the Far Eastern savage tribe called
the Lantsepoops. And until the revolution of 1917 there was a
rather exclusive club in Vladivostok whose membership was
limited to the descendants of the region's early Russian settlers,
which was known as the "Lantsepoops Club."

On July 25, 1894, Japan attacked China and won the war in
a whirlwind campaign that proved the absolute helplessness of
the Chinese against any well-organized enemy. It also demonstrated the surprising military prowess and modern organization
of the Japanese. As the result of the peace treaty signed in Shimo-
noseki on April 17, 1895, Japan received a part of the Liatung
Peninsula, the Formosa and the Pescadore Islands, and secured
the nominal independence of Korea, under Japanese tutelage.
Suddenly and dramatically, Japan became a world power, and
the number-one threat to the Russian Far East.

The St. Petersburg government realized that the defense of
the Far East, and all of eastern Siberia, was absolutely impossible
without a communication line across Siberia to Vladivostok.
Plans were hastily drawn up and the construction of a single-
track railway started in 1897. It was a tremendous engineering
feat of the time, and to facilitate the task Russia negotiated a
concession from China to build the eastern part of the line across
Manchuria rather than go along the round-about route north
of the Amur River.

TRANSIBERIAN R.R. ████████████

This disturbed Japan. But when the Russians got an additional concession to lease two Chinese ports on the Liatung Peninsula, Port Arthur and Dairen, for 99 years, and built a branch railroad there, Japan decided to act.

On the night of February 7–8, 1904, Japan attacked without a declaration of war, sank three Russian warships which were in the Pacific, and laid siege to Port Arthur. (Thirty-seven years later, Japan repeated this kind of attack at Pearl Harbor, even to the exact timing of the blow—i.e., early morning on Sunday when most of the officers and men would be off duty.)

Port Arthur held, despite savage attacks. Russia mobilized a huge army and started moving it into Manchuria. But supplying it by a single-track railway, which constantly kept breaking down proved to be impossible. The Russians suffered a number of defeats. Port Arthur held out until January 2, 1905, while the Russian armies continued to battle with the Japanese in Manchuria. Both sides suffered frightful losses. But the Russians thought that they had an ace up their sleeve. Their combined Baltic and Black Sea fleets were en route for the Far East, sailing around Africa and across the Indian Ocean, with Vladivostok as their destination.

The Japanese fleet, lightly regarded until then, set an ambush for the Russians in the Tsushima Strait between Japan and Korea. In a spectacular naval battle, the Japanese completely destroyed the Russian armada, sinking 14 heavy warships with a loss of 10,000 Russian lives.

This shook Russia, and the world: for the first time Japan was revealed as a major naval power. Vladivostok and the entire Siberian Pacific coast lay defenseless against possible Japanese landings. Russia sued for peace even though her land armies in Manchuria were more than holding their own in that spring of 1905. The United States' President, Theodore Roosevelt, offered his good offices as a mediator, and during the negotiations rendered Russia an invaluable service by bringing pressure upon Japan to be reasonable. The Peace Treaty of Portsmouth, New Hampshire, was comparatively favorable to Russia considering the size of her military and naval disaster. Japan got the two Chinese ports, the southern half of Sakhalin island, and the bleak Kurile Islands stretching all the way from the tip of Kamchatka to the northern tip of Japan's Hokkaido island. The Russians were now bottled up in the Pacific, but they were permitted to keep the Chinese Eastern Railway connecting Siberia with Vladivostok—something which Japan had originally demanded.

Russia now had a new enemy, Japan, and a new friend, the United States. She also had a brewing internal revolution of her own which all but overthrew the Tsar's government in 1905–1906.

It is interesting to note that the historical role played by the United States toward Siberia is not forgotten today. The Siberians like to stress the affinity between themselves and the Americans, and there is no people more admired in Siberia than the Americans, despite all the political difficulties. The old Siberians also remember that if it had not been for the American pressure, the Japanese militarists would probably have annexed the Amur provinces in 1917–1922, and would have attacked Russia during the last war.

I have spoken to many Siberians and almost all of them expressed their consternation about the present strained relations between Russia and the United States which they all consider to be a major historical misfortune.

"America is the only world power with which we have never been at war in our history, and it is inconceivable that we should ever fight each other," was the consensus.

For whatever reasons, the peace Japan imposed upon Russia in 1905 was surprisingly reasonable. Vladivostok, which many Japanese jingoists described as "a dagger aimed at the heart of Japan," remained in Russian hands, as well as the railroad leading to it. No wonder that many Japanese felt that it was a shameful peace.

The disastrous Russo-Japanese war and the revolution which swept Russia afterward was a profound shock to the St. Petersburg government. From this point on the Far East was given special attention as a defense bastion. All garrisons there were greatly strengthened. Demobilized soldiers were urged to settle in the "Pre-Amur Government General" which included not only the Amur, Khabarovsk, and Maritime Provinces, but also the entire seaboard of the Sea of Okhotsk, the Chukchi, the Kamchatka, and the northern half of Sakhalin island. Some did, bringing their families from Russia, but not many. Then the construction of the Amur Railway began. It was planned to go through Russian territory all the way to Vladivostok, a line almost twice as long as the direct route cutting through Manchuria via Hailar and Harbin. Though the actual labor was performed by Chinese gangs from across the Amur, construction brought a degree of prosperity to the region. Vladivostok, as the main Russian military and naval base of Siberia, had close to 50,000, not counting military personnel.

But this growth was primarily administrative. No attempt was made for industrial development of the region or for a survey of its natural resources. Further north no progress was made at all. At the time of the revolution the population of Petropavlovsk, the capital of the huge Kamchatka peninsula, was 2,000, and Okhotsk and Anadyr, two other centers, barely had that many people together. The country twenty miles north of the Amur Railway line remained a wilderness.

In the revolution of 1917, the Far East quickly declared itself on the side of the Soviets. But it was a shortlived declaration. In April of 1918, a strong detachment of Japanese troops landed at Vladivostok and quickly moved along the Amur and Chinese Eastern Railways. Fortunately for Russia, the Japanese did not have a free hand. Almost immediately some U.S. troops landed as well, followed by smaller detachments of British and French troops, as well as a token force of Italians. Soviet power was overthrown. Local counterrevolutionaries took control. Within a few days all of Siberia was in the hands of counterrevolutionaries. Not only Siberia, but the Ural regions were seized and Soviet power overthrown. In Kazan, "white troops" captured intact the bulk of the gold reserve of Russia—over 700 million gold rubles (350 million gold dollars).

The Far East found itself in the deep rear of the anti-Soviet front and under virtual Japanese occupation.

Meanwhile the civil war was being lost by the "whites," despite foreign support. By 1920, all foreign troops, with the exception of the Japanese, evacuated the Far East. But the Japanese had no intention of leaving. The Red Army came face to face with them, and had to stop: to provoke a war with Japan at that point would have been suicide for the weakened Soviet state. Japan, under pressure from the Allies, and particularly from the United States, did not want a full-scale war, but did want to preserve its foothold in the Russian Far East. To avoid a showdown, a so-called Far Eastern Republic was set up, ostensibly independent. The capital was Vladivostok. This puppet "government," though non-Communist on the surface, was nonetheless directed by the Soviets. It did everything in its power to foster guerrilla warfare against the Japanese. Early in 1922, its own troops joined the guerrillas for a concerted attack on the Japanese, and by the end of the year forced them to evacuate the Far East, with the exception of Sakhalin island. On October 25, Vladivostok was liberated. In November 1922 the Far East joined the Russian Federation. In the course of this struggle, the remnants of the white troops who had escaped into Mongolia were wiped out, and Outer Mongolia broke away from China and formed an independent Soviet-type republic.

Japan, now starting its Manchurian adventure with the aim

of ultimately conquering China, temporarily abandoned her designs on the Russian Far East, and occupied Manchuria instead.

The Far East was left in shambles: its population decimated, its small industry destroyed, its agriculture disrupted. Russia, though giving priority to the reconstruction of the devastated European part of the country, nonetheless had to strengthen the three provinces bordering Japanese-occupied Manchuria. Some important reconstruction work was begun in the early 1930s.

In 1936, the Far East was declared to be the first "All-Union Komsomol Shock Development Area." The movement was led by one Valentina Khetagurova, the young wife of an officer stationed in Khabarovsk. She made an appeal to young men and women of the Soviet Union to come to the Far East, and her call was given tremendous play by the Soviet press. Thousands and thousands of young volunteers started to pour into the Far East. In a short time the brand-new city of Komsomolsk-on-Amur was built, 180 miles north of Khabarovsk. This was the first of such new cities built in Siberia, and it had the usual drawbacks of such early cities, and rather monotonous architecture. But it had a beautiful scenic location, and dense forests all around it, with hazelnut, oak, birch, and fir. There were great stretches of lilacs and bird-cherry bushes, and the Amur lianas and wild vines gave the forests an almost subtropical appearance. This is one of the oddities of the region, the mixture of northern and southern flora and fauna; some types of plants and animals seem to be completely strange to the severe winter climate, but flourish in this beautiful country.

Today Komsomolsk-on-Amur is a thriving city of over 200,000 souls—the first of the completely new cities built in Siberia.

Other cities of the regions have had a vigorous growth, with new railroads and roads opening up new regions for colonization and cultivation. The available population figures for the three main cities give an idea of the development of this once desolate though delightful region. Blagoveshchensk, has close to 150,000 people today. Khabarovsk, perhaps the most beautiful and modern city of Siberia, has over 500,000 people, and it is the fastest growing city in the Far East. Vladivostok has almost 450,000 and has been developed into a great new naval base.

The Khabarovsk Institute of Rail Transport, a building very typical of modern Siberian architecture.

The development of the three southernmost Far Eastern provinces was unusually fast for Siberia in the period between 1922 and 1945. Until recently, information about the area was considered classified matter, because of the strategic importance of the area. It was primarily a military area controlled by the Special Far Eastern Army, a distinct, autonomous military establishment of the Soviet Defense Department. Only after the elimination of Japan as a world military power in 1945 did the outside world have a first glimpse of the area. But then, because of worsening relations with Mao Tse-tung's China, the Far East provinces once again assumed special military importance, and became a tightly controlled frontier zone.

At present only the city of Khabarovsk and the port of Nakhodka are open for foreign travel.

Khabarovsk, like Rome, is built on seven hills rising from the river which is particularly wide and majestic-looking here, with fine riverside boulevards flanking it. The city is green, with thousands of apple trees and birches lining its streets. It is an

A winter street scene in Khabarovsk, one of the few Siberian towns open to foreign travel.

important railway and industrial center, but the mills and factories are located well out of the city proper and do not mar the residential blocks and wide boulevards.

The sport stadium of Khabarovsk is the pride of Khabarovsk patriots. They consider it the most beautiful in the entire Soviet Union. This is also a science center with a number of important institutes of higher learning, including the Railroad Institute, which is known all over the country. Khabarovsk rates with the most modern cities of Russia, and in summer is the pleasantest big city in Siberia.

The naval base of Vladivostok is closed to foreigners, and all foreign travelers across Siberia end their crosscountry journey at the port of Nakhodka which was built entirely after World War II. It has a population of well over 100,000, and some of the most modern equipment of any port of the Soviet Union. It is located 50 miles southeast of Vladivostok, and all passenger and frieight traffic to and from Japan and other Pacific areas goes through it.

The latest available population figures are of January 1, 1967: Amur Province (the least developed) had 781,000 people, out of which 487,000 live in urban communities; Khabarovsk Province, 1,317,000, of which fully 1,050,000 live in cities and towns; and the Maritime (Primorski) Province, 1,641,000 with an urban population comprising 1,193,000. The above figures reflect the industrialization of the region rather than its development as an agricultural area.

Khabarovsk Province includes the ethnographic oddity, the Jewish Autonomous Region, with the city of Birobidzhan as its capital. The population of the region was 174,000 as of January 1, 1967, and is not believed to have increased much since then.

The Magadan, Kamchatka, and Sakhalin Provinces (the latter formed after 1945) are the other three provinces of the Siberian Far East.

Loading lumber at the port of Vladivostok.

The three southern provinces are rich in natural resources, even though less so than their northern neighbors; all have temperate climates by Siberian standards, and all are extremely picturesque and have the most unusual flora and fauna. Almost all the animals found in Siberia are abundant here but there are two species which are found nowhere else: the noble spotted deer (the producer of the priceless *panti*), and the famous Siberian tiger, the largest and the most spectacular member of the tiger family, much sought after by zoological gardens throughout the world. Unrestricted hunting and trapping almost destroyed this species, and it is estimated that at one point the entire tiger population of Siberia was 54 animals. For ten years, between 1956 and 1966, hunting or trapping Siberian tigers was completely forbidden, and it is believed that the tiger population is on the increase now, but no exact statistics are available: the Siberian tiger is a wary animal and not easy to track. Since 1966, one set of tiger cubs a year can be captured to be sent to one of the zoos of the Soviet Union. None can be killed. Ivan Bogachev, a hunter of Khabarovsk Province, is at present the only tiger-catcher in Siberia. He specializes in this peculiar vocation, and has 36 captured tigers to his credit, none of them harmed or killed, and all are at present on view in various zoos.

The seaboard of the Far East, as well as the entire Amur

The Siberian tiger, the largest in the world, is protected by law. None may be killed, and only one set of cubs can be taken alive each year for zoological gardens.

River, supplies much fish and fish products to Siberia and to the entire Soviet Union. Fishing and fish-canning industries flourish and fish products represent the largest exports of the region.

Among the vast natural resources discovered in the Siberian southeast are tin deposits, second only to Bolivia's. Gold has been found, as well as coal and iron. Hydroelectric development is the present bottleneck. The potential resources of the Amur River in this respect are enormous. But their development at present is much hampered by the political situation: much of the right bank of the Amur River is controlled by the China of Mao Tse-tung.

China has largely eliminated Russian influence in Manchuria, and the great Russian-built city of Harbin has lost much of its

A couple, who are tiger trainers in Vladivostok, taking a friend for a walk. A hundred years ago, tigers often invaded the city, killing cattle and domestic animals.

Russian aspect. During the past few years the Peking government has been promoting mass migration of Chinese into Manchuria. This has been unnerving to the Russians. However, Chinese immigrants from Central China find the severe climate of Manchuria not to their liking, and most of them return to their native provinces. Nonetheless, the political atmosphere remains charged. In all probability the Far East will remain "out of bounds" to foreign travelers for years to come.

The southern part of the Maritime Province has a considerable Korean minority, mostly Russified, but there have never been Chinese settlements in the Far East. The Chinese mainly went there as seasonal workers. But not now: the Far Eastern frontier is locked against all penetration.

On the face of it, the existence of the Jewish Autonomous Region in Siberia appears to be a geographical and historical oddity. It has not proved to be popular with Soviet Jews, and it is doubtful that more than 40,000 of its population are of Jewish stock. I could not get any accurate figures.

Located within a large loop of the Amur River the Jewish Autonomous Region is an administrative part of Khabarovsk Province. It borders Chinese Manchuria along its entire southern frontier and is at present a sensitive military area, and it is closed to foreign travel. It it popularly known as Birobidzhan, which is the name of its administrative center. This name is derived from two small tributaries of the Amur, the Bira and the Bidzhan, that traverse the region. The city of Birobidzhan is located on the main trunk of the Trans-Siberian Railway, some 100 miles west of Khabarovsk. It is a small modern town of neat apartment houses and office buildings built of prefabricated cement panels. Like all such production line towns, it has a rather monotonous appearance. It is a new Soviet town and unlike most others, its growth has been slow.

Here is a brief description of the region:

The territory, 13,900 square miles. The population stood at 174,000 as of 1967, and might be reaching 180,000 today. Seventy percent of the population is urban. The density of the population, about 13 per square mile, is considerable for Siberia. The city of Birobidzhan had a population of 47,000 as of January 1, 1968. The population is Russian, Ukrainian, and Jewish. Yiddish is the official language, but Russian is universally spoken.

The industries: mining (primarily tin), building materials, lumber, and light manufacturing. Besides tin, iron ores, graphite, and manganese have been found in some considerable abundance, and the prospects for increasing mining are good. About one-third of the territory, close to 2,500,000 acres, is covered by good-grade forests; larch, pine, fir, cedar, and birch. The principal agricultural crops are wheat, oats, soy beans, and potatoes. The animal husbandry: cattle, pigs, and sheep. There is commercial hunting and fishing. In 1966–1967 there were 39,700 schoolchildren of all grades, and there were 6 special technical schools of junior college level with an enrollment of 4,800. The proximity of the great educational center of Khabarovsk precludes the necessity for a local university. There are two national theaters, a national choir of considerable renown, 6 museums, 167 film installations, 80 public libraries, and 106 workers' clubs. There are 269 doctors and 1,880 hospital beds. Primary education is compulsory and illiteracy nonexistent.

The climate is continental: there are cold winters and hot summers, with about 160 frostless days a year, rather mild by Siberian standards. But though the town of Birobidzhan is located on approximately the same parallel as Seattle, Washington, its climate is considerably more inclement.

The Autonomous Region was set up on May 7, 1934. What was the reason for setting up this artificial ethnic entity and why in this strange location?

The Russian Empire had had a large Jewish population consisting of two uneven segments. The vast majority of this population was concentrated in the western part of European Russia —the Ukraine, Belorussia, the Polish regions under Russian control, and the southern Baltic regions. Certain territories were administratively set up by the Tsar's government as the Area of Jewish Settlement, or the Pale, and Jews were not allowed to leave those areas without police permission. About 80 percent of all Russian Jews lived within the Pale. The remaining 20 percent, representing Jewish intelligentsia, professional people and prosperous artisans and merchants, were spread out all over the country, including Siberia. This segment of the Jewish population was largely Russified and divorced from the Jewish religious tradition, which was extremely strong within the Pale.

Siberia was probably the only part of the former Russian Empire which never had any history of racial and religious discrimination of any kind. This attracted many professional people of Jewish faith as well as Jewish artisans and tradesmen. Also, many political exiles sent to Siberia for forced settlement were Jews. The Jews of Siberia were completely integrated into the economic and cultural life of the country and most of them had little if any connection with the Judaic theological tradition. Many of them were Russified, and in fact were part of the most educated and enlightened classes of old Siberia.

The Russian revolution brought drastic changes to the Russian Jews. All discriminatory laws and practices were abolished, and theoretically the Jewish community of the former Pale achieved complete legal equality with the rest of the Population. A large segment of this population lived in what was the newly created Polish State, and they were no longer under Russian control. The Communist revolution, however, even though confirming the absolute equality of all people of the country, played havoc with economic conditions of the Ukrainian and Belorussian Jewry and their traditional way of life.

Meanwhile, the Jewish intelligentsia dispersed throughout Russia welcomed the change, and a large number of early revolutionary leaders were Jews—a fact which was widely used by counterrevolutionary forces for propaganda purposes. The entire "white," counterrevolutionary movement was deeply tinted with anti-Semitism, and "pogroms" (mass killings) and other anti-Semitic excesses followed in the wake of all white armies. Only in Siberia did this not happen, and the propaganda found obsolutely no response.

The propaganda term "Jewish Bolshevism" was coined by the "whites," and this historical fraud proved to be hard to destroy. It was vigorously revived by Hitler and in World War II was used, with some success, in Nazi-occupied Ukraine, Belorussia, Poland, and the Baltic states. Some "pogroms" occurred in these territories during the German occupation, even before Himmler's Gestapo, with the active assistance of the German army, began the methodical extermination of the Jewish population in all such occupied territories.

Stalin's rise to power, after Lenin's death on January 21, 1924, played an important part in the history of Soviet Jews. Stalin, a member of a national minority himself, seemed to be obsessed with national questions—he was the Commissar for Nationalities in Lenin's original cabinet. With his growing influence in the Communist party, the process of ethnographic hair-splitting within the Soviet state was greatly accelerated—on a single day, December 10, 1930, not less than six "national regions" were set up in Siberia alone, in addition to the already existing Yakut and Buryat Autonomous Republics. The idea was to provide each more or less important ethnic minority with its own territorial national home. Some of these formations were historically and ethnographically sound, others less so. The small Siberian tribe of the Evenks, for instance, scattered all over Siberia, were given a national home of almost 300,000 square miles, i.e., larger than Texas, but even today the population of the entire region stands at 12,000, with only a few of them Evenks.

The status of these territorial national units has been repeatedly changed since then. Some national districts were upgraded to autonomous regions, some downgraded, some completely eliminated, others eliminated and then reconstituted again. In Siberia, two Buryat "national districts" were created as late as 1937, and the Tuva Autonomous Soviet Republic in 1961.

In the early 1930s, during the heyday of the ethnographic demarcation of the Soviet Union, the question of the national status of Soviet Jews was raised. Were they not, in fact, a distinct ethnic group deserving a national status?

For a while the Crimea was considered, and in fact some Jewish agricultural communes were set up there, but this led to a conflict with the Tartar minority who lived there and claimed the area for their own national home. So this movement petered out, and the idea was abandoned. (It is interesting to note that the Tartar "national home" in Crimea came to an inglorious end during the war of 1941–1945 when the local Tartars were accused of being too friendly to the Germans during the occupation, whereupon the territory was turned over to the Ukraine as one of her provinces.)

The idea of setting up a Jewish national home within the Soviet Union was a controversial one from the very outset. The only Jews who would welcome such a "home" were those steeped in religious tradition. Those who were fully integrated in the economic and cultural life of the country as a whole had no desire to be segregated in any way, least of all territorially: this reminded them too much of the old dreaded Pale.

But nonetheless the project was pushed ahead. When and under what circumstances Siberia was suggested as a likely national home is unclear, but the choice was an unhappy one. True, there existed a large tract of practically virgin, fertile land there; the country had never had any history of anti-Semitism, and the area was geographically far removed from the Pale, the center of theological Judaism. But the region was remote, the climate harsh, and Siberia had, under Stalin, again been given an unsavory reputation as a vast penal colony.

Many people to whom I spoke about it in Russia and in Siberia thought that Stalin personally was responsible for selection of Birobidzhan as the Autonomous Jewish Region. According to them, his idea was to separate the younger generations of Soviet Jews from the religious influence of their families, with dialectical materialism replacing the theological tradition of their ancestors. But whatever it was, the Jewish national "home" was set up in 1934, and widespread propaganda urged young Jewish enthusiasts to migrate there and start building their own state from scratch. It was to be based, of course, on the Marxist-Leninist-Stalinist principles, not religious ones. For a while this propaganda had some success, and some enthusiastic young Jews started off for Siberia, though the project was opposed from the outset both by the traditional Jewish community, and by integrated Soviet Jews, few of whom spoke Yiddish or had any desire to be segregated from their fellow citizens. So this migration never assumed a mass character, and many young migrants were disillusioned by harsh living conditions in the distant and lonely land, though some stayed, battling valiantly against nature, and achieving some noteworthy results.

So Birobidzhan has remained ever since what it was from the start—a sterile political idea devoid of any economic or emotional attraction to Soviet Jewry.

20.

Siberia's Fiery Frontier

IN the schools of old Russia, the least successful and the chronically bothersome pupils, among them myself, were relegated to the last benches in every class—a sort of exile. They were scholastic outcasts: to be assigned to the last benches, against the back wall, was tantamount to wearing a dunce cap. Those outcasts were known as the "Kamchadals," and their benches were known as "Kamchatkas." They just couldn't be pushed any further away. The next step would be dishonorable expulsion.

For in the world of a Russian child, Kamchatka was the end of the world.

Indeed Kamchatka was considered so remote and so Godforsaken in the old Russian scheme of things that even the most dangerous criminals and political exiles were never sent there. It would have been impossible to get anyone to guard them— no one would go to Kamchatka of his own free will.

Even among old-time Siberians, the Kamchatka peninsula was considered a most undesirable place to live. It was a cold, volcanic wilderness with just a few primitive Koryaks moving about with their deer herds. The only inhabited place of any significance in Kamchatka was the Russian administrative center of Petropavlovsk-on-Kamchatka, a log-cabin village which had less than 2,000 inhabitants in 1917. It is doubtful that there were more than 3,000 Russians then in the entire huge peninsula.

Kamchatka was the last part of northern Siberia to come into the Russian Empire, and one of a few places where the conquest was achieved by force of arms, for the few natives that lived there resisted bitterly.

Toward the middle of the seventeenth century otter skins became fashionable in Europe, and a call was sent out from Moscow to the Russian "land-farers" to bring in as many otter skins as possible. Until then otter was hunted only for food. But suddenly the skins which only the natives had used for clothing joined the list of the "soft gold" items. Like South African ostrich, the otter became a victim of fashion. A great orgy of extermination began.

Russian advances into northeastern Siberia, and later into Alaska, were in good part the result of this sudden demand for otter skins. With sable becoming more and more scarce, the otter was now king of the fur trade.

In 1647 a Russian Cossack, Dejnev, left Okhotsk, on the shore of the Sea of Okhotsk and went inland with his men to the high-waters of the Kolyma River. On makeshift rafts they went north, all the way to the Arctic Ocean, and then moved east to the Chukchi and the Bering Strait separating Siberia from Alaska. They had no idea that the two continents were separated. (This discovery was only made 80 years later, by Vitus Bering.) Since the strait was hard-frozen, Dejnev considered it land, a continuation of Siberia.

They found otters plentiful there, and so in 1648, Dejnev founded the Anadyr *ostrog* in the Chukchi which became a fur-collecting station under the administrative supervision of the Yakutsk *voyevoka*. Somehow the early Russians moved about without any proper equipment, without compasses or maps, without proper food, and miraculously succeeded in maintaining communication between all those lonely posts scattered all over northern Siberia. They must have been a special breed of strong men driven by a sense of discovery and adventure, and though many of them found graves in the north, a surprising number of them survived and prospered.

Anadyr, which is today the capital of the Chukchi Autonomous Region of the Magadan Province, was perhaps the loneliest of all such outposts of the era. Beyond it there was absolutely nothing. But eventually it became a base for the Russian conquest of the Kamchatka. That feat was performed by a single man, Vladimir Atlasov, who was not a Cossack, but a lowly clerk who spent his days counting otter skins brought to Anadyr by the natives.

It was from them that he heard about a huge land to the south which was always on fire, with its mountains shooting columns of flame high into the sky. And they said that this wild land was extremely rich in furs, not only otter, but sables, silver foxes, and beavers. These stories fired his imagination, and Atlasov appealed to the Yakutsk *voyevoda* asking him to back an expedition to the south. The *voyevoda* was sympathetic, but declined the offer. Atlasov decided to strike out on his own.

Possibly he was backed by some private fur traders of the Chukchi. He raised an "army" of 60 Cossacks, strictly on his own, and struck out into the unknown. In July of 1697, he went more than half-way down the Kamchatka peninsula and built the first Russian *ostrog* on the Kamchatka River, in the shadow of the towering Klyuchevskaya Sopka volcano, which rises 15,585 feet over the plain. It is the highest active volcano in Asia. He found the river valley pleasant in summer, and the few natives friendly, though this friendliness was not to last.

Leaving a few men at the newly built *ostrog*, Atlasov went to the west coast of the peninsula and then to its southernmost tip and even went across the strait that separates Kamchatka from the northernmost of the Kurile Islands, Shumshu.

Kamchatka's natives consisted of several feuding clans of nomads, and there were constant clashes among them. Atlasov succeeded in reconciling them, and was proclaimed by them to be their common prince. He was undisputed ruler of a huge domain, slightly larger than Texas. He found it a pleasant place in comparison with Yakutsk from which he originally came.

"The winters here are short and warm," he wrote in his first report to the Yakutsk *voyevoda*. "The sun is twice as near as in Yakutsk."

Also this was a peculiarly beautiful land. There were smoking volcanoes and large valleys with spouting geysers and clouds of steam. There was also an abundance of "soft gold" and of fish.

After collecting 3,000 otter, fox, and beaver skins, Atlasov left a deputy in charge of the new country, and headed for Russia to present the Tsar with a new domain.

The Krymsky volcano erupting. The peninsula is dotted with active volcanoes.

Somehow he succeded in reaching Moscow in 1701, and Kamchatka was graciously accepted by Tsar Peter the Great into his realm. Atlasov was given 100 silver rubles for his exploits, and a letter to the Yakutsk *voyevoda* ordering him to give Atlasov 100 Cossacks, necessary arms, and merchandise for barter. Whereupon he was sent home. But traveling through Siberia, Atlasov's sketchy knowledge of geography was his undoing. Not far from Yakutsk he met a Russian merchant coming from China with some goods. Believing that he was already in "his" Kamchatka, Atlasov seized the merchant's shipment. The man arrived at Yakutsk and complained, and when Atlasov got there he was arrested for armed robbery, flogged, and thrown into jail, where he spent the next four years. That was the end of his career.

Meanwhile things in Kamchatka were not going well. Other adventurers had arrived and had undone much of Atlasov's good work. They antagonized the natives, who then united against the Russians. There were bloody clashes all over the peninsula with the Cossacks and the Kamchadals stalking and killing each other. When Atlasov fiinally returned to Kamchatka after his prison term, he found his "army" in mutiny and the peninsula in turmoil. He was dismissed from his post and died in obscurity.

The armed struggle between the Russians and the Kamchadals continued for thirty years, into the 1730s. Finally the natives were practically exterminated, and the few survivors retreated into the wilderness. Their descendants are the present Koryaks, but even today they number only 6,300 people while another native Kamchatka tribe, the Selcups, numbers only 3,800.

In the autumn of 1740, two Russian gunboats dropped anchor in the Avancha Bay on the east coast of the peninsula, and the city of Petropavlovsk was founded, thus officially confirming Russian domination over the peninsula. This newly born town, the most eastern point of Russia, was then officially proclaimed to be the capital of the province. The "governor" and his staff went ashore. The modern story of Kamchatka had begun.

There is an amusing story that demonstrates the remoteness of the new province. Tsarina Elizabeth, a woman of highly romantic imagination, expressed her desire to have a few maidens

Two girls of the Koryaks, the natives of Kamchatka.

from her Kamchatka domain at her St. Petersburg court. Five young Koryak girls were sent off to St. Petersburg in the charge of an officer. The party had to stop in Irkutsk while all the girls gave birth to mixed-blood children. The officer in charge was dismissed and another appointed, but by the time the girls arrived in St. Petersburg, they were all pregnant again. It is not clear if they were ever presented to the Tsarina, although she probably would not have objected: her own love adventures were notorious.

The St. Petersburg government then forgot all about Kamchatka, and during 177 years of Tsarist rule the capital of Petropavlovsk only grew to 2,000 inhabitants by 1917. By 1939, the population of Petropavlovsk reached 35,000: the search for gold in Siberia was the cause of the increase. Growth was swiftly accelerated after 1945 when the Kurile Islands, annexed by Japan after the Russian defeat of 1905, were returned to Russia.

Petropavlovsk, renamed Petropavlovsk-Kamchatsky,* had 126,000 people on January 1, 1968. Petropavlovsk is the largest city of the Siberian seaboard after Vladivostok, and the fastest growing city in northern Siberia, with the exception of the great polar metallurgical center of Norilsk.

What has made it grow faster than other and more famous northern communities such as the "golden" Magadan, and even the "diamond" Yakutsk?

For one thing, the climate. It is severe, but not as severe as that of Yakutsk and not as uncomfortable as that of Magadan. Petropavlovsk is not nearly as northern as many other northern cities. Lying at 53° North latitude, it is only slightly north of Berlin and London. Too, Kamchatka is a romantic land; its remoteness and peculiar geography make it attractive to young Soviet migrants. Not only is it the last frontier, but it is an exciting frontier as well, unexplored, mysterious, and unusual. There are 28 active volcanoes and over 100 dormant ones. The whole peninsula rests on a bed of thermal waters that emerge in the form of numerous geysers and hot springs. There is great potential useful energy in these masses of often boiling water. Kamchatka is a laboratory of hydrothermics for the entire north of Siberia. The city of Petropavlovsk, just like Reykjavik, is centrally heated by the thermal sea under it.

Kamchatka is an extremely rich land, although only partly surveyed. The deposits of sulphur, mercury, rare metals, and gold are said to be truly gigantic. But the biggest wealth of Kamchatka is in the water around it. Due to some peculiar biological conditions the fish population around the peninsula is enormous; over 170 varieties of valuable food fish have been identified in commercial quantities. And the most valuable crab

---

* The renaming craze has been slowed down at present and some renamed cities got back their historical names. In one of the Soviet magazines a writer bitterly complained recently about it when he found fully 400 streets of Odessa renamed without any apparent reason, with some of them simply "trading" their names with each other. The newest rule precludes naming any city after any living person.

Volcanology students in Kamchatka are stringing electric wires. Tapping volcanoes for electric power is under intensive study in Siberia.

beds in the world are located here and around the Kuriles, the king crab of the Pacific which made the "Chatka" brand of canned crabmeat a household word throughout the world. These resources are practically inexhaustible since the biological balance of the Kamchatka waters seems to favor the valuable varieties of fish. Kamchatka exports several seafood products not only to the entire Soviet Union, but abroad as well, and with the food supply of the planet growing short, the importance of Kamchatka as a seafood factory of the world will become more and more striking.

Enormous herds of otter, walrus, and seal live on the shore, and the off shore rocks, and the interior of the peninsula teems with valuable fur-bearing animals: blue and silver fox, squirrel, polar hare, and mink.

Because of the presence of thermal waters, large-scale hothouse agriculture is feasible and inexpensive. Today Kamchatka fills its own needs for fresh vegetables, something undreamed of in

The famous king crab of Kamchatka, known all over the world.

other regions of northern Siberia. At Puzhetsk a large hydro-thermal electric station is nearing completion, and it will become the center of a more extensive hothouse agricultural complex. The use of volcanic power for producing electric energy is being studied at present, and it may solve the power needs of Kamchatka and of Eastern Siberia in general. Both coal and oil have been found. The industrial future of the peninsula looks extremely bright.

Kamchatka's potential has been barely scratched, and the peninsula has everything needed to create a full and prosperous life. It is an ideal place for young families. Petropavlovsk has a higher percentage of young brides than any other city of the Soviet Union, and more than twenty percent of them are below the age of 20. And, of course, Kamchatka, like the rest of Siberia, is teeming with children.

The present population of the province is still small. But the rate of new migration is high. Every region and every nationality of the Soviet Union is represented here, though Russians predominate. Almost two-thirds of the province is set aside as the Koryak National District. These tribes, once dying out have been rescued by the Soviet government from biological extinction. By special decree in 1930 the Koryaks, then numbering less than 1,000 people, as well as the Selcups, an even smaller tribe, were given special privileges: all Koryak and Selcup children were declared to be the state's wards, and up to this day the government pays their entire support until they complete their education. Siberian ethnographers and linguists have created a written Koryak language which is being taught in all schools of the region (along with Russian, of course), and illiteracy has been eliminated completely among the younger age groups. With the government paying all the expense, all Koryak and Selcup families can afford to have children and to educate them.

The native "Kamchadals" are fishermen and hunters. Some nomadic reindeer herding is still practiced, but more and more of the natives become settled in villages and small towns.

In time, Kamchatka will become a great tourist attraction— even today thousands of visitors arrive every summer from all over the Soviet Union. The airport of Petropavlovsk is large and modern, and it is a busy place, with regular flights from many Siberian towns. The dramatic sight that greets all new arrivals is the smoking volcano, Koryakskaya Sopka, an 11,339-foot-high furnace, one of the highest active volcanoes in the world. It is an unforgettable sight. But Kamchatka volcanoes, even though they are active, have had no disastrous eruptions in known history, and the volcanologists study them at stations set at the very edges of the craters.

The geographical continuation of Kamchatka is the chain of Kurile Islands that stretch from the southern tip of the peninsula all the way to Japan for almost 800 miles. There are 40 active volcanoes in this chain of volcanic islands. There are 30 large islands in this group, and hundreds of smaller ones, just rocks jutting from the ocean floor. There are 17 navigable straits leading from the Sea of Okhotsk into the Pacific, 17 gates of Siberia that open into the outside world. Several different ocean currents meet here and form mighty whirlpools, and unfortunately most of these currents are cold. Even though the Kuriles' southernmost island is located almost on the same parallel as Nice, the climate is inhospitable. The winters are cold and stormy, with snow often piling up in great drifts. The summer is short, cool, and rainy, and the only pleasant season is the autumn, which is warm, clear, and sunny.

A Siberian frontiersman: Vassili Nanaun, one of the few natives who live on icebound Wrangell Island.

After the Kurile Islands were returned to Russia by Japan, they were divided into three administrative regions, as part of Sakhalin Province. Japan did not exploit them in any way except for their fishing grounds. There was not a single permanent settlement there. At present there are five sizable modern towns, and a number of villages. The population of the islands is believed to be slightly over 35,000 at present, with thousands of temporary workers arriving from Sakhalin and the Siberian mainland during the seasonal fish runs, when the water around the islands "boils" with fish.

Considerable agriculture has been developed during the last few years, enough for the needs of this volcanic Siberian outpost. The flora of the islands is unique, with purely southern plants and far northern varieties growing side by side; bamboo and cedar, magnolia and pines, wild vine and lianas with northern lichens. There are over 1,060 varieties of plants that have been identified, and more are identified each year.

Wildlife is abundant. Blue and silver fox are found on all the islands, and it is estimated that on the island of Iturup there are six bears to every human being. There are considerable lumber resources, with the northern islands more forested than the southern, the effect of the warm current, the Soya touching the chain at that point.

The Kuriles are a virtual laboratory of volcanography; the entire island chain is alive with volcanic activity. Permanent departments of the All-Union Geographic Society and the Academy of Sciences are located on the islands. Forty volcanoes have been found to be fully active. The highest of them, the Alaid on the Alaid Island, rises to 7,674 feet. Some volcanoes are located on the sea bottom and their activity causes frequent earthquakes and disastrous *tsunami*, or tidal waves. Some volcanoes are corked up by cold lava; hot gases and steam break out from their sides. All the islands abound in hot springs, many of which have been found to possess curative properties. A strange steaming river on Paramushir Island deposits many tons of iron and aluminum ore into the sea each hour. At present there is a project for fishing out these minerals as they flow towards the sea.

All the towns on the islands are heated by thermal waters. On Kunashir Island, at the foot of the Mendeleyev volcano, there

One of the beautiful beaches in the Kurile Islands—where the bathing season is only a month!

is a unique boiling beach. Multicolored steam rises from the sand, and the part of the beach washed by the sea hisses like a hot griddle. A tea kettle buried in the sand here will come to a boil in ten minutes, and fish and crab can be cooked on the spot.

On the same island the geologists have found a boiling underwater lake with a water temperature of $+480°F$. The first geothermal electric station is being built here, with the used and worked out warm water to be used for swimming pools and hothouses.

There is a famous curative spa in operation at the foot of the Mendeleyev volcano. It is known through eastern Siberia, for

The Kurile Islands—peaceful-looking landscape.

its sulphurous waters which are said to cure the most stubborn cases of arthritis and eczema.

However, like Kamchatka, the real wealth of the Kuriles now is from the sea. The fish runs here are gigantic, with salmon and herring in enormous schools. Since 1959, a special type of Pacific sardine known as *saira* has become the most important item of all; millions of tons are caught and processed each year. Large fish-processing and canning factories produce countless millions of cans of seafood, including the finest crabmeat packaged anywhere. The Kurile salmon is famous all over Russia, and the species is restocked as well as caught: the fish hatchery on Iturup Island, the largest salmon hatchery in the world, plants up to 100 million salmon eggs annually.

Whaling and seal-hunting are also important. There are large herds of otter on the islands, but otter hunting is forbidden now in order to allow the depleted supply of this valuable aquatic animal to rebuild. There are several types of seal not found anywhere else. The Kostrikum rocks of Urup Island are set aside as the preserve of the so-called kalans seals, who produce probably the most valuable fur in the world. In early Siberian times, when the kalans were comparatively numerous, their pelts were sold by weight on a par with gold. They are rigidly protected at present: killing a kalan brings a 10-year prison term. In 1945 there were just about twenty-five of these animals left in the world. Today there are about 2,000, all on the Kostrikum rocks. The herds grow slowly; a female kalan produces a single offspring a year, and not every year at that.

In 1963, another and completely new kind of seal, known as antur, was identified, and also placed on the protected list.

The first Russian settlers who arrived in the Kuriles in 1946 were unfamiliar with the volcanic peculiarities of the islands. In 1952, the first Russian town founded there, Severo-Kurilsk, was wiped out by a catastrophic tidal wave, a *tsunami*. A fairly sharp earthquake preceded this catastrophe. The people ran out of their houses, and some of them ran up into the hills. Soon the shocks ended, but another and much more terrifying phenomenon was taking shape. The sea receded as much as half a mile, and then a tidal wave 35 feet high rushed in, smashing everything. It was followed by a second wave, this time 60 feet high,

In 1963 some Siberian zoologists noticed an unusual type of seal found along the Kamchatka and the Kurile Island coasts. Careful study has disclosed the fact that the antur was a distinct and heretofore unknown type of animal. The antur grows to be over six feet long and may weigh as much as 450 pounds. Its body is covered with coarse hair, and the color varies from dark yellow to dark brown, with white circle markings. It is believed that there are between 5,000 and 6,000 of them in existence.

which made the hills shake. When it receded there was not a sign of the town left.

The town was rebuilt on higher ground.

Because of the frequent earthquakes, all houses in the Kuriles are built of logs rather than stone or brick. There are stairways that lead from every village up into the hills. There are special warning signals all over the islands to alert the population to the approach of *tsunami*. The last alarm was sounded in 1966 during the Aleut Island earthquake, but no really catastrophic *tsunami* has hit the islands since 1952.

The Kuriles are a prosperous place. The average family income there is twice that of families on the mainland, and a new generation of Russian Kurilians is now taking over, with most of the original settlers retiring on pension, and many going back to their original homes.

Even though the beacon on Shikotan Island has the colorful name of "the End of the World," the Kuriles have daily air service with Sakhalin, Kamchatka, and Vladivostok. Many ships stop there in the warm season. Small boats and helicopters connect all the islands, too.

The island of Sakahlin was once the most dreaded name in Siberian prison lore. In 1905, the southern part of the island was annexed by Japan. It was returned to Russia in 1945. During the Japanese occupation, southern Sakhalin had only a single Japanese settlement, a small fishing town called Taiohara. Northern Sakhalin was also completely undeveloped. After the Russian revolution the former prison colonies had been liquidated, and most of the involuntary settlers had left the island. Though the Sakhalin waters were extensively fished by Japanese fishing fleets, there was no industrial activity, and the entire population of the island did not exceed 10,000, a figure that included the nomadic aboriginal tribesmen called the Nivkhi. (The census of 1959 listed only 2,100 Nivkhi.)

The Soviet development of Sakhalin was begun in the late 1940s, and during the last twenty years the island has undergone a complete change. Today it is a well-developed industrial and cultural center, with a population of about 700,000 which is rapidly increasing. The old Japanese village Taiohara is no more. In its place has been built the new, modern, and handsome city of Yzhno-Sakhalinsk which has about 100,000 people, predominantly Russian and predominantly young. Two-thirds of the people of the island are in their 20s.

Yzhno-Sakhalinsk is one of the model cities of Siberia. It is the administrative center of the new province, and Yzhno-Sakhalinsk is notably a city of students. Fully 34,000 of its people

Bathing in one of the natural warm-water pools of Sakhalin Island.

go to school, many at night because they work during the day. The Khabarovsk Railroad Institute and the Moscow Law Institute have branches here, in addition to the local Pedagogical College and 4 junior-college type schools—pedagogic, music, forestry, and trade. There are 8 technical schools and 35 grade schools. There is a theater of drama, a Philharmonic orchestra, a House of Culture and 11 film theaters. Like everywhere else in Siberia, women work along with men, and over 50 percent of the people of the island are women. (In Yzhno-Sakhalinsk this percentage goes up to 52.3 percent.)

The southern half of Sakhalin has a series of new industries: paper-cellulose, food-processing, and machine-building plants. Important coal fields have been found, and there are large oil and natural gas fields in the northern part of the island; a gas pipeline across the Tatar Strait delivers gas to the mainland. The island, particularly its southern part, has a well-developed railway network, and there are modern airports at Yzhno-Sakhalinsk, Aleksandrovsk, and Okha. There are scheduled daily flights to the mainland.

The Far East fishing fleet on the move.

Fishing and fish-processing industries are well developed: large fishing fleets operate from all ports.

The climate is somewhat milder than the mainland.

Some Japanese remained on the island after it was turned over to Russia in 1945. The Japanese government paid for the evacuation of the Japanese population until 1949, but 112 Japanese families chose to stay on the island and become Soviet citizens. Altogether less than 1,000 Japanese were evacuated.

The average income of Siberians has been rising during the last ten years, but the rise has not been spectacular. But the prices, especially for food, have come down, and certain community services became cheaper. This seems to be the general policy of the Soviet Government: purely monetary increases are not considered as important as the general improvement of living conditions, and particularly the care of those who have reached retirement age. A very large part of the Soviet budget is expended in this connection, and the mass pension scheme is the most striking feature of the Soviet internal economy. It is proving to have a profound influence on the thinking of the people—in Siberia particularly, because of the lower retirement age there.

Does this lower efficiency and productivity? Undoubtedly, in some cases, more among the older workers than the young. To combat this, the Soviet industry is switching more and more to the new plan under which productivity reflects upon the income of the workers in each enterprise—a certain concession to human nature.

Any comparison between the socialist and capitalist systems in purely monetary terms does not give an accurate picture. In Siberia the comparison should really be made between the general welfare of the people, say, twenty years ago, and today. On this basis, the Siberians are enjoying an unprecedented prosperity boom. Would they have fared better under a capitalist system? Of course this question is academic, but old Siberians remember conditions as they were under the Tsars, and few of them pine for the "good old times." The fact is that Siberia has made gigantic progress in all spheres of life. And within the last ten years, the progress has been accelerating at a dizzy pace.

"Today is already our yesterday," is the most common saying in today's Siberia. This sort of overall optimism for the future is the most striking feature of the new Siberia which differentiates it from the rest of the Soviet Union and, generally, the rest of the world.

21.

Conclusions

THIS book does not pretend to present a complete story of today's Siberia. This is impossible to do in a single volume. But it does contain some of the impressions of a man who knew the country half a century ago and then revisited it. All the facts and figures in it are as accurate as possible.

The reader might feel that the author is partial to the Soviet system. This is not so. The author recognizes not only the accomplishments of the system, but its failures as well. This is not a pro-Soviet book, but it is a pro-people one—the author approached the theme with honest good will toward the men and women involved in the development of Siberia, not so much trying to find faults in the process as to understand the dynamic creative forces behind it.

The author believes that what is happening in Siberia today has a profound significance for the entire world. It demonstrates that the Soviet people are building their future without any designs on other people or any other country. It also demonstrates that peace in the world is not only their ardent desire, but an absolute necessity for them: without it all that is being done in Siberia will be a wasteful absurdity. The colossal investment of capital and effort in Siberia implies that peace will be the national policy of the Soviet state for generations to come. This is a good thing to know at a time when any major armed conflict may well mean the extinction of humanity.

The development of Siberia to its full economic potential will require a century or more, and by that time the world is bound to find other means of solving international differences than universal suicide.

Siberia is very young, and is being developed by young people. This is another all-important factor for a world still run by older generations poisoned by intolerance, mistrust, prejudice, and bigotry. In Siberia all the tragic mistakes of the past can be avoided, and it is the author's firm belief that most of them will be avoided. If ever a new and better human community can be created, it can be created in Siberia, the largest and richest piece of almost completely undeveloped real estate on this swiftly-shrinking planet.

The fact that the development of Siberia is directed primarily by scientists is another important factor. During the last half-century, science has made advances rendering obsolete most of the old concepts of politics and life. The preoccupation of today's Siberia with science and education is the most heartening facet of the country's development.

In the new Siberia the author did not find an ideal society, but he did find a land of young people looking forward and building for tomorrow, unhampered by antiquated traditions or prejudices of the past, and if one believes in a better future, one must believe in Siberia. There is no man living today, and no child who will be born tomorrow, who would not benefit from the peaceful development of this great and empty land. This is why the present young builders of Siberia deserve universal good will, and it is with this good will that the author has approached the fascinating Siberian scene in this modest work.

George St. George

Notes

1. Traveling in the U.S.S.R.

ALL foreign travel in the Soviet Union is handled by Intourist, the government tourist organization. But it should be arranged through a travel agency, many of whom work with Intourist.

The entire cost of travel must be paid in foreign currency, including transportation, hotel accommodation, and food for the duration of the proposed trip. (The trip can be extended and the itinerary altered while in the Soviet Union by arrangement with Intourist there, but still all such arrangements must be paid for in foreign currency.)

There are three classes of accommodation available—deluxe, first, and tourist class. There is also organized group travel at reduced rates.

The deluxe class is expensive and might come to 30 dollars per person per day, in addition to first-class transportation to and from the Soviet Union. It includes, besides the first-class hotel accommodation and additional food allowance, the free use of a car, and an interpreter's services for four hours per day.

First class provides first-class transportation, first-class hotel accommodation, and food allowance, but no car and no interpreter. However, these can be obtained at the hotel when needed, at an extra charge. The cost of this class of travel is substantially lower than for the deluxe, and comes to about 20 dollars per person per day.

Tourist class provides the economy fare transportation, tourist-class hotel accommodation, usually without a private bath, and basic food allowance. The cost is about 15 dollars per person per day.

It is possible to have a combination arrangement, i.e., tourist class transportation and first-class accommodation while in the Soviet Union. This is recommended for economy-minded travelers.

All classes include free baggage handling, free transportation from the airport or railway station to the hotel and back (at departure time), and free medical and dental care while in the Soviet Union. Medicines must be paid for, but prices are very nominal. There is no charge for local telephone calls and the cost of public transportation, including taxis, is very low.

Each tourist is met by a representative of Intourist who speaks English, French, and German, who will assign the tourist to the hotel and arrange his transportation there. Since all accommodations are handled on a pooling basis, there is no way of knowing in advance to what hotel the traveler may be assigned. However, those who wish to specify any particular hotel in advance may do so, at an additional charge of 25 dollars per person. The recommended hotels in Moscow are: the National, the Rossya, the Ukraina, the Moskva, and the Metropole. All the Intourist hotels are comfortable and clean.

Upon arrival at the hotel, each foreign tourist must register at the hotel Service Bureau, which is staffed by personnel speaking foreign languages. Then he is assigned a room and issued food coupons. These coupons represent the money value marked on them, and can be used in any desired way, i.e., two or three breakfast coupons may be used to pay for lunch or dinner, etc. Unused coupons may be cashed back into foreign currency on leaving the country.

Each hotel has a money exchange office. The current rate is 90 kopecks for $1.00. (One ruble is 100 kopecks.) All unused Russian money can be changed back into foreign currency before leaving by presenting the exchange slip issued every time the tourist spends foreign currency. All such slips must be kept as a proof of lawful currency transactions.

Each traveler is requested to fill out a custom's declaration listing all the foreign currency assets brought into the country, as well as gold articles, jewelry, etc. On leaving another declaration must be made, listing all the unspent money. Theoretically, the travelers must be in possession of documentary proof showing when and where his foreign assets were spent while in the Soviet Union. In practice such proof is rarely asked for, but it is wise to keep all the exchange and purchase slips.

Russian currency cannot be taken in or out of the country. All unused rubles must be converted back into foreign currency when leaving the U.S.S.R., except coins, which are considered souvenirs.

In most large Soviet towns there are special stores where all purchases must be paid for in foreign currency. This is a great boon to foreign travelers, since the prices in such shops are low: A quart of whiskey, for instance, sells for under 3.00 dollars, and a package of American cigarettes for 33 cents. There is a large assortment of Soviet products as well, vodka, wines, liquors, chocolate, food items, cigarettes, cigars, watches (a marvelous value), cameras and photo supplies, fur articles, and souvenirs of all kind, sold at about one-third of their regular price in rubles. It is unnecessary to bring such articles from abroad—they are substantially cheaper in Russia than at home, provided they are paid for in foreign currency.

If some small gifts are brought into Russia for friends they should be inexpensive items which are currently in short supply in the Soviet Union, such as ball point pens, gas cigarette lighters, Scotch tape, or kitchen gadgets.

Things not to bring: expensive gifts such as jewelry, foreign printed matter (especially of political nature), letters addressed to anyone within the Soviet Union, and of course, Russian money. Theoretically, no gifts should be brought in, but the customs people will not object to some inexpensive items even if declared. There is no limit to the amount of foreign currency brought in, but all must be declared. Since the Soviet Union is a document-conscious country, all documents such as visas, customs declarations, purchase slips, etc., must be kept. It is a good idea to have a special large envelope to keep them in.

All tourists are strongly advised not to change their foreign money through any private persons, no matter how attractive the rates might be, and not to sell any articles to strangers. This is illegal and can lead to serious trouble.

In the event of any difficulty, foreigners should go to the Service Bureau for help and advice. The people who work there speak foreign languages and are generally very helpful.

All travelers are required to have a valid passport and a Soviet entrance-exit visa which is a special document, not just a passport stamp. The visa can usually be obtained through your travel agent. A short questionnaire must be filled out and three photographs supplied. This procedure may take some time; up to two weeks in the summer tourist season, about five days in winter. No ticket to the Soviet Union may be sold without a hotel confirmation from Moscow, so travelers are advised to make their travel arrangements in advance, especially during the summer season. Exit arrangements should also be made in advance in Russia through the Service Bureau, and usually, three to four days is enough.

The Soviet visa is issued free of charge.

Generally, your travel agent can give you all the additional information. It is advised to make all travel arrangements through a good agency. Attempts to make the arrangements on your own will cause delay and confusion.

People traveling to Europe can make all arrangements there, since the European travel agencies usually have more experience in these matters and can save travelers time and money. This is especially important for tourists from smaller towns in the United States where local agents might have no experience and where there are no Soviet consulates.

While in the Soviet Union, it is best to follow the advice of the Service Bureau in all matters. They are trained to advise and to render whatever help foreign tourists require. Do not hesitate to call on them even for small matters. They are there to help you.

Special Points

Tipping: theoretically this is not required, but in all larger towns tips are accepted and appreciated. No service charge is added to restaurant bills, so tipping about ten to fifteen percent of your bill is in order. Taxi drivers should be tipped, as well as the hotel personnel when leaving. Small gifts, like liquor or candy or foreign cigarettes bought in the foreign-currency shops are highly appreciated. Since they cost little, that is a good way to tip. There is a floor attendant on every floor of all hotels. A collective tip for the entire personnel can be given to her when leaving the hotel.

Laundry and shoe-repair service are fast and good. Shirts given out in the morning are usually returned at night or the next morning. Since the laundering is often done by the chambermaids it is a good practice to tip them when the laundry is returned.

Medical help may be summoned at any time, day or night. There is no charge.

In all other matters consult the Service Bureau in your hotel.

Traveling in Siberia

The following places in Siberia are at present open to foreign travel:
Novosibirsk (including Akademgorodok)
Irkutsk
Bratsk
Khabarovsk
Nakhodka

The fact that other Siberian cities are "not open" to foreign travel means that Intourist as yet has no contractual arrangements with local hotels, and therefore, no facilities to guarantee the traveler's proper comfort and, especially, no advance reservations. It is expected that some other cities will shortly be included in this list as new hotel facilities are constructed.

Permission to visit other cities may be requested and is usually granted, but this a protracted procedure.

The very best way to see Siberia is to go by train, at least one way. The trains are comfortable and pleasant, and the fares are comparatively low. Here they are, in "soft" or first class:

Moscow to Novosibirsk—38.70 rubles

Moscow-Irkutsk—57 rubles

Moscow-Khabarovsk—91.80 rubles

All fares are computed on a per kilometer basis with no extra charge for stopovers and no reduction for roundtrips.

Bratsk is best reached from Irkutsk by air—a flight of 1 hour 30 minutes.

Nakhodka, the port on the Sea of Japan, is recommended only to those who plan to go to Japan, and to the United States across the Pacific. It is reached by train from Khabarovsk. The fare is 12.80 rubles.

The time element is important. The train trip from Moscow to Khabarovsk takes six days and six nights.

All the arrangements for all these trips must be made in Moscow through Intourist—unless they were made in advance. (There are Intourist offices in all Soviet tourist hotels.) All hotel reservations must be secured in advance and visas adjusted to include the places to be visited. Intourist will provide all the additional information, but the arrangements take time, and at least three days should be allowed.

All charges must be paid in advance in foreign currency at the rate of about $1.10 per ruble.

Hotel rates in Siberia are about 30 percent lower than in Moscow or Leningrad. All other costs and prices are fairly standard throughout the Soviet Union.

Traveler's checks are readily accepted, but American credit cards cannot be used. There is an American Express office in Moscow, the only one in the Soviet Union.

The best time to go to Siberia is from the beginning of May to the end of September. No special clothing is required in summer, but some heavy winter clothing including overshoes and a fur hat with ear flaps is a must in winter, and can be bought in Moscow at one of the foreign-currency shops. The Service Bureau has all that necessary information.

Travel guides, books, and pamphlets are available in English at every tourist hotel.

The language barrier may be a problem in Siberia. Outside the Intourist hotels, a foreigner will find few people who speak foreign languages. Sightseeing is best done in a group with a guide-interpreter. Such guides are available through Intourist offices in all the towns open for foreign travel. Bring a good Russian phrase book with you; finding one in the Soviet Union can be a problem.

Each foreign tourist in the Soviet Union must remember that Intourist is responsible for his welfare during his entire stay in the country. It is a surprisingly efficient organization considering the size and scope of its activities.

With patience and good will, foreign tourists will experience no difficulties. The Siberians particularly are extremely hospitable and friendly and will go out of their way to help a stranger.

"Schastlivogo puti!"

Meaning, of course, a pleasant journey.

II. *The Structure of Siberia Today*

SIBERIA is a multinational state—there are about thirty non-Russian and non-Slavic nations and tribes that can be considered as the original pre-Russian Siberians.

But it would be historically incorrect to consider Siberia a Russian colony. None of the Siberian nationalities ever had independent state-hood in their history, and all of them joined the Russian state more or less voluntarily, or certainly without any serious resistance. Almost all of them have been a part of the Russian state for well over 300 years, with one notable exception—the Tuva, which joined Siberia, and Russia, in 1944. Present-day Siberia is a part of the Russian Federation, the Russian Soviet Federated Socialist Republic, or the R.S.F.S.R., and today the non-Slavic and non-Russian population of Siberia represents only 3 percent of the entire population of the country.

If the policy of the Tsarist government toward the native Siberians was that of utter, almost criminal, neglect (the Tsarist administrators were actually unconscious of the existence of some of the tiny ethnic minorities), the policy of the Soviets was to bend the other way by giving even the smallest minorities a sense of national identity and the widest possible autonomy. This policy often bordered on ethnographical hair-splitting, but it must be admitted today that it has saved some of these ethnic groups from biological extinction.

Siberia came under Soviet rule considerably later than the rest of Russia. It was not until October of 1922 that the whole of Siberia came under Soviet control. But even while the Soviet army was marching across Siberia, the autonomous Soviet republics, regions, and national districts were being set up. There have been considerable changes and status-alterations since then. This is how the national structure of Siberia appears today:

As we said, the entire territory is included in the Russian Federation, and all Siberians are the citizens of the R.S.F.S.R. as well as of the Soviet Union. But within the structure there are three autonomous Soviet socialist republics, three autonomous regions, and eight autonomous national districts—fourteen territories nominally expressing the ethnic composition of their population. We say "nominally" because in many of them the local national element does not represent the majority.

The Autonomous Soviet Socialist Republics are full-fledged states with their own constitutions, their Councils of Ministers, and their citizenship (in addition to the Russian and All-Union).

The three of them are:

The Buryat A.S.S.R.,

The Yakut A.S.S.R., and

The Tuva A.S.S.R.

(Also popularly known as Buryatia, Yakutia, and Tuva.)

Let us describe them briefly:

The Buryat A.S.S.R. was constituted on May 30, 1923, shortly after the end of the civil war. It is located in Transbaikalia, along the eastern shore of Lake Baikal. It has a land area of approximately 135,500 square miles, slightly larger than that of New Mexico (121,666 square miles), and a population of 789,000, or roughly that of Washington, D.C. This is the most populous of all such republics, but the Buryats do not represent the population majority; the Russians outnumber them. The capital of the republic is Ulan-Ude (formerly Verkhneudinsk on the Trans-Siberian Railway).

The Buryats are people of almost pure Mongolian stock, and they voluntarily joined the Russian state 310 years ago.

No written Buryat language existed before the revolution. It has been developed using the Russian alphabet. Now Buryat is taught in all schools along with Russian.

Four-fifths of the territory of the republic is covered by forest, and lumbering and lumber processing are the most important industries. The largest paper-cellulose plant in the Soviet Union is now being built in Buryatia. There are important mineral resources—gold, coal, molybdenum, tungsten, bauxite, asbestos, graphite, etc. The coal production is important—1,249,000 tons were mined in 1966, compared with 39,000 tons in 1944. In Ulan-Ude there is a large locomotive and rolling-stock building plant, a very large meat-processing combine, and thermal-electric plants. The industrial production of Buryatia has risen 139 times its prerevolution level.

Agriculture and animal husbandry are important. Wheat, rye, and oats are grown. The farm animal population in 1966 stood at 448,000 cattle, 200,000 pigs, and 1,580,00 sheep and goats. These figures have considerably risen since then, but no later figures are available.

Before the revolution the Buryats were almost totally illiterate. There were no Buryat schools. In 1915–1916 there were 13,500 school pupils of lower and middle grades with almost 100 percent Russian enrollment. There were no schools of higher education.

This situation has been drastically altered. Illiteracy has been practically eliminated. Education is compulsory and universal.

In 1966–1967 there were 715 general education schools with 201,000 pupils, 397 kindergartens with 33,700 children, 22 special schools of the junior-college type with 18,400 students, and 4 institutes with 16,200 students. There are three national theaters—one of opera and ballet, and two of drama: a television center at Ulan-Ude, 2 museums, 433 public libraries, 604 workers' clubs, 746 film installations (646 of them in rural districts), and approximately 90,000 radio receivers. In 1966, 121 books were published with an aggregate printing of 534,000 copies. There are 30 newspapers, including 13 in the Buryat language with a yearly overall circulation of 36,943,000 copies.

In 1966 there were 1,400 doctors in Buryatia (as compared with 440 in 1940) and 8,200 hospital beds (as compared with 2,300 in 1940). No earlier or later figures are available.

All in all, Buryatia enjoys a balanced economy and brisk industrial and cultural growth, about average for the Soviet Union.

The Yakut A.S.S.R. is the oldest autonomous republic of Siberia— it was constituted on April 27, 1922, and in many respects it is the most remarkable.

First of all, territorially it is a giant. Located in the northeast of Siberia in the basins of the Lena, Yana, and Indigirka Rivers, and in part of the basin of the Kolyma River, it has a land area of 1,198,000 square miles—more than four times that of Texa (267,339 square miles). In addition, it is the coldest country in the world. Two Yakut towns, Verkhoyansk and Oimyakon, claim the distinction of producing the lowest thermometer readings of any inhabited place. Paradoxically, the summers in Yakutia are quite hot—hotter than in Moscow or in most European capitals, and substantially hotter than in San Francisco, for instance. Readings of +100°F are not unusual in July and August. But those summers are short.

Despite what is probably the most uncomfortable continental climate in the world, Yakutia has made near-fantastic progress since the revolution.

Even though Yakutia voluntarily joined Russia more than 350 years ago, it was considered an absolutely useless place by the Tsarist government. Probably if Seward could have spent a few more million dollars, he could have bought Yakutia along with Alaska. Yet today Yakutia is the greatest foreign-currency earner of the Soviet Union—even though its colossal natural resources have barely been scratched.

Now let us look at Yakutia as it is today:

It is a huge and largely empty place—its population is 662,000 (the estimate on January 1, 1968)—roughly the population of New Orleans. Some 56 percent live in towns, primarily in the capital city of Yakutsk which had 98,000 people at the latest estimate and is growing at a brisk rate. More than half are Russians—the pure Yakuts numbered only 237,000 in the 1959 census. There are several minor far-north tribes who consider themselves Yakuts, but are in fact distinct though tiny ethnic entities.

But other figures are much more impressive.

Before the revolution only six Yakut men in 1,000 could read (Russian, of course, since there was no written Yakut language), and only two Yakut women were known to be literate. Since the revolution, a written Yakut has been created using the Russian alphabet, and the Yakuts have proved to be most avid scholars. Illiteracy has been completely stamped out. Almost all the world classics, including Shakespeare and Edgar Allan Poe have been translated into Yakut, a surprisingly rich and well-developed language of Turki origin. There are 745 general education schools with 149,000 pupils. 774 kindergartens with 43,300 children, 18 higher (mostly technical) schools with over 10,000 students, a state university with 4,700 students, the Yakut branch of the Academy of Science, and a number of research institutes including the unique Permafrost Institute. There are three permanent theaters of opera, music, and drama, a television center, 821 film installations (653 in rural districts), 7 museums, 521 public libraries (376 in rural districts), 680 workers' clubs, and 99,700 radio receiving installations. (All those figures are for 1966, and have been substantially increased since then.) In 1966, 175 book titles were published with an aggregate printing of 816,000 copies. There are 43 newspapers (27 of them in the Yakut language) which have a yearly circulation of 38,725,00 copies. The Yakut Union of Writers has 50 members writing in both Yakut and Russian.

And the president of the Supreme Soviet of Yakutia, the republic's highest executive, is a woman, one Alexandra Yakovlevna Ovchinnikova, a full-blodded Yakut, a graduate engineer, and a Doctor of History.

The once dismal fur-trading town of Yakutsk is being completely rebuilt with modern buildings despite the great difficulty presented by the permanently frozen subsoil, which in this region reaches a depth of almost 1,000 feet. Therefore the buildings are constructed on steel piles driven into the permafrost to a depth of 25 feet, and rise some 6 feet above the ground so that the warmth of buildings will not melt the foundation.

What has caused this outburst of activity? The fact is that incalculable riches have been found in the frozen ground—gold, iron ores, oil, natural gas—and just ten years ago, what are probably the richest deposits of industrial and gem diamonds in the world. Today Yakutia is the second largest producer of diamonds in the world, almost matching South Africa, and exceeding it many times in already known, but still untouched, reserves.

In addition, Yakutia is the largest fur producer in the export trade, and possesses immense lumber resources as well as hydroelectric potential for the creation of a tremendous industrial empire. To meet the needs of the future, there is a plan for the construction of the most gigantic hydroelectric plant ever conceived, in the Lower Lena, with a capacity of 20,000,000 kilowatts of electricity—an amount fully sufficient to satisfy all the needs of a highly industrialized nation of 50 million people. (In comparison, the largest hydroelectric plant in the United States at Grand Coulee has a capacity of 1,900,000 kilowatts, and the largest working plant in the world, at Bratsk in Siberia, has 3,800,000 kilowatts.)

So this is the potential future of this frozen land. And it is in Yakutia that the first fully enclosed town is being built at Aykhal, an experiment in which the population will live in a permanently controlled spring-like temperature.

There were 1,500 doctors in Yakutia in 1966 (compared with 311 in 1940) and 8,500 hospital beds (1,400 in 1940). No later or earlier figures are available.

The Tuva A.S.S.R. is the youngest member of the Russian Federation and the Soviet Union. Until 1921, Tuva was one of the most backward nomadic regions of Asia, nominally under Chinese control. The population was 100 percent illiterate, and no records of any kind had been kept.

In 1921, Tuva broke away and became an independent state, Then in 1944, it voluntarily joined the Soviet Union as an autonomous region, and on October 10, 1961, was constituted as an autonomous republic within the Russian Federation.

Tuva is the southernmost region of Central Siberia, located at the headwaters of the mightiest of all Siberian rivers, the Yenisei. It is the smallest of all the autonomous republics of Siberia. It has a land area of

66,000 square miles—a shade smaller than the state of Washington
(68,192 square miles)—and a population of 222,000 on January 1,
1968, about one-half native Tuvans, the rest Russians and small Altai
tribes.

The capital is Kyzyl. Once a small trading post, its estimated present
population is 48,000. There are several other towns, all of recent origin.
There were no urban settlements in Tuva before 1921.

Altogether Tuva has been under Soviet rule for only 25 years, but
its progress is considerable. Some important natural resources have
been found—iron ores, copper, polymetals, cobalt, mercury, rocksalt,
asbestos, and coal. Mining is the main industry—coal (319,000 tons
were mined in 1966), rocksalt, asbestos, and cobalt.

The nomadic population has largely settled down. There are 14 state
and 37 large collective farms. Animal husbandry is the main pursuit
(sheep predominating), but there is some agriculture as well—882,000
acres were under cultivation in 1966.

But it is in the field of education that progress has been more remarkable. The written Tuvan language (of Altai-Turki origin) has been
developed using Russian characters, and the basic 8-year education is
compulsory and universal. Illiteracy among the younger age groups has
been completely eliminated. There are 194 general education schools
with 51,900 pupils, 137 kindergartens with 9,000 children, 5 special
junior-college type schools with 3,1000 students; and a pedagogical
college at Kyzyl with an enrollment of 1,400. There is a national theater
of music and drama, 193 film installations, 131 public libraries, and
175 clubs. (All the above figures are as of January 1, 1967.) In 1966,
79 book titles were published with an aggregate printing of 294,000
copies. There are three newspapers with the yearly circulation of
9,673,000 copies, all in the Tuvan language. (The Russian newspapers
are flown daily from Krasnoyarsk and Irkutsk.)

In 1966 there were 440 doctors and 2,700 hospital beds. (In 1950
the respective figures were 138 and 600.) Before 1921, no modern
medicine was practiced.

Let us now consider the so-called autonomous regions. These regions
enjoy considerable national autonomy within the regular provinces.*
They are administered by the regional Soviets, but are subordinate to

---

* Within the R.S.F.S.R., the provinces are known as *oblast* or *krai*. The distinction is purely semantic; there is no difference in administrative structure. They were
known as *gubernias* before the revolution. The present definitions were adopted to
differentiate them from the Tsarist bureaucratic administrative usage.

the provincial Soviets. They were set aside to provide the local national minorities with an opportunity for national cultural identification, although in practice the local population is not necessarily in the majority. However, the local languages are taught in all schools along with Russian.

There are three such autonomous regions in Siberia:

The Gorno-Altai Autonomous Region;

The Khakass Autonomous Region; and

The Jewish Autonomous Region.

The Gorno-Altai A.R. is the part of the Altai Province. This region was constituted on June 1, 1922, and was known as the Oyrot Autonomous Region until 1948 when it was given its present name.

It is a small region located in the Altai mountains of southern Siberia. It has a land area of 42,790 square miles or roughly that of Ohio, and a population of 168,000, or slightly less than Nashville, Tenn. The capital is Gorno-Altaisk, a small town of about 32,000. The urban population is predominantly Russian. The rural population is Oirot—an Altai people of Turki origin.

There is some industry. Gold is mined. Animal husbandry is the main rural pursuit—sheep, cattle, yaks, and mountain deer. Agriculture is primarily concerned with raising animal fodder.

In 1965–1966 there were 41,500 pupils of all grades. There were 5 special schools with 4,200 students and a pedagogical college with an enrollment of 3,700. There is a national theater, 251 film installations, 136 public libraries, and 119 clubs. In 1966 there were 204 doctors and 1,620 hospital beds. The Altai language uses the Russian alphabet. Russian is universally taught and spoken.

The Khakass A. R. is a part of Krasnoyarsk Province (Krai) of Central Siberia. It was constituted on October 20, 1930. Its area is 23,800 square miles, roughly that of West Virginia and its population stood at 466,000 by January 1, 1968—roughly that of Atlanta, Ga. The regional center is Abakan, with a population of 80,000 in 1968.

This is a well-developed industrial region of southern Siberia. The main industries are mining and smelting: coal, iron ores, non-ferrous metals, etc. There is an important food-processing industry and agriculture. The economy is well balanced.

There has been created a written Khakass language on the basis of the Russian alphabet. Illiteracy has been almost totally eliminated. In 1959–1960 there were 107,400 pupils of all grades. There were 6 schools of junior-college level with 7,500 students and a pedagogical college with 3,500. There is a dramatic theater, television center, 386 film installations, 193 libraries, and 41 clubs. In 1966 there were 515 doctors and 4,510 hospital beds. (All the above figures have grown since then.)

The Jewish A. R., a part of Khabarovsk Province (Krai), is an experimental oddity. It was created on May 7, 1934, to provide the Jewish population of the Soviet Union with a national home, a Yiddish national language, and national identification outside the theological tradition. It has not been a success because the majority of the Jewish population of the Soviet Union (2,268,000 according to the 1959 census) did not avail themselves of this opportunity.

The geographical location may have something to do with this. Also the fact that, according to the same census, only 21.1 percent of Soviet Jews knew the Yiddish language in addition to their local language.

The region is located along the left bank of the Amur river bordering Manchuria (China). It has an area of 13,900 square miles—roughly the combined areas of Massachusetts and Connecticut, and a population of 174,000—roughly that of Nashville, Tenn. It is believed that less than 30 percent of the population is of Jewish stock, even though Yiddish is the national language of the region. The capital is Birobidzhan, with a population of 48,000.

The region has both industry and agriculture. Since over one-third of the territory is forest, lumbering and wood processing are important, and tin is extensively mined. Wheat, oats, soy beans, and potatoes are the principal crops. Fishing is conducted on a commercial basis.

The region has 39,700 schoolchildren of all grades and 4,800 students in 6 junior colleges. There are two national theaters, a national choir, 6 museums, 167 film installations, 80 libraries, and 106 clubs. There are 269 doctors and 1,880 hospital beds.

In addition to the autonomous republics and autonomous regions, there are so-called national districts to provide smaller nationalities with national and cultural identification. There are ten such districts in the R.S.F.S.R., and eight of them are located in Siberia.

Here are the national districts in alphabetical order:

The Aga Buryat-Mongol N.D. is located in the Chita Province (Oblast) of Transbaikalia close to the Buryat A.S.S.R., but separated from it geographically. It has an area of 7,344 square miles—roughly that of New Jersey, and a population of 62,000 (in 1967). The regional center is the town of Aginskoye.

Predominantly a rural region, only 19 percent of its population is urban. The principal branch of economy is agriculture and animal husbandry. Tungsten, lime, and marble are mined on a limited scale.

Buryat is the national language. In 1966 there were 16,200 pupils of all grades in addition to 300 students in the Aginskoye Pedagogical College. There are 38 public libraries, 51 clubs, and 50 film installations. There are 60 doctors and 440 hospital beds. This is still a backward region by new Siberian standards.

The Chukchi N.D., constituted on December 10, 1930, is a part of the Magadan Province (Oblast) and is located in the extreme northeast of Siberia, facing Alaska. It has a territory of 280,000 square miles, slightly larger than that of Texas, and a population of 97,000, more than 75 percent of whom live in towns, primarily in the capital of Anadyr (45,000).

This is one of the most promising gold-producing regions of Siberia and is generally known as the "Golden Chukchi." New gold strikes are reported constantly, but the climatic conditions make mining difficult as the mining here requires heavy machinery. Very important deposits of coal and tin have been found as well.

The written Chukchi language (of Paleoasiatic group) was created after the revolution. The Russian alphabet is used. During 1965–1967 there were 15,000 schoolchildren in all grades, and over 100 students in the Anadyr Pedagogical College. There are 72 public libarries, 112 clubs, 156 film installations, 342 doctors, and 1,250 hospital beds. This is a "gold rush" region with all the characteristics of such regions, including a swiftly growing population.

The Evenk N. D. is a part of Krasnoyarsk Province (Krai) and it is the "emptiest" of all such regions. It has a land area of 257,850, almost that of Texas, and a population of only 12,000. The small town of Tura is the "capital."

The Evenks, one of the most ancient races of Siberia, are spread all across the country and are in effect the most authentic Siberian aborigines. They have been actually saved from natural biological extinction by the revolution—it is doubtful that there were more than 1,500 of them in the whole of Siberia in 1918. They are of Tungus-Manchurian origin and probably migrated north in prehistoric times.

Since the revolution a written Evenk language has been created (with the Russian alphabet), and at present there are 2,300 pupils of all grades in the region in addition to 120 students at the Tura Medical School. There are 23 public libraries, 26 clubs, 27 film installations, 46 doctors, and 300 hospital beds.

The Evenks are traditional hunters and trappers—sable, squirrel, polar fox, muskrat, and kolinsky are the main furs produced. There is some deer-herding and fur animal farming. Some garden vegetables and potatoes are grown.

The Khanty-Mansi N.D., formed on September 26, 1930, is a part of the Tyumen Province (Oblast), is also an ethnological rescue operation —to preserve those two ancient Siberian tribes from extinction. These people of Finnish-Ugor origin had been dying out from sheer neglect during the Tsarist administration.

The district has an area of about 200,000 square miles twice that of Colorado, and a population of 250,000 (in 1967), 68 percent of whom live in towns, and are mostly Russians. The regional center is Khanty-Mansisk.

About nine years ago, immense oil and natural gas deposits were discovered here—the whole region may be actually resting on a "sea of oil." Despite the difficult climatic conditions and lack of communications, oil drilling and oil and gas pipline construction are going on incessantly; the region may well become the Texas of Siberia. Lumbering and fishing are important, but oil is king. The region produces furs—squirrel, polar hare, fox, ermine, etc. Reindeer-herding, some limited agriculture —rye, potatoes, and truck farming are also practiced.

A written Khanty-Mansi language has been created (with the Russian alphabet). In 1966–1967 there were 47,000 pupils of all grades, and 1,200 students in the pedagogical and medical colleges. There are 205 public libraries, 195 clubs, 189 film installations, 288 doctors, and 2,250 hospital beds.

The Koryak N.D. is another example of ethnological hair-splitting. Created on December 10, 1930, it is a part of the Kamchatka Province (Oblast), and in fact occupies two-thirds of the province. It is located in the extreme northeast of Asia, below the Chukchi, and it occupies the northern half of the Kamchatka peninsula, some outlying areas, and Karaginski Island. It has an area of 120,000 square miles—roughly that of New Mexico, and a population of 39,000 (in 1968). The regional center is the small town of Palana.

Fishing and seafood processing are the industries, as well as hunting —sable, ermine, fox. Some very limited dairy and truck farming is developing.

A written Koryak language has been created (of Paleoasiatic origin) using the Russian alphabet. In 1966–1967 there were 5,600 school pupils of all grades. There are 41 public libraries, 63 clubs, 63 film installations, 130 doctors, and 630 hospital beds.

The Taimyr (Dolgan-Nenets) N.D. was also created on December 10, 1930, as a part of the Krasnoyarsk Province (Krai). It is located in the extreme north of Central Siberia and some parts of the Central Siberian plain. It has a huge land area of 335,600 square miles (Texas has 267,399 square miles) much of it polar desert, and a population of

37,000 people. It also has well over 500,000 small lakes in addition to the huge Lake Taimyr.

Iron-ore mining has become important because of the close proximity of the huge metallurgical center of Norilsk, the largest city beyond the Arctic Circle in the world. Reindeer herding and hunting are the occupations of the rural population—about 35 percent of the entire population of the region are so employed.

The regional center is the town of Dudinka.

This is another ethnological rescue operation—the Dolgans and the Nenets had been dying out. Now a written language (of Finnish-Ugar origin) has been created using the Russian alphabet. In 1966–1967 there were 6,800 school pupils of all grades and over 100 students in the Dudinka Zoological-Veterinary Institute. There are 33 public libraries, 38 clubs, 68 film installations, 123 doctors, and 750 hospital beds.

The Ust-Orda Buryat N.D. was created on September 26, 1937, to provide national identification to the Buryats living in the Irkutsk Province (Oblast) and separated from Buryatia by Lake Baikal. It is the smallest of all national districts with a land area of 8,500 square miles—roughly that of Massachusetts—and a population of 151,000—roughly that of New Haven, Conn. The district center is the small town of Ust-Ordynski. The population is predominantly Buryat and rural. Only 18 percent of the people live in urban centers.

The district has a balanced economy. Coal and gypsum are mined, dairying is important (milk and cheese), as well as animal husbandry. Agriculture is developed—wheat, oats, and barley are the main crops.

The Buryat is the national language. In 1966–1967 there were 43,200 school pupils of all grades in addition to 500 students in the medical and pedagogical colleges. There are 137 public libraries, 321 clubs, 304 film installations, 80 doctors, and 1,030 hospital beds. This territory has been a part of the Russian state for over 350 years, and Russian culture has made a strong imprint—almost all Buryats are bilingual.

The Yamal-Nenets N.D. was created on December 10, 1930, (the great year for national district creation) and is a part of the Tyumen Province (Oblast). It is located in the northern part of the West Siberian plain and possesses immense oil resources, at present being developed. It has an area of 291,300 square miles, and a population of 74,000, 43 percent of whom are urbanized. The district center is Salekhard.

At the present time fishing, fish-processing, fur animal farming (blue polar fox, mink), reindeer herding, and hunting (polar fox, squirrel, muskrat) are the principal industries.

A written Nenets language (Finnish-Ugor group) has been created.

The Russian alphabet is used. In 1966–1967 there were 15,700 school pupils of all grades. There are veterinary, medical, and pedagogical colleges with an enrollment of 1,300. There are 73 public libraries, 77 clubs, 81 film installations, 186 doctors, and 1,080 hospital beds.

So much for the "native" Siberians. It may appear that Siberia is extremely heterogenous, but in fact this is not so. The Soviets' extremely conscientious national policy should delight all ethnologists, but since Siberia has been basically Russian for over 300 years, and since Russia, penetrating into Siberia, came into a statehood vacuum, the tribes have become staunchly loyal to Russia, and accepted Russian culture, even under the Tsarist policy of neglect. There have never been any interracial animosities in Russian Siberia among the Siberian aborigines, or between them and the Russian settlers. There certainly has been enough room for everybody.

Undoubtedly the Soviet government has performed a tremendous historical task in saving many small Siberian nationalities, none of whom, for instance, had a written language before the revolution. These nationalities have probably been the greatest beneficiaries of the revolution. It has given them education, above everything else, and has drawn them into the mainstream of Soviet life. There is some disagreement among ethnologists as to the end result of this process: Will it tend to obliterate the national identity of some very small nationalities rather than strengthen it? Only time will tell.

Now let us look at the ethnic composition of Siberia outside of administrative divisions. This is the list of non-Slavic and non-Russian nationalities of Siberia based on the last Soviet census of 1959:

Buryats	253,000	
Yakuts	237,000	
Tuvans	100,000	(est.)
Khakass	57,000	
Altaians	45,000	
Evenks	24,000	
Nentsi	23,000	*
Khanty	19,000	
Dolgans	19,000	
Chukchi	11,700	
Evens	9,100	
Nanaitsi	8,000	

* Since the Nentsi live on both sides of the Urals only some 30 percent of them live in Siberia.

Mansi	6,450
Koryaks	6,300
Selcups	3,800
Nivkhi	3,700
Ulchi	2,100
Udegheitsi	1,400
Itelmeni	1,100
Eskimos	1,100
Orochi	800
Nganasani	750
Aleuts	400
Yukaghir	400
All others (est.)	1,000
Grand total	835,800

The latest estimate of the population for all of Siberia shows the figure of 25,231,000 (probably it is closer to 25,500,000 at this writing) so the percentage of non-Russian population is a shade over 3 percent. The rest of the population is predominantly Russian—with the Ukrainian and Belorussians, and other Soviet nationalities, representing a very small minority. Many non-Russian Siberians have become completely Russified during the last 350 years. So much so, in fact, that during his recent trip to Yakutsk, the author found educated Yakutians speaking better, more literary, and more precise Russian than is generally spoken in the streets of Moscow.

There is one point which must be made clear—no other nation and no other culture has ever made any contribution to either the welfare of the Siberian peoples or to their cultural or educational development. This includes the Chinese who have made moral claims to certain Far East territories. Even though some of those territories had been from time to time nominally under Chinese rule, this rule was exercised by the Manchurians who had imposed their dynasty upon China. The Manchurians were later overthrown by the Chinese and dominated by them. Almost no Chinese have stayed in any of the Siberian territories for any length of time, nor settled there in numbers. So this claim has no more historical validity than claims of the Russians to California—because, once upon a time, the Russians reached the Russian River above San Francisco and built a fort there.

While we are on the subject of the administrative structure of today's Siberia, we might as well take a closer look at it—using the very latest available figures (Jan. 1, 1968), though some may be slightly out of date.

Here it is—going from west to east:

THE WEST SIBERIA REGION

The Kurgan Province (Oblast)

Area: 27,410 square miles   Population: 1,081,000
Capital: Kurgan   Population: 222,000

The Tyumen Province (Oblast)

Area: 501,000 square miles   Population: 1,379,000
Capital: Tyumen   Population: 256,000

This region includes:

The Khanty-Mansi National District
The Yamal-Nenets National District

The Omsk Province (Oblast)

Area: 53,900 square miles   Population: 1,829,000
Capital: Omsk   Population: 800,000

The Novosibirsk Province (Oblast)

Area: 68,750 square miles   Population: 2,470,000
Capital: Novosibirsk   Population: 1,079,000

Novosibirsk is often referred to as the capital of Siberia. Even though it has no such administrative distinction, it is the largest city of Siberia, and its industrial, cultural, and educational center. Known as Novonikolayevsk until 1922, it had a population of 120,000 in 1926.

The Altai Province (Krai)

Area: 101,000 square miles   Population: 2,723,000
Capital: Barnaul   Population: 418,000

This province includes:

The Gorno-Altai Autonomous Region

Capital: Gorno-Altaisk   Population: 32,000

The Tomsk Province (Oblast)

Area: 122,350 square miles   Population: 795,000
Capital: Tomsk   Population: 334,000

The Kemerovo Province (Oblast)

Area: 34,900 square miles   Population: 3,005,000
Capital: Kemerovo   Population: 372,000

This region has been developed into the largest coal-mining and metallurgical center of Siberia since the revolution. Its growth can be judged by the fact that the city of Kemerovo had a population of only 22,000 in 1926, and the largest city of the region, Novokuznetsk, with over 495,000 population in 1968, had only 4,000 in 1926.

THE EAST SIBERIA REGION

Many old Siberia hands consider this the true or traditional Siberia. However, this is an emotional rather than geographic or economic definition.

The Krasnoyarsk Province (Krai)

Area: 927,000 square miles   Population: 2,939,000
Capital: Krasnoyarsk   Population: 592,000

This province includes:

The Khakass Autonomous Region

Capital: Abakan   Population: 80,000

The Taimyr (Dolgan-Nenets) National District
The Evenk National District

The Tuva Autonomous S.S. Republic

Area: 66,000 square miles   Population: 222,000
Capital: Kyzyl   Population: 48,000

The Irkutsk Province (Oblast)

Area: 298,000 square miles   Population: 2,281,000

Capital: Irkutsk   Population: 428,000

This province includes:

The Ust-Orda Buryat National District.

The Buryat Autonomous S.S. Republic

Area: 135,500 square miles   Population: 789,000
Capital: Ulan-Ude   Population: 235,000

The Chita Province (Oblast)

Area: 166,800 square miles   Population: 1,090,000
Capital: Chita   Population: 208,000

This province includes:

The Aga-Buryat-Mongol National District.

THE FAR EAST

This is the traditional appellation given to the eastern part of Siberia. (Some geographers do not include these regions in Siberia, but to the Siberians this *is* Siberia.)

The Amur Province (Oblast)

Area: 140,500 square miles   Population: 782,000
Capital: Blagoveshchensk   Population: 125,000

The Khabarovsk Province (Krai)

Area: 318,000 square miles   Population: 1,336,000
Capital: Khabarovsk   Population: 448,000

    This province includes:

    The Jewish Autonomous Region.

Area: 13,900 square miles   Population: 174,000
Capital: Birobidzhan   Population: 48,000

The Primorski (Maritime) Province (Krai)

Area: 64,000 square miles   Population: 1,669,000
Capital: Vladivostok   Population: 410,000

The Magadan Province (Oblast)

Area: 462,600 square miles   Population: 340,000
Capital: Magadan   Population: 85,000

    This province includes:

    The Chukchi National District

The Kamchatka Province (Oblast)

Area: 182,250 square miles   Population: 281,000
Capital: Petropavlovsk-Kamchatsky   Population: 129,000

    This province includes:

    The Koryak National District

The Sakhalin Province (Oblast)

Area: 33,600 square miles   Population: 639,000
Capital: Yuzhno-Sakhalinsk   Population: 93,000

The Yakut S.S. Republic

Area: 1,198,000 square miles   Population: 662,000
Capital: Yakutsk   Population: 98,000

(All the population figures are the official Soviet estimates as of January 1, 1967.)

It is interesting to note that there is a disagreement among geographers as to the exact size of Siberia, since there is some question about the exact border between Europe and Asia. Also, as we said, many geographers do not consider the Soviet Far East as a part of Siberia. Also there is some question about the territories acquired by the Soviet Union from Japan after the last war (the southern half of the Sakhalin island and the Kuriles), even though these territories were earlier annexed by Japan from Russia in 1905 after the Russo-Japanese war. There is also a tendency not to include the Tuva S.S. into the count, even though it became a part of the Soviet Union in 1944.

The National Geographic Society gives the size of Siberia as 4,403,100 square miles. This does not agree with the official Soviet figures which indicate that Western Siberia, Eastern Siberia, and the Far East region (even without the provinces of Chelyabinsk and Kurgan) occupy the area of 12,765,900 square kilometers, or about 4,928,943 square miles.

The development of Siberia has been slow. There are many reasons for that. The cruel climate, of course, has been a deterrent. Then much of Siberia is unsuitable for agriculture, and the vast majority of migrants during the Tsarist regime were agriculturists: there were practically no industries in the country. Many of them went back to Europe after failing to raise the crops in Siberia with which they were familiar. Too, the Tsarist practice of treating the country as a sort of vast penal colony gave Siberia a bad name for some 300 years—and it did not improve very much during the period of the so-called Stalinist repressions.

Recent history has not been good to Siberia either. After the end of the civil war the rebuilding of the devastated European part of the country had an absolute priority in the Soviet economy. The main industrialization efforts also favored the European U.S.S.R.—and Siberia had to wait her turn. Then World War II shattered much of European Russia and the entire Ukraine, the industrial heart of the country. Once again, the gigantic job of postwar reconstruction left Siberia waiting. So the new age of Siberia did not arrive until some fifteen years ago when industrial development of the country was begun in earnest. What has been done since then is impressive, what is being done is even more impressive, and what is planned is very exciting.

As new industrial projects were built, they attracted a new population which was mostly urban. A number of brand-new cities have been built—such as Komsomolsk-on-Amur which had 207,000 people in 1966; Norilsk with 127,000; Angarsk with 179,000; Bratsk with 113,000; Nakhodka with 92,000; Magadan with 82,000; Anzhero-Sudzhensk with 118,000; Belovo with 115,000; etc. Others, even though they existed before, have grown enormously—Novosibirsk, with 60,000 in 1920 jumped to 1,049,000; Petropavlovsk-Kamchatsky went from 2,000 to 119,000; Cheremkhovo from 9,000 to 111,000; Prokopyevsk from 11,000 to 291,000; Novokuznetsk from 4,000 to 484,000; Kemerovo from 22,000 to 358,000.

People are settling in Siberia and this process will accelerate as new industries are developed and new productive regions open for development. And Siberia, properly developed—as it *is* being developed now—can certainly accommodate them all. It is waiting for new Siberians. How many? According to Soviet economists, it can comfortably support a population of 250 million—on the basis of known resources.

So, indeed, Siberia is a land of tomorrow.

Index

915.7
S14   **Date Due**
